MOTHERING MATTERS

The sources of love,
and how our culture harms
infants, women, and society

Dr Peter Cook

MB, ChB, MRCPsych, FRANZCP, DCH

Foreword by Steve Biddulph

Published in 2011 by
Freedom Publishing
35 Whitehorse Rd,
Balwyn, Vic. 3103
Phone (03) 9816 0800
Fax (03) 9816 0899
Email: books@freedompublishing.com.au

Mothering Matters: The sources of love, and how our culture harms infants, women, and society
is an updated and extensively revised second edition, that replaces
Mothering Denied: The sources of love, and how our culture harms infants, women, and society published on April 24, 2009.

ISBN 978-0-977-56993-9

Copyright © 2011 by Peter S. Cook
All rights reserved.

Cartoon: *Thoughts of a baby lying in a child care centre.*
© 1995 Michael Leunig. Used with permission

Peter Cook is a doctor who has specialised in psychiatry and has been working in the field of child and family mental health for decades. In this book he has created something of great value. He summarises much research, making it accessible to those who wish to know more, as he draws on over half a century of thinking and learning about human infants and their mothers and fathers.

Steve Biddulph
Psychologist
Author of *Raising Babies*

Peter Cook presents much evidence that there is a natural, 'best fit' pattern of human mothering; he asks his readers to consider some ways in which significant departures from this pattern can harm infants, women, and society, and so contribute to emotional, behavioural, and health problems.

An increase in conduct disorders and aggression in young people, and changes in societal behaviour, have been the shared experience of many professionals dealing with such problems.

A mother has a relationship with her child which no one else can share. At birth the total growth of the child's body and brain has been the result of environment supplied by the mother. The rapid growth of the brain and body of the infant, and the acquisition of communication skills, are also largely the result of the intimate interactions of mother and child.

Fathers play an increasingly significant part in the infant's life, with the expanding ability of the child to communicate and learn through new experiences, usually mediated through play with the father and other family members in a safe and supportive environment.

I urge everyone with a social conscience to heed Peter Cook's sage words about early childhood. Failure to do so can only result in further damage to the young and the fabric of our society.

Forrester Cockburn
Emeritus Professor of Child Health
University of Glasgow, Scotland

What Peter Cook has to say in this most thoughtful volume is certainly not politically correct, and so may not prove widely popular. But that is not to say that he is mistaken or even misguided.

Unlike many, Peter Cook acknowledges, even heralds, evidence that underscores the fact that for many infants and women life does not provide what they want—and perhaps even what nature planned for them. Not all will agree with Peter Cook's analysis, but that is not a reason to ignore it. Open minds will most certainly be enriched. As for closed minds ...

Jay Belsky, Robert M. and Natalie Reid Dorn Professor
Department of Human and Community Development
University of California, Davis, California

The pervasive triumph of consumerism will be damaging us for generations to come. We now have a world where many new mothers and fathers see no choice but to work, even for a minimum wage, while their baby is cared for by someone else—anyone else.

The movement for women's liberation, rightly aggrieved by unfair patriarchy, and seeking emancipation and equality with men, chose to deny the fundamental importance of mothering, equating it with fathering, parenting or 'caregiving'.

When will the logic and evidence marshalled by Peter Cook in this book have its influence on the world of new babies? Not until all of us opt for a way of life beyond the envy and greed of consumerism, and revalue the many things that matter most for human wellbeing.

As I said in 1996 of his *Early Child Care: Infants and Nations at Risk*, "This small book should be dropped like leaflets all over the country to get past the ubiquitous network of the now-entrenched daycare propagandists, to reach the parents who have never heard the whole story."

Elliott Barker, MD
Forensic psychiatrist
Founder, Canadian Society for the Prevention of Cruelty to children
Editor, *Empathic Parenting*

About the author

Peter S. Cook was born in Japan, spending his early years there and in the UK before going to live in New Zealand. Having qualified in medicine at Otago University, Dunedin, in 1950, he studied adult and child psychiatry in London, mostly at the Maudsley Hospital and the University of London Institute of Psychiatry from 1952 to 1956. He gained the Diploma of Psychological Medicine in 1955 and the Diploma of Child Health in 1956. He is a member of the Royal College of Psychiatrists in the UK and a Fellow of the Royal Australian and New Zealand College of Psychiatrists.

He practised adult and child psychiatry in Christchurch, New Zealand, from 1957 until 1964, and then worked in Sydney, Australia, at the Royal Alexandra Hospital for Children, becoming Director of the Department of Psychiatry.

In 1974 he became a senior consultant in child psychiatry with the New South Wales Department of Health at the Queenscliff Health Centre in Sydney, and was advisor on child mental health to the Regional Director of the Northern Metropolitan Health Region. From 1982 he was in private practice until his retirement.

His many publications have been mainly concerned with primary prevention in child and family mental health, and also with conservation, environmental sustainability, and related issues.

Foreword

Every era in human history has naturally assumed itself to be the most modern, progressive, and advanced. There is no deeper myth in our history than the myth of progress, the idea that things get better. It may well be our most dearly held illusion.

Just recently, with the growth of technologies that can look inside the living brain, and video cameras that can watch the tiny movements and gestures of mothers and infants, we have realized that in our basic assumptions of Western industrial life, we were terribly wrong about something very important. We thought that minding babies was a casual, inconsequential thing that could be left to underpaid teenagers, or done in bulk with one person to five babies or ten toddlers, without any problem.

It now appears that mother-baby interaction, in the first year especially, is the very foundation of human emotions and intelligence. In the most essential terms, love grows the brain. The capacities for what make us most human—empathy, co-operation, intimacy, the fine timing and sensitivity that makes a human being charismatic, loving, and self-assured—are passed from mother to baby, especially if that mother is herself possessed of these qualities, and supported and cared for, so that she can bring herself to enjoy and focus on the task.

Just as we were wrong, in our industrial culture, about almost everything related to sustainable and happy living on this earth, we were wrong about childhood. It is entirely possible that in our civilisation we have been getting worse, as parents, for many hundreds of years. Of course these are dramatic, sweeping overstatements. But the trends are there.

Peter Cook is a doctor who has specialised in psychiatry and has been working in the field of child and family mental health for decades. In this book he has created something of great value. He summarises much research, making it accessible to those who wish to know more, as he draws on over half a century of thinking and learning about human infants and their mothers and fathers.

I'd like to say read and enjoy, but it's more a case of read and weep. Or better still, read this body of work to find confirmation and a spur to put love back at the top of the list for building a human race that is still here in a century's time; because if we don't learn to love our babies, our earth, and each other, very fast, we will disappear. It has already begun, and there isn't a moment to lose.

Steve Biddulph

Psychologist and author, *Raising Babies*

Thoughts of a baby lying in a child care centre

THOUGHTS OF A BABY LYING IN A CHILD CARE CENTRE

I can't believe it! My *own* mother — who I want to be with more than anything in the world; my mother — font of all goodness and warmth, dumps me here in this horrendous crèche. I can't believe it!

Call her a cruel, ignorant, selfish bitch if you like, but I will defend her. She is my mother and I think the WORLD of her.

She is above reproach! She is my wonderful, only mother. The failure is mine. I take full responsibility. Clearly I haven't got what it takes to keep her hanging on. It's my problem. I'm such a bore! Such a nerd.

After all, let's face it, she's got her life and, well, — the writing's on the wall — I'm not that attractive to her which is hardly *her* fault — in fact I'm fairly repulsive come to think of it. I *must* be.

I hate myself for this. I'm angry at myself for being so slack and stuffing up the relationship. I'm so STUPID I've lost her and it's all MY FAULT! I can't believe it! What a fool!

One thing's for sure. I'm going to get myself back for this one day. I'll punish myself! And serves me right too. She might like that. She's a good woman.

Leunig

© **1995 by Michael Leunig**. Used with permission.

Cartoonist's interview

Late Night Live: **Dec 5, 2007**
Australian Broadcasting Corporation

Philip Adams: I'm talking to Australia's most remarkable cartoonist, Michael Leunig.... The most hated cartoon of yours was the one that had a baby speculating on its absent mother. Could you remind the listener of this incredible attack on feminism and political correctness?

Michael Leunig: Without having it here in front of me, it was my way of kind of illuminating this emerging disaster I thought was happening in the culture of maternity and early childhood emergence and development. I thought 'There's a disaster shaping up here, and it's the abandonment of babies, essentially, and the abandonment of mothering,' and so I made this little tale of the baby and its imagined thoughts, as mother puts it in the crèche and goes off to pursue her career—it was a female baby, you see. So I was picking up—it's a very elaborate idea and a cartoon can't handle such a complex question. And lo and behold, there wouldn't be too many early child development psychologists and people who have studied this who would disagree with it. They would say 'Y-yes; the mother leaves, and something starts to change.' And a lot of this came from my concern for the work of the great Donald Winnicott—the very wonderful British psychoanalyst of the 40s and 50s, the man who did the great work—he was England's answer to Freud and Jung and everyone else—so many women know the truth of this anyway.

Creativity, women, and parenting

For most of the past century, concepts of intelligence have been dominated by the attributes that psychologists identify and measure in tests. However, this view ignores the very different and crucial qualities involved in emotional intelligence and creativity. These are important in parenting and can be actively developed by the parenting experience.

The dormant creativity of many adults is awakened through imaginative interaction with their children. Many characteristics typical of creative people are readily evoked in parenting—for example, humour, playfulness, curiosity, flexibility, high intrinsic motivation, sensitivity, spontaneity, tolerance of incongruity, and experiencing deep emotion. Life with young children provides continuous opportunities for identifying problems and solving them creatively. Since young children are often unable to indicate their purposes or problems clearly, the parent's challenge is to clarify the problems experienced by the child and negotiate solutions.

The value of love and dedication in parenting is universally recognised. If we also placed a high value on the emotional intelligence and creativity involved in sensitive parenting, the social status accorded this role would rise. The insight and skills required for managing emotions and relationships are increasingly valued in the workplace. Men and women who use their interpersonal skills in the public arena are applauded. Yet those who use such skills in the private world of parenting are so lacking in status that they may wonder how to explain this period of their lives in their CVs.

Parenting is currently in a state of flux where, more than ever before, each individual chooses whether to become a parent, and then what sort of parent to become. It is a special opportunity for personal development wherein you can become a creative artist, choreographing your own dance in partnership with your child.

Jenny Cullen

Table of Contents

Synopsis
Part One: Five lines of evidence for natural, 'best-fit' mothering   5
Part Two: When the environment does not match early needs   6
Part Three: Conclusions and what can be done   8

Introduction   9

Part 1: Five Lines of Evidence for Natural, 'Best-Fit' Mothering

1. Our pedigree for success in mothering
Facts deduced by considering direct maternal ancestors   13
The nature of baby girls, boys, and young children   15
Our paternal ancestors   17
How our genome developed: the evolution of mammals & humans   18
The length of our maternal pedigree   19
Human babies as exterogestates – 'kangaroo care' and carrying   21

2. Breastfeeding and its health significance
Breastfeeding   23
The many benefits of breastfeeding   24
Breastfeeding and intelligence   26
Breastfeeding, love, and brain development   28
Breastfeeding, the economy and 'working' mothers   29

3. Attachment, John Bowlby, and pre-war London doctors
Attachment essential for all mammals   33
Attachment, separation, John Bowlby and James Robertson   34
Attachment, separation, in Swedish study of reactions to childcare   38
Webcams in daycare?   39
Pre-war London doctors' conclusions supported by recent research   40

4. Mothering, hormones, brain activities, and love
Early Years Study 2 – Mothering and brain development   43
Early formation of brain pathways, languages, and early memories   46
Brain studies of mothering in humans and other mammals   48

5. Comparing some effects of mother-care and daycare
Studying the effects and risks of early non-family childcare   51

The NICHD Longitudinal Study into effects of early childcare	53
Security of infant-mother attachment	54
Ideology masquerading as science	55
Wider societal effects of early non-maternal childcare	56
Inherent problems of research into early non-family childcare	56
Absence of normal infant-carer 'joint attention sequences'	57
Raised cortisol levels during childcare still abnormal at age 15	58
Such experiences disrupt brain architecture - "we see it happening"	60
Can high quality non-maternal childcare be harmful?	60
A report on raising childcare staff-infant ratios from 1:5 up to 1:4	61

Part Two: When the Environment Does Not Match Early Needs

6. How 'eco-genetic' mismatch can affect health

Mismatch between our environment and our biology	64
Health implications of hunter-gatherer genes	65
Eco-genetic mismatch, pregnancy and early child development	66
Our socio-cultural environment in a biological perspective	67
Eco-genetic mismatch and social settings relevant to parenting	68
Nature's rewards and satisfactions	70

7. Early civilisations and environmental change

Males, aggression, power, psychopaths, slavery, and war	73
The Tragedy of the Commons	74

8. Are children born as Jesus saw them, or with original sin?

Christianity and children	77
The doctrine of original sin–misinterpreting the nature of the child	78
Some 20th century versions	82
Psychoanalytic theory and the misreading of the normal baby	83
Two contrasting approaches to childrearing	87

9. The fateful hoaxing of Margaret Mead

Margaret Mead and her influence	90
Cultural Determinism – an antidote to Social Darwinism?	91
The hoax, and *Coming of Age in Samoa*	93
Mead tells of her lies, in a book called *All True!*	99
Was Mead's *Coming of Age in Samoa* "just plain rubbish" ?	100
On being a heretic – follow the facts	102
Freeman's "swept clear the faulty foundations of his discipline"	103

10. Social sciences detach from biology

Is sociology "a mess"? 105
How the 'blank slate' theory of the child, and behaviourism,
influenced childrearing 106

11. Equality feminism – and mothering denied

"Women should not have that choice" 110
Feminist icons recant 110
Mothering denied 112
The removal of "mothering" from the lexicon of family policy 113
The juggernaut of "the childcare industry" 114
Is the term 'childcare' for infants often a euphemism? 117

Part Three: Conclusions and What Can Be Done?

12. What conclusions may we draw?

Was women's liberation misled by dogma and ideology? 120
Management of childbirth – "Like a snowball rolling downhill" 121
Can we evolve new humans to fit the childcare environment? 122
Love, alloparents, & compartive costs of childcare and mothercare 122
Potential costs of total 'collateral damage' in childcare policies 125
Universal, affordable, high quality childcare is an 'abstraction' 127
Professionals privately think mother-care is best in the early years 128
Mothering needs maternity leave and support 128
Mothering needs appropriate environments 130
Fathers' natural roles 130
Nurturing the natural child in the 21st century 131
It takes a child to raise a village 132
Normal infancy involves a love affair – it cannot be re-run later 133

Summary

Part 1: Five lines of evidence for natural, 'best-fit' mothering 136
  1. Some facts deduced from the pedigrees of maternal ancestors 136
  2. Evidence about the values of breastfeeding 137
  3. The importance of attachment between mother and baby 138
  4. Comparative behavioural and brain-imaging studies in humans 139
  5. Research into effects of early centre-based childcare during infancy 140
Part 2: When the environment does not match early needs 142
Part 3: Conclusions and what can be done 144

Notes

Note 1. When is an infant no longer an infant?   146
Note 2. Genes, chromosomes and DNA   147
Note 3. Infant distress and disturbance in Swedish childcare   151
Note 4. Bevan-Brown and Baby's Point of View   153
Note 5. Dr Truby King's ideology   155
Note 6. Abstract: Childrearing, culture and mental health
   Table: Comparing approaches   157
Note 7. Margaret Mead and Samoa: Freeman *was* right after all!   160
   7 A. The film by Frank Heimans, *Margaret Mead and Samoa*   160
   7 B. Margaret Mead tells of her lies, in a book called *All True!*   163
   7 C. Mead's 'hunches' that went on to influence feminism   164
   7 D. Derek Freeman's health   165
   7 E. Cultural relativism and women's rights   165
Note 8. De Beauvoir – Two concerns
   8 A. "No woman should have that choice"   166
   8 B. "I am astonished when I realise how thoroughly I was cheated."   168
Note 9. Why daycare centres can't offer "high quality" infant care   171
Note 10. Child Psychiatrists' Daycare Memorandum of 1971   175
Note 11. A two-year-old's mother goes to hospital   176
Note 12. It takes a child to raise a village   179

References   180

Acknowledgements   193

Author's note   195

Postscript   198

Appendix 1. Do effects of early childcare extend to age 15?   200

Appendix 2. The dollar costs of suboptimal breastfeeding in US   202

Appendix 3. Six months breastfeeding lowers infection risk   203

Epilogue   205

Synopsis

Although the American Psychological Association has long declared that the word 'mothering' should generally be avoided, the facts of life remain unchanged. It seems that there is a natural, biologically based, best-fit pattern of human mothering that includes breastfeeding, carrying, secure attachment, mutual rewards, enjoyment, and empathy – that is, a mother's sensitivity to her baby's feelings and her appropriate response. Mutual playfulness and joy help to sustain healthy development if the environment is supportive and meets basic human needs. Five different lines of evidence now converge and complement each other to support this proposition. This is an example of 'triangulation,' where greater validity is achieved when multiple streams of evidence come from different directions and disciplines to support the same conclusion.

Part One: Five lines of evidence for natural, 'best-fit' mothering

1) The facts about each person's line of direct maternal ancestors lead to some basic deductions about our human genomic inheritance and its relationship to mothering, infancy, human nature, and health. The word 'infant' is here used in its original meaning of a child in the preverbal stage of life.

2) Human breast milk has many unique short-term and long-term values for the health of human babies; no other milk is so well matched to the needs of human infants. Mutually satisfying breastfeeding brings many benefits for both mother and child, and it helps them to achieve their highest potential for physical and emotional health.

3) Secure attachment between a mother and her infant has been essential for the breastfeeding and survival of all mammals, including humans, during most of their life on earth.

4) In enjoying and caring for their babies, human mothers show a number of basic behaviour patterns that correspond to those that have been studied in other mammals, and human mothering depends on the same neuro-hormonal reward systems that are seen in these animals. Live brain-imaging techniques show that during mothering the same

brain centres are active, deep in the 'mammalian brains' of both humans and other mammals.

5) In comparison with the long-term development and wellbeing of children reared mostly by their mothers during infancy, there is increasing evidence that the placement of infants in non-family daycare during their early years involves risks to their healthy emotional and behavioural development. The more hours spent in childcare, the greater the risk of adverse effects. These include increased aggressiveness, disobedience, and abnormal blood levels of the stress hormone cortisol. In vulnerable infants, rearing in non-family childcare disrupts many processes that depend on normal mothering. The quality of family life is the most significant influence on a child's development, and non-family childcare is only preferable if the alternative would be worse.

Part Two: When the environment does not match early needs

The basic needs of infants arise from their biology, and this in turn is based on their human genes. If the conditions of the environment or ecology do not adequately meet the genetically based needs of the infant, the resulting mismatch may be termed an 'eco-genetic mismatch.' Disturbed development can arise when departures from the natural patterns of mothering involve a mismatch to the extent that it disrupts important biological mechanisms. Some of these mechanisms are sensitive and vulnerable, and many of the adverse effects of non-family childcare can be better understood when seen as arising from this kind of mismatch.

For humans, eco-genetic mismatches can lead to risks at any stage in life, but they can be especially risky when they interfere with normal biological processes during pregnancy, childbirth, and infant care. Such a mismatch can occur in other areas of life, and may arise from ignorance, customs, or misconceived social policies, advocated by proponents who, however well meaning, failed to understand matters that today are accepted as basic facts. Two that are considered here are still influential in Western societies, and can have ill effects on infants, families, health, and social wellbeing.

1) Though contrary to all the recorded sayings and actions of Jesus relating to children, the doctrine of original sin, with its strongly negative ideas about the basic nature of the infant, eventually became

authorised teaching in Western Christianity from 529 AD. It viewed the child's nature as inherently sinful, with great risk of awful and eternal consequences. Similar ideas have permeated much religious and secular advice about childrearing up to and including the present, and they also appear to have shaped psychoanalytic theory. Sometimes they have been sadly counter-productive, leading to disturbed parent-child relationships, psychological and behavioural maladjustment, and child abuse. Moreover, as this cultural process undermined many of the natural rewards of mothering and fathering, it, together with other societal changes, prepared the way for another, compounding, set of problems.

2) The much-needed movement to 'liberate' women might have fought for a maternal feminism that included equal rights for women. However, 'equality feminism' focused on equality with men, legally and in the workplace. It denied that there was any special value in early mothering, and this was (and often still is) regarded as being no different from fathering. 'Mothering' and 'fathering' were replaced by words with a different meaning – 'parenting' and 'caregiver' – and it has become politically correct to require the use of these words.

In their agenda for the advancement of women, equality feminists relied on cultural determinism – an ideology that denied the influence of biology in most aspects of human nature and behaviour. Unfortunately, cultural determinism was itself fundamentally misconceived, because it depended on anthropological information that was untrue and arose from a hoax.

Instead of seeking support for mothers who had become separated from their extended families by societal changes, equality feminists engineered social policies that pressured women back into the 'workforce,' mostly against their real wishes, as if rearing infants only involves 'work' when you are not the mother. Ignoring research evidence about the risks and possible ill effects that are involved, some childcare advocates still talk as if infants, even from a few weeks of age, can be safely reared in institutional daycare centres. A powerful and costly childcare 'industry' has developed, with vested interests in early childcare and early learning, and it often has large public subsidies.

Part Three: Conclusions and what can be done

While there has been an explosion of interest in 'early education,' it remains very important to distinguish the needs of children approaching school age from those of infants, whose primary needs revolve around good early mothering. Since support of mothering cannot so readily become an academic or government activity, or a profit-making industry, it has received much less attention. These needs are best met by a healthy mother and, hopefully, an empathic father, within a supportive environment.

There is much that we might do. We could aim to bring our society – that we *can* change – into better harmony with our biological 'givens' that we *cannot* change and would therefore do well to accept. This involves allowing maternity leave for up to three years, and supporting healthy mothering, breastfeeding and attachment. The natural patterns of mothering work best if help is available through an extended family and/or social group in a suitable environment. There are models we could follow that include other family-friendly provisions for mothers and fathers, and these are likely to have long-term benefits, even for 'the economy.'

It is necessary to work with Nature and not against her if we are to promote health and wellbeing in young children, their mothers, and society. We were all babies once, and a normal mother-child relationship is a love affair that needs the right conditions to flourish. Infancy cannot be re-run later.

Introduction

This book is partly a sequel to, and an update of, my book, *Early Child Care: Infants and Nations at Risk*, published in 1996. As updated in 1997, it remained in print for ten years. Since then the early childcare situation has worsened in some ways, but there has also been an explosion of new research, activity, and concern. This book outlines how increasing bodies of evidence converge from different disciplines to support its main thesis about the nature of healthy mothering during infancy, and its long-term importance. It also describes how our culture became seriously deviant in some ways that have adversely affected infant nurture. Finally it offers suggestions as to what we might do about it.

Since 1900 there have been vast increases in knowledge about our biology, our health and how we relate to other living creatures on the earth. Yet, in the West at least, the management of crucial stages of development in babies and young children is still greatly influenced by notions and social policies deriving from ill-informed ideas of the past, rather than from evidence-based understanding of healthy development and how to offer the best chance of raising emotionally healthy children and families.

The debate about early non-parental childcare and whether we should promote it, usually involves quoting studies of its various effects.[1] Yet, although millions of dollars have been spent on rigorous research, disputes continue about what the findings mean and whether ideological bias is influencing the studies and their interpretation. Moreover, early institutional childcare is likely to have effects that we cannot yet measure validly or at all (Cook, 1996: 58–73).

---

1. The words 'daycare,' 'childcare,' 'child-care' and 'child care' are all in current use to refer to the non-family, centre-based care of young children. It seems important to keep the two separated words 'child care' to cover their broader, literal meaning—the care of children in general. Thus 'child care' may include care by mother, father, a relative, family day care, or the institutional daycare of young children, after-school care, or indeed the whole subject of the care and welfare of children. The word 'daycare' can be used to include the care of persons of various ages in various contexts. In this book the word 'childcare' has usually been used, but where 'child-care' or 'child care' appear in quotations this spelling has been retained.

Throughout this book the word 'infancy' is used in its original sense, meaning 'without speech.' This does not cover just the first 12 months after birth but the whole pre-verbal period of childhood – that is until a child can understand speech and also communicate her point of view in words.[2] The term 'infant' comes from the Latin word *infans*, meaning 'without speech.' In the 1968 *International Encyclopedia of Social Sciences*, infancy is defined as the preverbal period of a child's life. On this developmental criterion, infancy may last for two and a half to three years (Rheingold, 1968; Room, 1999; Cook, 1996: 74–5; also see Note 1).

There is rapid expansion in the evidence about some of the material presented here, but there is little reason to expect that our broad understanding of the history of our species and the basic patterns of mothering by humans and other mammals will be invalidated by new information.

The book is in three parts, as outlined below. Before the main text there is a synopsis, and after the main text there is a fairly full summary that follows the same sequence as the main text, but without the references.

Part 1 consists of five chapters outlining the evidence from five different directions and disciplines that complement each other to support the same biologically based understanding of healthy mothering and the management of infancy.

Part 2 considers how mismatch between the environment on the one hand, and genetically derived biology on the other, can lead to failure to meet genetically based needs. The term 'eco-genetic mismatch' is proposed for this kind of disturbance, and it is suggested that this is a valid way of understanding some health and relationship problems that arise in human mothering, infancy and child development.

Part 3 offers some suggestions about what we could do to increase health and wellbeing for mothers, families and society.

---

2. The pronouns, he and she, his and hers etc., are used throughout to represent both sexes, except where the context makes it clear that the reference is either to a boy or a girl.

PART ONE:

FIVE LINES OF EVIDENCE
FOR NATURAL, 'BEST-FIT' MOTHERING

1

Our pedigree for success in mothering

All the world loves a baby, so it is said. We as a society do not act that way. A newborn baby is a re-affirmation of the miracle of the creation of life. Most infants are near perfect at birth and possess enormous potentialities for bringing deep joy to themselves and others.
—Joint Commission on the Mental Health of Children, 1969

The new evidence is a celebration of what good mothering has done for centuries. Parents have always known that babies and young children need good nutrition, stimulation, love and responsive care. What is fascinating about the new understanding of brain development is what it tells us about how good nurturing creates the foundation of brain development and what this foundation means for later stages of life.
—The Early Years Study, 1999

We must learn to work with Nature, not against it.
—Ian McHarg

It used to be generally acknowledged that infants in the early years need good mothering, but today, the words 'parenting' or 'caregiving' are used instead, and anyone can be a 'caregiver.'[3] Yet there is a mass of evidence affirming the nature and lifelong benefits of good early mothering. Fathers, relatives, and others who love the child can give valuable nurture during infancy, but there is no successful long-term precedent for raising infants in 'daycare' or 'childcare' institutions for most of their waking hours, without being cared for by anyone who will have an enduring relationship with them.

Although the American Psychological Association (American Psychological Association, 1995; 2005) has long declared that the word 'mothering' should generally be avoided, the facts of life remain unchanged. It seems that there is a natural, biologically based, best-fit

---

3. See Chapter 11: The eclipse of 'mothering.'

pattern of human mothering that includes breastfeeding, carrying, secure attachment, mutual rewards, enjoyment, and empathy – that is, a mother's sensitivity to her baby's feelings and her appropriate response. Mutual playfulness and joy help to sustain healthy development if the environment is supportive and meets basic human needs.

Five different lines of evidence now converge and complement each other to support this biologically based understanding of healthy mothering and the management of infancy. This is an example of 'triangulation,' where greater validity is achieved when multiple streams of evidence come from different directions to each support the same conclusion.[4] The first line of evidence is outlined in this chapter.

Some facts that may be deduced by considering our direct maternal ancestors

The genes of many plants and animals in use today have been selected by humans to bring out some characteristic that they valued, but this does not amount to a pedigree. For an animal to have a pedigree means that its ancestors have been selected by humans over a number of generations because they possessed some desired quality, and there is a record to prove it. For a thoroughbred racehorse to have a pedigree means that there are papers to show that its ancestors were winners over a number of generations – the more, the better.

Our own pedigrees are different and they were not selected in this way. Most generations were not recorded, but each of us actually has a long, direct maternal pedigree and a paternal one as well. Each woman in this pedigree was successful in the biological sense that she passed on her genes to the next generation. If we think about what must have happened in the lives of each of these women, we can deduce some

---

4. Triangulation—to find a point in space derived from three measurements—has long been used in surveying and map-making. Accuracy is confirmed if additional readings lead to the same point. The term is now widely used in other disciplines. The *Oxford Dictionary of Sociology* says: "Triangulation is an approach to data analysis that synthesizes data from multiple sources. Triangulation seeks to quickly examine existing data to strengthen interpretations and improve policy and programs based on the available evidence." Also "The use of at least three, but preferably multiple studies, theoretical perspectives, investigators, and data-sets for research on one issue or theme." www.enotes.com/oxsoc-encyclopedia/triangulation

basic and almost self-evident facts about mothering, infancy, health and some aspects of human nature.

Many people who lived in the past have no direct descendants alive today. Yet each person now alive had a mother who also had a mother, and so on, back through many generations. Each of these women was selected by Nature (and good luck) to win her place in our respective maternal pedigrees. She did this by giving birth to, and in most cases rearing, a healthy baby girl who grew up to do likewise.

If you imagine walking back in time past a line of your own direct maternal ancestors, you may picture each one of them as a woman, or as a little girl, or as a baby. If you imagine four of them in each metre (39.4 inches) and allow 25 years for each generation, then in one metre you would see your maternal ancestors over a period of 100 years. In twenty metres (22 yards) you could see all your maternal ancestors for the past 80 generations – back to the time of Jesus, 2000 years ago.[5]

Even if a woman died after childbirth, each woman was 'successful' in the biological sense of having passed on her genes to the next generation. To the extent that genes influence mothering, it follows that each woman in our respective lines of direct maternal ancestors had a pedigree for being well-equipped in her genes and biology to be a mother.[6] By this process through many generations, there was selection for those women whose genes best enabled them to survive successfully in the environmental conditions in which they lived.

Often the going must have been hard. If a baby or a little girl lost her mother, she needed to be appealing enough for her mother's sister or some other woman in the group to want to adopt and breastfeed her – otherwise she would have died. Their success was determined by having

---

5. James Ussher (1581–1656), who was Archbishop of Armagh in Ireland, and a man of vast learning, calculated that the world and its creatures were all created in 4004 BC. This date was long accepted with little question, although it does not appear in the text of the Bible. Right into the 20th century it was sometimes printed above Genesis Chapter 1 in the King James Authorized Version of the Bible. Some people still believe this date, but even within this time frame, the line of direct maternal ancestors would stretch back 60 metres—past 240 generations of women, each of whom won her place as a direct maternal ancestor by her success in a process of natural selection, without necessarily involving any evolutionary theory.
6. Nevertheless, in the absence of modern obstetrical care, a number of births can have serious, and sometimes fatal, complications.

the genes that were needed for good health in the environment prevailing at that time, and they also needed to be lucky. Good genes couldn't always protect them. These genes prescribed their biology and that of their infants so as to enable them to be as well equipped as possible to thrive in the conditions of their environment in that time and place.

The pedigrees of the men in our lines of paternal ancestors are considered only briefly here. They were selected simply for success in fathering a male infant who grew up to do likewise. For each of them, biological success was probably more likely if they supported the mother of their child, but this was not a prerequisite.

The genes that all humans have in common – the human genome – are a blueprint that comes with an implicit 'instruction manual,' because success does not come automatically. The healthy working together of all these genes, in the biochemistry and biology that they help to create and organise, depends on having a facilitating environment, both materially and socially.

For humans, the environmental necessities include fresh air, drinkable water, exercise, food matched to human needs, and shelter, all within a liveable climate. Our ancestors also needed the social support and protection of others, because the long dependency of young humans meant that it was not sustainable for mothers and infants to survive on their own, as some mammals – for example, bears – can do.

Returning to the implicit 'instruction manual,' we accept that any complicated mechanism must have inputs and usage that match its design specifications if it is to give long and reliable service. Even a tough, well-engineered Mercedes limousine will become sick if you ignore its instruction manual and design specifications, give it the wrong oil and fuel, and then use it like a tractor. If many people did this, it would not be a sensible solution to call on the government to provide more special Mercedes garages, and train more specialist mechanics to work in them. Yet our societies often do something like this with human health problems.

The nature of baby girls, boys, and young children

Our pedigrees also give important clues about the basic nature of babies and little girls. Although each woman was selected for her success in being a mother, she first had to succeed as a baby and then as a little girl. To do this she must, at each stage, have given enough rewards and pleasure to her mother, and perhaps to her father as well, for it to have been worth their while making all the sacrifices involved in rearing her. She must have done this through her appearance, her behaviour, and her generally appealing and rewarding qualities.

From birth, each infant had to give her mother powerful emotional rewards; otherwise why, over all those eons of time, would each mother without fail have done all that mothering? Nobody *made* them do it. Acceptance at birth and during infancy was not guaranteed. In some human groups a variety of factors – such as lack of appeal, too many other offspring, or a scarcity of resources – led to decisions as to which babies were worth the big investment needed to rear them. Eliminating unwanted babies sometimes occurs today, and it probably goes back long before human records. It is known to occur in many other species that regulate the number of their offspring according to the supply of resources likely to be available to sustain them (Hrdy, 1999).

So each little girl was selected for having genes from her ancestors that best enabled her to gain the love and nurture of her mother *and* the support of the social group in which she lived. The same logic applies to little boys.

There is therefore a biological basis to argue that while human babies are, like all living creatures, born with primary drives for self-preservation that must necessarily be 'selfish,' *they have also been selected for being rewarding, appealing, and innately social*. In other words, they are well made for social living. This is contrary to the assumptions underlying much writing about the need to 'socialise' the child, and it has far-reaching implications for more healthy ways of rearing infants and cooperative young people. Clearly, the impulses arising from these two primary drives must sometimes be in conflict with each other; an essential part of parenting is to help the toddler resolve these two conflicting urges so as to achieve a socially acceptable outcome in the long run, not necessarily immediately (Cook, 2005a).[7]

---

7. Cf. "The longer a creature stays young, the more perfect it is when it's finished" (Anon).

Our paternal ancestors

We each have a corresponding pedigree of direct paternal ancestors, and each one of them was successful in competing with other males to father at least one baby boy. This must have happened because that line of males survived through to the present time, as each of them passed on to his son a copy of his unique Y chromosome. Your father's Y chromosome had been passed on by each father in your direct line of paternal ancestors, and from generation to generation these Y chromosomes were copied without change, except very rarely when a mutation occurred.

However, there was no biological advantage in a man being a mighty hunter unless at least one of his own babies, and preferably also the baby's mother, survived. A precondition for the continuation of his line of Y chromosomes was that he had a baby son who had enough mothering, protection and support.[8] So the children of those fathers whose biology encouraged them to respond to their baby's cues and help the mothers rear them would have had an advantage in being selected to pass on their genes to the next generation.

Fathers do not have such powerful parenting help from hormonal influences as those that prepare a woman during her pregnancy, childbirth and breastfeeding to receive pleasurable rewards and good feelings from mothering. However, caring for infants can lead to some of the same hormonal responses in men and these help to increase their satisfactions in nurturing an infant (Hrdy, 1999).

The genes of a father who remained healthy and able to support the mother of his child were more likely to be carried on by his descendants because the loss of a father decreased the chances of his child's survival – especially if the mother took another mate, as is still the case today (Hrdy, 1999: 236).[9]

---

8. In the direct line of fathers, each passed on his Y chromosome to a son, while each mother passed to her daughter the DNA in her mitochondria—energy structures that are inside the cell but not in the nucleus. As a result, Y chromosomes can be traced back down the male line, and mitochondrial DNA can be traced back down the female line. In each case these are unchanged unless altered by a mutation, and this occurs very rarely (see Note 2).
9. Hrdy writes: "Child homicide in civilized societies is very much against the law and uncommon. Nevertheless, in North America when the father of offspring under two years of age no longer lives in the home and an unrelated man or stepfather lives there instead, this rare event is seventy times more likely to occur."

Whereas a woman knows that a child is her own, a man sometimes cannot be as certain that he is indeed the father of her child. In Nature, the female's interests lie in securing the sperm of the best male she can attract (mate selection), and in seeking quality rather than quantity. A male's interests lie in increasing his chances of having as many successful sons and daughters as possible (Tooley, 2002).

How our genome developed: the evolution of mammals and humans

In 1859, Charles Darwin concluded *The Origin of Species* with this paragraph:

> It is interesting to contemplate an entangled bank, clothed with many plants of many kinds, with birds singing on the bushes, with various insects flitting about, and with worms crawling through the damp earth, and to reflect that these elaborately constructed forms, so different from each other, and dependent on each other in so complex a manner, have all been produced by laws acting around us. These laws, taken in the largest sense, being Growth with Reproduction; Inheritance which is almost implied by reproduction; Variability from the indirect and direct action of the external conditions of life, and from use and disuse; a Ratio of Increase so high as to lead to a Struggle for Life, and as a consequence to Natural Selection, entailing Divergence of Character and the Extinction of less-improved forms. Thus, from the war of nature, from famine and death, the most exalted object which we are capable of conceiving, namely, the production of the higher animals, directly follows. There is grandeur in this view of life, with its several powers, having been originally breathed into a few forms or into one; and that, whilst this planet has gone cycling on according to the fixed law of gravity, from so simple a beginning endless forms most beautiful and most wonderful have been, and are being, evolved.

As outlined above, the biological givens that we inherit through our genes are the outcome of a long process of natural selection for being well made to survive in the environment of the time. This is not to overlook the fact that Nature makes 'mistakes,' since no such genetic copying is 100% accurate and abnormal mutations can arise from various causes.

Exceptions to being genetically well made are now surviving because some who would have failed to reproduce in earlier times are now being rescued by scientific medicine, including those who would otherwise perish in childbirth. But we cannot remake our genome and the biological mechanisms that it prescribes. So how was this genome refined, and under what conditions does it work well to give us good health?

The length of our maternal pedigree

Science provides abundant evidence that our maternal pedigree of baby girls who became successful mothers is of very ancient origin. Returning to the image of walking back in time past the line of your direct maternal ancestors (with four in each metre), then within 100 metres (110 yards) you would have seen each of your direct maternal ancestors over the last 10,000 years.

Most people at that time, and many since then, lived as hunter-gatherers, and before about 11,000 years ago they all did. In *The Seven Daughters of Eve*, Bryan Sykes (2001) tells how we know that most European women are descended from one of seven female ancestors; they lived at different times in what we now call The Middle East. The earliest of these women lived about 45,000 years ago.

We last shared a common ancestor with chimpanzees about 6 million years ago, after which our ancestral lines diverged.[10] Estimates vary on these figures, but the principles remain. To review your maternal ancestors back to this time, you would need to travel about 60 kilometres (37 miles) past a single, unbroken line of females, each of them being one of your direct maternal ancestors.

With rare exceptions, they would all have carried, played, worked, and slept with their infants, often skin-to-skin, and breastfed them frequently over as long a period of time as was mutually desired. Such feeding generally continued for long after the first year – often to age three or four, supplemented with other foods after teeth appeared. Such patterns

---

10. This raises the intriguing picture that our ancestral female at this 'fork' in the lineage must have been one of two sisters who had a small, but momentous, genetic difference. Our maternal ancestor had a mutation that led to her descendants becoming the line that led to humans, while her sister may have been 'the mother of all chimpanzees.' Their mother was ancestor to both!

of frequent suckling, day and night, tend to space siblings several years apart by delaying the return of ovulation.

Each pair was a nursing couple who would mostly have enjoyed each other's company within an extended family or social group, many of whom shared in the care of the infants. Most of our maternal ancestors did this under conditions that were in many ways less favourable by our standards than those widely available today; and yet, while many lines of inheritance dropped out, ours all succeeded.

It is awesome to realise that, as this planet was making its last six million cycles around the sun, there was always at least one of your direct, more or less human, maternal ancestors on earth being alive and successful. Such a continuum must command our respect. There was also a successful direct paternal ancestor somewhere, but the selection pressures for men were different.

Complex life on earth had been evolving for around 400 million years when the extinction of the dinosaurs 65 million years ago left a major ecological niche. Much of this was taken up by animals that were warm-blooded, and built to a plan that had been developing on earth for many millions of years. The mothers fed their babies with milk, and most of them developed breasts or mammae, so we call them mammals. Over time, some of them adapted to living in trees, and they developed grasping thumbs to live more safely in the branches, and binocular vision to judge distances more reliably. These animals – the primates – include lemurs, monkeys, and apes. The apes include us, and also chimpanzees, who are our nearest living evolutionary relatives. Their DNA is about 98.5% the same as ours.

However the significance of this figure is not clear, and as a great deal of DNA has no known function it was termed 'junk DNA' by some geneticists. In 2007, it was reported there are many differences between humans and chimpanzees in their junk DNA, and this called for a major re-think about how this junk DNA may have more important roles than previously understood (Note 2).

In this 'ascent' toward modern humans, there was a progressive development and expansion of the cerebral cortex – the outer part of the brain – but the more central anatomical and physiological features of the brain continued with relatively little change. These include the deep structures concerned with mothering – the 'maternal brain.' Nature is economical, and since the maternal brain had been tested and refined over millions of years and was working very successfully, it needed little modification to meet the needs of humans also. This is why we can learn much about our own patterns of health and disease from research with rats, mice and monkeys.

Human babies as exterogestates – 'kangaroo care' and carrying

Kangaroos and other marsupial mammals, instead of having a placenta, have a kind of exterior gestation, so they may be called 'exterogestates.' After birth, the tiny baby wriggles into its mother's pouch, latches onto a nipple and stays there until he is big enough to come out and explore the world. Then, if there is any sign of danger, a young marsupial can jump back into his mother's pouch until he has become too big. Attachment bonds still keep him near his mother, and if she is neglectful he is less likely to survive.

Of all the mammals that have a placenta, human babies are born at the most immature stage of development. After the nine months following conception, their brains continue to grow rapidly. If they stayed in the uterus any longer, there would be major problems for both mother and baby. To deliver a baby with a larger head, a woman would need a larger pelvis, but this would create other problems, such as making it harder for her to run. So Nature settled on the best available compromise.

Human babies are in some ways like exterogestates, since they are born more helpless than the babies of any other *placental* mammal. To survive in hunter-gatherer societies, as well as in more recent times, they each needed a mother who had a reliable attachment to her baby, and the baby, in turn, had to become strongly attached to the mother. A baby chimpanzee could cling to his mother's coat or walk soon after birth, but human babies needed to be carried for much of the time during this long 'in-arms' stage of development; this may be seen as one of their 'expectations' and it has been described as 'kangaroo care' (Liedloff, 1975; Adderly and Gordon, 1999). When infants could toddle or walk, survival still required that they stayed near their mothers until they could manage safely when she was not nearby.

A woman carrying a growing baby could not survive alone. To have the best chance of survival she needed the protection and support of her extended family and/or social group. This suggests that *the prolonged dependency of humans during infancy and childhood determined the type of social structure that gave them the best chance of surviving.* So humans must have been selected for surviving well within the competition of a generally cooperating social group. In her book, *Mothers and Others: The evolutionary origins of mutual understanding,* Hrdy (2009) shows how the long dependency of human infants, in requiring the help of "alloparents", also gave a survival advantage to those who were able to understand each other's feelings, as well as share and reciprocate in ways that are not seen in other primates (Hrdy, 2009).[11] As seen above, having an interested father increased a child's chances of survival – as is still the case today.[12]

Many human groups lived as hunter-gatherers until well into the 20th century. Despite great geographical differences, their infants all had similar experiences if they were living in a tropical or semi-tropical environment. Their mothers carried and slept with them, breastfeeding them frequently and joining in the work and play of their social group. These babies were in physical contact with someone for much of each day and night (Werner, 1972).

Before the revolutionary scientific advances of Western, evidence-based medicine in the 20th century, both children and adults perished easily, so they were familiar with tragedy and early death. Since the ancestral line of everyone alive today consists only of survivors, we may conclude that humans have been selected to have babies and little children who normally give pleasure, love and sometimes joy (all of which they receive in return) because their survival depended on it. They also needed good health, but they could not achieve all this success and good health unless their environmental conditions were sufficiently well matched to their genetically based needs.

---

11. Hrdy (2009: 22) defines alloparent: "An alloparent (from the Greek 'allo-' for 'other than') refers to any group member *other than* the parents who helps them rear their young."
12. See Footnote 9, this chapter.

2

Breastfeeding and its health significance

> Human milk is uniquely superior for infant feeding and is species-specific.... Exclusive breastfeeding is the reference or normative model against which all alternative feeding methods must be measured.
> —American Academy of Pediatrics, 2005

Breastfeeding

The three broad groups of animals that suckle their young are all called mammals.[13] The largest group have a placenta that nourishes the baby inside the uterus, so that by the time of its birth it has developed to a much greater level of maturity than occurs in the mammals that feed their babies in pouches – such as koalas and kangaroos.

Breastfeeding has been fundamental for the survival of all placental mammals, and the composition of their breast milk reflects their infant-care style. Some of them (for example, foxes) cache or hide their young while the mother goes away to hunt for food, and so she must feed them at longer intervals. They have evolved breast milk that is quite different in composition from that of mammals that carry their young and suckle them more frequently. The composition of human breast milk places us at the extreme end of those who carry their young and suckle them frequently (Blurton Jones, 1972). In primates, the larger the brain, the earlier the stage of development at which the birth has to occur. Humans have the largest brains, and hence they have the most helpless babies. Therefore other powerful methods are required to ensure survival.

A human baby who might cry could never be safely hidden in a nest or hollow while his mother went away in search of food. So suckling is not just for milk; it also has a comforting function that is sometimes called

---

13. The three kinds of mammals are: i) the monotremes, represented today only by the platypus and the echidna; they lay eggs, and after birth, their tiny young are suckled inside a pouch; ii) the marsupials, such as koalas, kangaroos, and many others; iii) the placental mammals.

'non-nutritional' sucking, and it helps to silence a baby. A pacifier or 'dummy' is an artificial substitute, as are other cuddly objects that sometimes become very important to infants.

During eons of natural selection, frequent breastfeeding over several years delayed the conception of the mother's next baby. This natural spacing of children could increase a mother's wellbeing in many ways. For example, it made her life easier if she had only one infant needing to be cared for and carried at any one time; this also gave the child a better chance of survival. Because each human baby needs such a large investment of maternal care and resources, the *quality* of the offspring was much more important than their *quantity* in the human struggle for survival. Over this long period, the composition of human breast milk became exquisitely matched to the changing needs of babies as they developed.[14] Some of the mass of evidence showing that breastfeeding has far-reaching importance for good health in childhood and throughout life is summarised in four authoritative reports outlined below.

The many benefits of breastfeeding

Three major reports about breastfeeding were outlined in *Equal opportunity for babies: breastfeeding as a strategic priority* (Cook, 2005b). These reports advocated breastfeeding for 12 to 24 months, and then for as long as mutually desired by both mother and child, with suitable complementary feeding after about 6 months of age. They say that such breastfeeding improves a child's prospects for physical, intellectual, and emotional health in childhood and throughout life. It also promotes bonding between a mother and her child, laying a foundation for a lifetime of wellbeing. Breast milk varies so that it contains the correct balance of nutrients, enzymes, and antibodies to suit different ages and stages.

The WHO and UNICEF published their *Declaration on the Protection, Promotion and Support of Breastfeeding* in 1990. They urged that:

> All governments should develop national breastfeeding policies and set appropriate national targets... creating an appropriate

---

14. Yet a mother's milk may still upset her baby if she eats exotic foods with chemistry outside the 'expectations' of her baby's 'design specifications.'

environment of awareness and support so that women can breastfeed in this manner.

In 2003, The National Health and Medical Research Council of Australia, in their *Dietary Guidelines*, said:

> The total value of breastfeeding to the community makes it one of the most effective prevention measures available and well worth the support of the entire community.

In 2005, the American Academy of Pediatrics (AAP) updated its policy statement, *Breastfeeding and the Use of Human Milk*. It could hardly be more emphatic, citing a large body of evidence in support of the benefits of breastfeeding for child and maternal health:

> Human milk is uniquely superior for infant feeding and is species-specific; all substitute feeding preparations differ markedly from it, making human milk uniquely superior for infant feeding. Exclusive breastfeeding is the reference or normative model against which all alternative feeding methods must be measured with regard to growth, health, development, and all other short- and long-term outcomes. In addition, human milk-fed premature infants receive significant benefits with respect to host protection and improved developmental outcomes compared with formula-fed premature infants.

The policy statement also described health benefits for the mother. Breastfeeding increases her level of the hormone oxytocin after delivery, resulting in less bleeding and more rapid recovery of the uterus; it also reduces the risk of ovarian and breast cancers later on. The cessation of menstruation during breastfeeding prevents blood loss and gives a mother better recalcification of her bones, reducing her risk of fractures later in life.

In 2007, the content and recommendations of these three reports were endorsed and extended in the Report to the Australian Parliament: *The Best Start: Report on the inquiry into the health benefits of breastfeeding* (House of Representatives Standing Committee on Health and Ageing, 2007). It concluded:

> These benefits are diverse, relating to the psychological, nutritional and cognitive aspects of infant development as well as maternal wellbeing... [they] are immediate and also persist until later in life.... Breast milk is also an environmentally friendly

product.... There is solid evidence for the protective effect against... gastrointestinal illnesses and middle ear infections.... The longer a baby is breastfed, the greater the protective effect against infections.

It said that breastfeeding may help to reduce sudden infant death syndrome, some childhood leukaemias, urinary tract infections, celiac disease, Type 1 diabetes, and obesity. The Report reiterated that breastfeeding also helps to protect against a range of chronic illnesses that can develop when the child becomes an adult. These include Type 2 diabetes, obesity, heart disease, atherosclerosis and high blood pressure. It adds, "these long-term health benefits can also have more pronounced effects at the population level, *with broader implications for economically sustainable health care.*".[15] Unfortunately, it logically follows that formula feeding increases the risks of all these disorders.

Again, evidence of health benefits for the mother is cited. The 2007 Report said that breastfeeding promotes recovery from childbirth and delays the return of menstruation and fertility. The extent of the maternal recovery process and suppressed fertility depends on the duration, intensity and frequency of breastfeeding. Emotional benefits are also described:

> The emotional closeness generated by breastfeeding benefits both the mother and the baby. It is a pleasurable and positive skin-to-skin interaction. The hormones oxytocin and prolactin are stimulated, reducing maternal stress and fostering emotional bonding.

Thus breastfeeding can benefit both mother and infant by increasing her satisfaction and pleasure in mothering her baby.

Breastfeeding and intelligence

In 2008 Kramer and his colleagues reported the findings of a major study, with the strongest possible evidence that breastfeeding does indeed *cause* an increase in intelligence.[16] They studied 13,889 babies

---

15. Emphasis added.
16. Many studies of infant feeding and intelligence show an IQ disadvantage for those who are formula-fed, but these studies are not able to 'prove' that formula feeding *causes* lower IQ, because the design of the studies comparing breastfed with non-breastfed babies should ideally control for differences such as the family background or parents'

children born at 31 maternity hospitals across Belarus between 1996 and 1997. They had previously randomly selected half of the hospitals to adopt supportive breastfeeding practices modelled on the WHO/UNICEF Baby-Friendly Hospital Initiative, while the other half of the hospitals continued to offer their usual postnatal advice to the mothers, and their babies were followed as the control group.

As each infant reached three months of age it was recorded whether or not that baby was still being exclusively breastfed. Of the babies whose mothers had received the usual post-natal advice (the control group), only 6.4% of these babies were still being fed solely on breast milk at three months of age. But among the babies whose mothers had given birth in hospitals implementing the Baby-Friendly Hospital Initiative program, 43% (*nearly seven times as many*!) of these babies were still being fed exclusively on breast milk at three months of age.

Each child was then tested at six and a half years of age; those who had been in the breastfeeding promotion group scored an average of 7.5 points higher in verbal intelligence tests, and 5.9 points higher in overall IQ tests, compared with the children in the other (control) group. Their teachers also rated the children who had been fully breastfed at three months as being more advanced in reading, writing and solving mathematical problems (Kramer et al, 2008).

---

intelligence in both formula-fed and breastfed babies. If breastfed babies have more intelligent parents because breastfeeding is an intelligent choice, then the breastfed babies could be smarter because of their genes, not because of what they were fed. The answer to this research problem is to do an experiment that *randomly* allocates babies to be breastfed or formula-fed, and then see if the children in the formula-fed group have lower average IQ than those in the breastfed group. However, because the importance of breastfeeding for babies' nutrition and health is so well established, this kind of experiment is not considered ethical. The cluster randomised design of the Belarus study therefore provides the most powerful evidence that is possible in this kind of research because, by randomly allocating the hospitals to be breastfeeding-friendly or not, the researchers could compare the average effect on the children's cognitive development of the resulting higher breastfeeding rates that eventuated in the two types of hospitals. In this sort of study, the results are not biased by differences in such variables as the mother's intelligence or her way of interacting with her baby because there is no reason to expect the mothers giving birth in the randomly selected 'experimental' BFHI hospitals were different in any way (for example, in age, education, intelligence, etc.) to those who happened to give birth in the 'control' hospitals. *So this experimental study provides strong possible scientific evidence that there is indeed a causal relationship between breastfeeding and higher intelligence.*

Breastfeeding, love, and brain development

These reports, like the Canadian report *Early Years Study 2*, and the research by Swain and co-workers (outlined in Chapter 4), all say that breastfeeding is a powerful aid in establishing a strong loving attachment bond between a mother and her baby. Much more is happening than just filling a baby with the best food. Nature has packaged many benefits into one essential activity and relationship. When breastfeeding does not go well, excellent relationships can still flourish, but either way, feeding her baby allows a woman to stay still and relax. In both animal and human studies, lactation hormones such as oxytocin and prolactin support and reinforce mothering behaviour (Uvnas-Moberg et al., 2001; Brunton et al., 2008).

Breastfeeding is not simply a matter of supplying better milk. In 1999, in *Reversing the Real Brain Drain: The Early Years Study*, McCain and Mustard, described the importance of sensory experiences during breastfeeding, including the opportunities for skin-to-skin contact. When a baby is being breastfed, cuddled and rocked in his mother's arms as she smiles and coos at him, his brain is busily receiving signals through sensations of warmth, touch, taste, sight and smell. There can be uniquely valuable moments of playfulness and mutual enjoyment (McCain and Mustard, 1999).

If a mother cannot breastfeed, then it is best if she can obtain another woman's milk to feed her baby.[17] She can still hold and cuddle her infant, offering warm skin-to-skin contact and attention during feeding.[18] Some mothers have been surprised to find that they have unexpectedly 'fallen in love' with their babies. This is another way of describing what the London pediatrician/psychoanalyst Donald Winnicott termed "primary maternal preoccupation." The quality of this early nurturing has long-term effects. In the first three years, when the

---

17. There are reports of increased employment of wet-nurses. The services of wet-nurses are reported to cost around $1000 per week in the US. In China the wealthy reportedly pay wet-nurses around $2,000 to $10,000 p.a. Also, there are human milk banks in several countries, including Australia, supplying donated milk from breastfeeding mothers.
18. When a baby is suckling from the breast in skin-to-skin contact, it is interesting to watch his hands as they explore and fondle the breast or any skin in that area. This may also happen with bottle-feeding, if the baby is held close to the skin. Corresponding movements may be seen in other mammals, as when kittens 'paw' the mother's breast to stimulate it as they suckle.

trillions of connecting pathways between the brain's billions of cell are being formed (or 'wired'), an infant's experiences during breastfeeding help to develop structures and functions of the brain in ways that enhance the child's sense of security and social relationships. This *sets the base* for many lifelong patterns, such as those of learning, behaviour and emotion. Breastfeeding also benefits the child's endocrine and immune systems by tempering the responses to stress, and so reducing the risks of disease throughout life.

Breastfeeding, the economy and 'working' mothers

In the 2007 Australian Government report, *The Best Start*, the House Standing Committee on Ageing and Health accepted evidence showing some far-reaching *economic* benefits of breastfeeding. Julie Smith, PhD, pointed out that it would be more accurate to say that these so-called 'benefits' are really the biologically *normal* level of health, and the effects of formula feeding are departures from this norm, with short-term and long-term health *risks* for infants and mothers. This is another way of putting the 2007 AAP Policy Statement's judgment that "Exclusive breastfeeding is the reference or normative model against which all alternative feeding methods must be measured with regard to growth, health, development, and all other short- and long-term outcomes" (Smith, 2004).

Some companies have found that a number of benefits can follow when suitable arrangements are made for mothers to bring their babies to work and breastfeed them if they wish. But it is difficult for a mother to breastfeed and care for her infant while she is employed in most of the paid jobs available to her. The facts and recommendations outlined above do not fit in easily with a mother's return to 'the workforce' in the early months, and they are studiously ignored in most discussions about the pros and cons of early childcare – perhaps because the case is unanswerable.

An Australian study of new mothers found that returning to work on a part-time or casual basis in the early months presents almost as much of a barrier to breastfeeding as working full-time. In a study of almost 3700 mothers six months after giving birth to their babies, 56 per cent of the women who were not working were breastfeeding, but this figure dropped to 44 per cent for women who returned to work part-time, and 39 per cent for women working full-time (Cooklin, et al., 2008).

A systematic review of evidence on the effectiveness of support for breastfeeding reported that mothers of premature infants were about *sixty* (60) times more likely to breastfeed successfully if they were referred to support groups run by women who have themselves breastfed (such as the La Leche League or the Australian Breastfeeding Association), when compared with mothers who received conventional standards of care (Renfrew, 2009).[19]

In some Western societies, for the sake of 'the economy,' women are urged, or feel pressured, into taking paid work outside the home in ways that prevent them from breastfeeding and mothering their own infants. Economists typically focus only on conventional market values, ignoring other economic values, and they therefore exclude the value of all the benefits that flow from the breastfeeding and healthy mothering of infants (Smith, J., Ingham, L.H., 2005). They continue to make the costly error of regarding such mothering as of no *economic* value to the community. As a small example: money spent on expenses associated with feeding modified cow's milk are seen as adding to the economy, while a woman who feeds her infant with her own breast milk and nurtures her family is seen as adding nothing to the Gross *Domestic* Product.

Although economists regard the GDP so highly as a measure of the health of the economy, it is a seriously defective measure of a nation's wellbeing. For example, if most of the things we buy were designed to fail or fall apart twice as quickly, and then had to be thrown away, it would boost a country's economy, its GDP, and its pollution; but not the happiness and wellbeing of its people or their environment. Some would benefit (temporarily) but the rest would have to run faster and faster just to stay in the same place (Cook, P., Coombs, J., 1975; Cook, 1995). Policy priorities based on such partial perspectives of economic value

---

19. Based on review of a number of studies of peer counselling interventions, including three randomised trials. The definition of 'standard care' varies from study to study—a problem generally in this kind of research, Standard care can be very different in different projects/locations/countries. In these particular trials, the intervention was compared with standard care defined either as Baby Friendly Hospital Accreditation only, or standard care including access to lactation consultants (Renfrew, 2009:48).

are distorted and biased against families' investment of time and effort in building human capital.

Implementing policies to support breastfeeding

In Norway in the 1970s, many active feminists also were amongst those who actively supported breastfeeding, so their work was mutually reinforcing (Austveg, B., Sundby, J. 1995). From the mid-1970s, the concerns of community-based support groups were quickly acknowledged and incorporated into national policy at the highest level.

High rates of bottle-feeding in Norway concerned Dr Gro H. Brundtland, who had trained as a physician and specialised in public health. She entered politics in 1965, and between 1974 and 1989 she served for various periods as Minister for Environmental Affairs, and then as Norwegian Prime Minister. She introduced measures that enabled mothers to raise breastfeeding levels toward world best practices. When, as an alternative to childcare, mothers were offered the option of long maternity leave and appropriate support, most preferred to stay at home, breastfeeding their babies for much of the first year rather than placing them in childcare and returning to paid work. Dr Brundtland saw this as the simplest and most strategic step she could take to bring many benefits to her country with just this one change in national policy. She went on to become Director-General of the World Health Organization.

In 2004 it was reported that in Norway about 98% of new mothers initiate breastfeeding, and 80% are still breastfeeding at 6 months. Around 75% of births are in hospitals that have been accredited as "breastfeeding-friendly", compared with just 30% in Australia, and even fewer in the US (European Commission. Directorate, Public Health and Risk Assessment, 2004).

Implementing such policies means ensuring that all women who wish to mother and breastfeed their babies have the opportunity and support that they need. There is ample evidence that implementing breastfeeding policies, as recommended in the reports discussed in this chapter, is the simplest and most far-reaching step that any government in a developed country can take to improve the health and intelligence of its people.

A study by Duijts et al. published in June 2010 in *Pediatrics*, the official journal of the American Academy of Pediatrics, concluded: "Our findings support health-policy strategies to promote exclusive breastfeeding for at least 4 months, but preferably 6 months, in industrialized countries." (see Appendix 3).

3

Attachment, John Bowlby, and pre-war London doctors

> Intimate attachments to other human beings are the hub around which a person's life revolves, not only when he is an infant or a toddler or a schoolchild but throughout his adolescence and his years of maturity as well....
> —John Bowlby, 1981. Concluding words in his trilogy, *Attachment and Loss*

Attachment essential for all mammals

Throughout the long history of mammals, it is self-evident that breastfeeding has depended entirely on the successful working of mechanisms for keeping a mother and her young near to each other. In humans, the attachment of a mother to her infant, and later of the infant to the mother was essential for continued breastfeeding and for the young to be protected and taught the skills needed to survive. Infants without such bonds of attachment would soon have perished.

Genes specify the mechanisms for this attachment through biochemical, hormonal, and neurological processes that create rewards, such as feelings of mutual attraction, satisfaction, joy, delight and love. The appeal of babies can work across species; the young of many animals appeal to humans, and sometimes to mothers of other species, as when a young animal is adopted and reared by a quite different mother. Many pets bought for their appeal when young become less appealing as they grow older.

Genes probably 'communicate' with us through promptings like maternal intuition, which must be much more ancient than language or culture. For example, film and video recording techniques have revealed the amazingly sensitive 'attunement' that occurs in normal mother-baby relationships. Their facial responses to each other can occur in fractions of a second, helping to harmonise the interactions of mother and baby from the earliest days. While the primary attachment is normally with mother, important secondary attachments occur if suitable people are available and dependable.

Since the separation of an infant mammal from its mother can be life-threatening, it sets off acute distress responses that take priority until the mother and her infant are reunited. For example, removing a tiny kitten from a litter can trigger a penetrating squealing, so that the mother is galvanised into action, leaving her other kittens huddled together while she retrieves her baby.

Attachment, separation, and the work of John Bowlby and James Robertson

The importance of attachment and separation in the development of humans and other mammals was established in the work of John Bowlby and James Robertson. Born in 1907, Bowlby gained experience in institutions for emotionally disturbed children, became a doctor, and trained as a psychiatrist and a psychoanalyst. Like the pre-war London doctors described below, he came to think that some of the serious disorders of the emotional life that he encountered in young people might be based in real feelings about real early-life events, and not just in infantile fantasies, as orthodox psychoanalysts insisted. To seek evidence as to whether serious emotional disturbance could be related to early environmental traumas, he decided to study young people who had a clear history of complete separation from their parents during infancy. These were events that could be documented and perhaps related to disorders that his young patients presented.[20]

In 1940 Bowlby published *The influence of early environment in the development of neurosis and neurotic character*, and he followed this with *Forty-four juvenile thieves, their characters and home lives* (1944). After leaving army service, he became Head of the Department for Children and Parents at the Tavistock Clinic in London in 1946. During World War II many young children were separated from their families and some showed much emotional turmoil, so the World Health

---

20. Karen (1994) presents details of Bowlby's childhood, training, and disagreements with other psychoanalysts.

Organization invited him to review all the evidence about the effects of separation experiences in early childhood. His resulting monograph *Maternal Care and Mental Health* was published by the World Health Organization in 1951, and it became a major milestone. It is more widely known as *Child Care and the Growth of Love* – the title of the abridged edition published later.

Bowlby began to explore how emerging new studies in animal behaviour and evolutionary biology might shed light on his findings. The fruits of this quest led to his three-volume work about attachment and the effects of separation. *Attachment and Loss. Vol.1: Attachment* appeared in 1969, and it was followed by *Attachment and Loss. Vol. 2: Separation: Anxiety and Anger* in 1973. The final volume, *Attachment and Loss. Vol 3: Loss: Sadness and Depression,* was published in 1980. Much subsequent research has confirmed the far-reaching significance of early attachment and separation experiences.

A normal toddler explores the world from the 'secure base' of his mother, returning periodically to make sure that she is still there. If she is not there, he normally becomes anxious and preoccupied with searching for her. Secondary attachments – usually to father or related people – can provide additional security, but, unless good substitute mothering is available, prolonged separation of an infant from his mother can be a very stressful experience and may cause lasting psychological damage. This can occur even if all physical needs seem to have been met.

In his book, *Becoming Attached: Unfolding the Mystery of the Infant-Mother Bond and Its Impact on Later Life*, Robert Karen (1994) records the remarkable story of how the understanding of attachment and separation developed. Some of that story is summarised here.

Another early milestone, also in 1951, was when James Robertson, who had been working with Bowlby, made a short, silent, black and white film called *A Two-Year-Old Goes to Hospital*. Using a hand-held camera, and shooting at pre-determined intervals or on specified occasions, he portrayed a (randomly selected) little girl, Laura, aged 2 years and 5 months, as she was admitted to a London hospital for routine removal of her tonsils. This was a common operation in those days, and her mother saw her into her cot and stayed for a while, but eventually she kissed her goodbye. Laura was initially composed, but as she realised that her mother had left her there, the film poignantly showed how she developed acute and continuing distress. Visiting in those days was normally once a week, but at Robertson's special request the parents were allowed to visit every other day so that the child's reactions could be observed. When they visited, Laura pleaded to be taken home, but as her protests and pleadings were useless, they were gradually followed by despair. She became listless, unsmiling, and her traumatised emotional state was heart-rendingly clear, as she turned away from her mother on the occasions when she did visit the child during her eight days in hospital.

On return home, after some turmoil, Laura went through a period of anxiety and irritability, sleeping poorly, sometimes soiling herself, throwing tantrums and clinging to her mother. Five months later she had to stay with her grandmother for five weeks while her mother was in hospital. When her mother returned, she was greeted with a blank stare. A month later, Laura walked in on Robertson's screening of the film for her parents. She burst into tears and cried to her mother, "Where was you all that time?" (Karen, 1994: 79–80). Karen describes the reactions of doctors and nurses at professional screenings of this film. There was angry, and even furious, denial, with much abuse of Robertson and accusations that he had selected the moments of stress – something that he had carefully avoided doing. Eventually their eyes began to see what they had so long denied, and many wept. An elderly nurse told Bowlby, "This film brings back to me the first child I ever nursed in hospital. This child was a little boy. He grieved for his mother and it simply broke my heart. After that I never saw grief again until I saw this film."[21] *A Two-Year-Old Goes to Hospital* helped to initiate a revolution in the care of children in hospitals in the UK, and eventually the reforms became worldwide.

In the mid-1960s, James Robertson and his wife Joyce made a series of films called *Young Children in Brief Separation*. The first four films showed the reactions of four happy, healthy children in their second year who were cared for by Joyce Robertson in her home after they had already become accustomed to her, and their mothers were then hospitalised. They were much less disturbed through having one stable

---

21. Karen (1994) references this as cited from Tanner and Inhelder, 1971 p.223, but adds, "this is obviously not a direct quote, but Bowlby's memory of what she said."

mother-substitute; but the Robertsons concluded that "no matter how good the relationship, separation from the mother remains a hazard for the young child because of the discontinuity of the relationship" (Robertson, J. and Robertson, J., 1973, cited from Karen, 1994).

In 1969 the Robertsons released the film *John*. This showed how, despite being in a caring but large residential nursery, John aged 17 months deteriorated very seriously during a period of just nine days while his mother was having a baby. His efforts to establish a relationship with any nurses were dashed, as four different nurses cared for him, but they often had to attend to more clamorous children. By the fourth day he began refusing food, and by the time his mother came to take him home on the ninth day, he was a drastically changed child. He suffered emotional damage that was difficult to heal afterwards despite much psychotherapy.

Bowlby and Robertson described three phases in an infant's response to such separations. First came 'protest'; this was followed by 'despair,' and finally came 'detachment.' By this stage the infant appeared superficially settled, but a pattern of seeming not to care had also developed, and the child would turn away when approached by her mother. Some infants and little children also showed much emotional disturbance after returning home, and there are reasons to think that the residues of such painful separations can last for a long time. In the passage cited below, Bowlby vividly describes the typical reactions of a child between the ages of about twelve months and three years, when removed from his mother-figure to whom he is attached, and left full-time with strangers in a strange place:

> His initial response... is one of protest and of urgent effort to recover his lost mother. He will often cry loudly, shake his cot, throw himself about, and look eagerly toward any sight or sound which might prove to be his missing mother. This may with ups and downs continue for as long as a week or more. Throughout it, the child seems buoyed up in his efforts by the hope and expectation that his mother will return. Sooner or later, however, despair sets in. The longing for mother does not diminish, but the hope of its being realised fades. Ultimately the restless noisy demands cease; he becomes apathetic and withdrawn, a despair broken only perhaps by an intermittent and monotonous wail. He is in a state of unutterable misery.... A child's persistent longing

for his mother is often suffused with intense, generalised hostility (Bowlby, 1981: 9, 13).

Karen's book not only presents a detailed account of the development of attachment theory, but also the research and more recent perspectives that developed from Bowlby's studies. Mary Ainsworth developed a method of assessing the quality of an infant's attachment to her mother at around fifteen months of age. Called *The Strange Situation Test*, it was established as a valid and reliable instrument by the first studies of the Early Child Care Research Network (ECCRN) of the US National Institute for Child Health and Development (NICHD).[22]

Another easily preventable occasion of traumatic mother-infant separation used to occur quite frequently when a mother went to a maternity hospital to have another baby. She might stay there for up to 14 days 'rest,' but her two-year-old child was not allowed to visit her during this time. In *A two-year-old's mother goes to the maternity hospital*, three clinical accounts were presented and discussed. An account of this situation by the mother's sister is appended in Note 11. It appears that much of what had been seen as inevitable 'sibling rivalry' was a reaction initiated and fuelled by the preceding emotional upset when a two-year-old child was separated from his mother for up to 14 days. When she returned home *with another baby in her arms*, he was supposed to be pleased! As there was no scientific justification for preventing these young siblings from visiting their own mothers while they were in maternity hospitals, this custom was soon changed to allow infants and young children to visit their mothers in maternity hospitals (Cook, 1962; Cook, 1977; also see Note 11).

Attachment, separation, and Harsman's study of reactions to childcare

Though Bowlby's work and the Robertsons' films led to world-wide reforms in the care of children in hospitals and other institutions, many childcare advocates argued that these findings had no relevance to the briefer but repeated separations of institutional long-day childcare – especially if it was of 'high quality.' Realistic criteria for high quality in

---

22. This Network and its first study are outlined in Cook, 1996, and a postscript in the 1997 reprint summarized results up to three years. Some more recent NICHD ECCRN findings are in Chapter 5.

childcare were seldom specified, and much research has shown that claim to be untrue.

In 1994, Ingrid Harsman reported her observations of two matched groups of babies who, during their early months, were all cared for at home by their mothers and breastfed. She then described their progress as one group went into high quality Swedish daycare, while the other group of babies remained with their mothers. The two groups were matched and controlled, and the effects on attachment, relationships and behaviour in both groups were recorded in writing, but unfortunately *not* on film. The study had to finish after five months, but the results showed grounds for serious concern about the future of some of the childcare babies. Disturbing reactions were seen following admission to daycare at ages varying from 6 to 12 months, and fifty-two per cent "showed a negative change in mood during the initial period and they were assessed as sad and depressed in the daycare setting." Two or three of these infants "reacted in line with the classical phases of 'protest and despair.' " Overall, their developmental scores fell behind those of the infants who remained at home. The full Report is in Swedish, but a summary of the study and its findings, in English, is in *Early Child Care* (Cook, 1996: 102–106; also see Note 3).

Webcams in daycare?

James Robertson's film, *A Two-Year-Old Goes to Hospital,* opened people's eyes to the emotional reactions of a child during such an experience, and it initiated reform in the care of children in hospital. But a 'James Robertson' of childcare, who produces a film such as *A Two-Year-Old Goes to Childcare,* has yet to appear. He or she is urgently needed, as there appears to be no available film showing how infants, aged from (say) 3 months up to 24 months, react in the days, weeks, and months after placement in institutional childcare.

Today, with webcams, and cameras in mobile phones, it is easy for people to be observed almost anywhere. But this facility is not generally available to parents who leave their babies and young children in childcare. Nevertheless, there *is* a daycare centre where a webcam provides this transparent service to offer you peace of mind – you can watch your loved one with new friends, and enjoy the games they are playing, while you are at work. It can be seen how socialisation reduces separation anxiety and nervous behaviour; it also helps to maintain the highest quality and standards within the centre, making it a fun and safe environment for all to enjoy. Protected by a personal password, this webcam view is available on the Internet at any time. However, this access is strictly for clients of Dogs@Play Daycare, where all this and more can be learned about "Sydney City's most trusted and established Dog Daycare Centre" (www.dogsplay.com.au/daycare.html).

Perhaps modern technology offers a way of achieving a revolutionary advance in the quality of early childcare for young humans. In the interests of high quality assurance and parental peace of mind, the providers of daycare should be (and hereby *are*) challenged to make a comparable service available, particularly for parents of infants up to two years of age. This could help to bring baby's point of view and feelings into public consideration, as Robertson's film did for children in hospital in 1951. It could also lead to mothers being equally supported, whether they choose daycare or to nurture their babies at home and breastfeed them if they wish.

Pre-war London doctors' conclusions are supported by recent research

> The child must *feel* loved.
> —Bevan-Brown, 1950

Much of the general theme of this material was understood and published before and after World War II by a number of medical doctors who were associated with the Tavistock Clinic in London. While accepting the importance of Freud's findings, they dissented from some basic aspects of his theory, in that they adopted a more biological, eclectic approach that emphasised the importance of healthy early nurture for future mental health.

These medical pioneers in psychological healing included Dr J. A. Hadfield, who published from the 1920s into the 1960s. His *Psychology and Morals: An Analysis of Character* was published in 1923, while his *Psychology and Mental Health* appeared in 1950, and *Childhood and Adolescence* in 1962. "The mother: agent or object?" by Drs Ian and Jane Suttie appeared in 1932 in the *British Journal of Medical Psychology,* leading up to Ian Suttie's major critique of Freudian theory in *The Origins of Love and Hate*, published in 1935, around the time of his premature death. Suttie's Introduction to this book lists the references to eight of his papers that were published in reputable journals between 1922 and 1933.

In his preface to *The Origins of Love and Hate*, Hadfield wrote:

> The starting point of his [Suttie's] conception of human life and development is the 'need for companionship,' a fact that can be objectively observed in the behaviour manifestations of early childhood and in animals. Upon this need Dr Suttie founds his conception of love, and his insistence upon this factor, as against the Freudian theory of sex, is fundamental to his system.... His [Suttie's] view differs from Freud's in that it assumes only the one primal factor, love, and makes anger and hate the frustration-reactions of love.

Hadfield added, "Most of the disorders in early childhood, in our opinion, originate in a lack of security and love, rather than in incestuous desires;..." Dr Joyce Partridge was also in this group, and her little book *Baby's Point of View* was published in 1937 by Oxford University Press; it is a gem that has long been out of print (Note 4). Other publications followed, but in 1939 in *Clinical Studies in Psychopathology* H.V. Dicks wrote, "The leaderless eclectics in London have perhaps felt unnecessarily diffident about publishing systematisations of their views in the face of the homogeneous bodies of psychoanalysts and of other 'schools' all marching in step..." (Dicks, 1939; Dicks, 1947: 14).

Dr C.M. Bevan-Brown, who was associated with these colleagues in London for many years, returned to New Zealand in 1940. He published *The Sources of Love and Fear* in 1950, and emphasised the basic importance of a mutually satisfying early mother-infant love relationship, often centred in experiences during breastfeeding. He would ask, "how, when, and why did this person become ill?" Other issues relating to primary prevention in mental health, such as natural childbirth as pioneered by the obstetrician Dr Grantly Dick Read (1942), were also covered in *The Sources of Love and Fear*.[23]

In 1950, Hadfield wrote:

> In our experience *the basic cause of the psychoneuroses is the feeling of deprivation of love, the repressed craving for love*....

---

23. *The Sources of Love and Fear* was published in three countries, and second-hand copies may generally be found through www.abebooks.com.

> The most fundamental need of every child is for protection and security: this is involved in the very nature of childhood itself, for during infancy the child is helpless to care for itself and must have the protective love of others. The need is *biological*, for the child is in fact dependent on others for its very life, for its food, its warmth, its safety from danger. But this need is also *psychological*: for the child not only needs protection but *feels* the need of it. This need... is normally provided for in the care and tenderness of the mother... so that the mother's love becomes the central fact of the child's life... But because this protective love is first experienced in close contact with the mother it is also associated with sensuous pleasure, so that the mother becomes the main object of pleasurable desire. The main function of maternal love is to satisfy the child's needs for protection and security: the sensuous pleasure accompanying it both in mother and child encourages the mother to give such love and the child to seek it (Hadfield, 1950: 120–122, original italicisation). [24]

This was well before Bowlby published his works on attachment and separation.

As described in the next chapter, much recent research also supports conclusions published by Bevan-Brown in 1950, when he wrote:

> "a child's mother is, or should be, the first person in the world with whom he associates. She represents the first personal relationship, the first social relationship, the first sensuous relationship, the first love relationship... this relationship being the first, sets the pattern of all subsequent relationships." (Note 4).

---

24. Hadfield goes on to cite R.S. Briffault (1876–1948), a British medical anthropologist, who wrote *The Mothers* (1927), in which Briffault sought to show that all simply structured cultures are basically matriarchal.

4

Mothering, hormones, brain activities, and love

> Pregnancy and motherhood change the structure of the female mammal's brain, making mothers attentive to their young and better at caring for them.
> —Kinsley and Lambert, 2006

> Parenting behavior critically shapes human infants' current and future behavior.... An integrated understanding of the brain basis of early parenting has profound implications for mental health.
> —Swain et al., 2007

Early Years Study 2 – Mothering and brain development

Early in 2007, the Canadian Report, *Early Years Study 2: Putting Science into Action*, by Margaret McCain, Fraser Mustard, and Stuart Shanker, summarised extensive new evidence about the importance of early experiences for the full development of the *structure* of a baby's brain, and also for its *functions*, and its lifelong *settings* for coping with life.

It was a sequel to their 1999 Report, *Reversing the Real Brain Drain: The Early Years Study*, and they said that this Report had had an "electrical effect on the scientists working in the area of early child development." By 2007, it needed to be updated to take account of scientific advances in developmental neuroscience during the previous eight years. It also reported on the progress made in Canada to implement the recommendations of the 1999 Report.

Early Years Study 2 adopted an evolutionary approach to the infant and the lifelong importance for optimal brain development of natural mothering and fathering within a conducive social milieu. In essence, it advocates working with nature. The Study describes the vital importance of caregivers offering support to nurturing mothers, as they touch, hold, breastfeed, carry and enjoy their infants. It also documents the heavy price our societies pay – and will pay for generations – if we keep on failing to meet these needs. Reciprocal and mutual experiences in the relationship between infants and their mothers or mother-figures are not optional luxuries; they are essential for full brain development, because they build "pathways for learning and health.... Experiences in early life activate gene expression and result in the formation of critical pathways and processes. Billions of neurons in the brain must be stimulated to form sensing pathways that influence a person's learning, behaviour, and biological processes that affect physical and mental health."

The Study outlines the relevant areas of the brain in these words:

> Neurons are the basic building blocks of the brain. Based on genes and experience, neurons are connected to form networks. Networks that are underdeveloped are pruned. Each stage of the brain's development rests on another. The brain includes the cerebrum, brain stem, limbic system, and the cerebral cortex. The limbic system includes several structures that are central to a wide array of body functions, including the thalamus, hypothalamus, hippocampus, and amygdala. The cerebral cortex is divided into the frontal lobe (which includes the prefrontal lobe), parietal lobe, temporal lobe, and occipital lobe. The cortex in the human brain is significantly larger than the cortex found in other mammals, including monkeys and chimpanzees (p.18).[25]

For some areas of the brain there are critical periods during infancy. If healthy stimulation is not given at this time, then deficits occur in the development of the corresponding regions of the cerebral cortex. In the 'pathways' for vision, such deficits cannot be corrected later. In the hearing pathway there seems to be a similar critical period. Pathways for general coping are influenced by early sensory stimulation, including touch. Incoming sensory stimuli activate nerve cells deep in the

---

25. These brain areas, present in all mammals (but not reptiles) include the 'mammalian brain'. Diagrams and an account of their functions may also be seen in: Kingsley, C.H. and Lambert, K.G. (2006). The Maternal Brain. *Scientific American*, Jan 2006: 58-65. The rather forbidding anatomical names of these structures, being international, are derived from Greek and Latin. Thus, from Greek: *neuron*—nerve; *thalamus*—a chamber or receptacle; *amygdala*—amygdale, almond; *hypo*—under or below; *epi*—on, near, above, in addition; *nephros*—kidney. From Latin: *cortex*—bark or outer layer; *limbus*—border; *renal*—kidney; *pituitosus*—secreting, to separate. For diagrams see figures 1.1 to 1.4 in McCain and Mustard, 2007
action.web.ca/home/crru/rsrcs_crru_full.shtml?x=98547.

thalamus of the brain – a reception centre where incoming messages are processed so that alerting responses can be interpreted and integrated with other neural pathways.

Some signals go to nerve cells in the cortex – the outer and most recently expanded layer of the brain – to bring the message to conscious awareness. Other signals go to the amygdala – a deep brain centre that acts as a kind of sorting station. Through these centres, the capacity to cope and deal with daily life, its challenges, potential threats and new situations, is controlled by a set of interrelated neural pathways and hormonal systems, that are 'set' early in life.

The best known is the fight-flight-or-freeze response that operates immediately, primarily through the autonomic nervous system. The adrenal glands release into the bloodstream a shot of adrenaline (norepinephrine), and this rapidly increases the rate of the heart and respiration and also enhances the senses.

There is another pathway that acts more slowly. It is made up of the limbic system in the brain – the hypothalamus, the pituitary gland, and the adrenal glands; the authors refer to it as "the LHPA pathway." When aroused by incoming stimuli, nerve impulses trigger the hypothalamus to get the pituitary gland to send a hormonal signal to the adrenal gland to release another hormone – cortisol. This has a powerful impact on many bodily and brain functions to help them cope with emergencies and stressful situations.

Experiences early in life, particularly the quality of nurturing and sensory stimulation during infancy, establish lifetime *set-points* for coping with stress throughout life. Excessive or prolonged stress leads to wear and tear on tissues and organs, and can result in chronic physical and mental disease.

Early Years Study 2 summarised evidence that:

> Humans, like all other mammals, are born with a number of mechanisms to promote mother-baby attachment. New-borns are perceptually attuned to the human face, voice, touch, taste, and even movements, with a marked preference shown to the mother, or primary caregiver. Infants have reflexive behaviours that automatically evoke caregiver responses, the most important of which are crying, smiling, gazing, cooing, and imitation.

Caregivers exhibit a number of behaviours that suggest humans are pre-adapted to nurture our infants. Even in very noisy environments, mothers can hear their own infant crying, and distinguish between their own infant's smell and that of other infants; and they also unconsciously fine-tune their behaviours in order to help their infant master verbal, social, and cognitive skills.

A new infant, guided by smell, will search for the breast and begin rooting and suckling. This reflexive behaviour, which dramatically reduces infant crying, also triggers a surge of oxytocin in the mother, which is vital for attachment, and a gastro-intestinal hormone that enhances the mother's capacity to cope with the caloric demands of breastfeeding. But perhaps the most striking is the discovery that the newborn's 'search' for the breast enhances her olfactory learning about the environment. This effects the expression of the serotonin receptor genes that will affect adult behaviour and health and has an overall organizing effect on the development of the brain (McCain et al., 2007: 47–49).

Early formation of brain pathways, languages, literacy, and early memories

Although few people can remember any events from their earliest years, their far-reaching importance can be clearly seen in the way small children can learn two languages and speak them both without a foreign accent – an achievement beyond most people after childhood.

The *Early Years Study 2* says: "early experiences set up the architecture of the LHPA pathway and autonomic nervous system pathways. Lifelong patterns for coping with challenges and new situations become part of the brain's architecture.... There is a sensitive period in early life when the function of the LHPA pathway and related neural circuits in the brain are established. After the sensitive period has passed it is difficult to alter the function of these pathways.... Early experiences have a powerful influence on the neural pathways that underlie humans' capacity to use language, become literate, and understand the complexities of their environments."

The Study cites evidence that "by the time infants are a year old, they are no longer able to discriminate foreign contrasts in the same way that they were able to do at two to three months. Infants exposed to two languages (for example, Japanese and English) in the first seven to eight months of life will have little difficulty mastering the two languages and they will not have an accent.... Individuals who develop an understanding of two languages early in life have denser grey matter in the left hemisphere of the brain than individuals with monolingual backgrounds. They find it easier to learn third and fourth languages later in life. Neurons in the auditory cortex that respond to sound develop a sensitivity to the sounds of different languages in early life that make it easier to differentiate the sounds and develop the neurological pathways necessary for capability with multiple languages. Current research suggests that when a child is exposed to two languages or more from birth, both languages will be processed in the same neural systems, whereas when a child is exposed to a second language at a later point, different neural systems are used. The sound-sensing stimuli influence the architecture of the sound section of the cortex, particularly to the sounds that are heard during the first seven months." (These two *Early Years* studies are freely available online.)

It is much easier to see the enduring effects of early experiences on language ability, than to recognise that early *emotional* experiences, too, can have enduring effects. An 'overload' of emotional distress and pain can be too much to bear, and these feelings can be 'repressed' and 'forgotten,' so that they are no longer accessible to conscious recall, but that does not mean they have no continuing influence.

In *The Psychopathology of Everyday Life*, Freud (1901) gave many examples; but even today, such effects are not regularly recognised or taken into account. Post-traumatic stress disorder in adults is now often diagnosed, and yet – because they can only tell us with a cry, often followed by despair and emotional detachment – it is seldom recognised that babies and infants are much less well equipped to cope with stress and painful emotional experiences than are mature adults. Evidence outlined in Chapter 5, in the section 'Raised cortisol levels due to stress during childcare are still abnormal at age 15,' suggests that there is evidence that, under some circumstances, early institutional childcare can indeed lead to a 'post-traumatic stress disorder.' It is possible that this could have legal consequences, since earlier warnings have not been well heeded.

The *Early Years* studies have been used to support much activity and expenditure in early child 'education,' but our society is slow to acknowledge the sensitive emotional, as well as cognitive, learning that proceeds rapidly in babies. Traumas at this stage can exert dynamic influences over the later emotional and intellectual life, colouring attitudes, perceptions and behaviour in ways that become blended into the personality.

Behavioural and brain studies during mothering in humans and other mammals

Evidence extending that described in *Early Years Study 2* was presented in a major review, *The brain basis of early parent-infant interactions, psychology, physiology, and in vivo functional neuroimaging studies*, by Swain, Lorberbaum and others (2007). It summarised much robust evidence about the psychology, physiology and brain circuits underlying mothering. They described evidence showing how the same neural centres in the brain can be seen to be active during live imaging of the brains in humans and some other mammals when they are mothering their infants. Within a long abstract, the authors say:

> Parenting behavior critically shapes human infants' current and future behavior. The parent-infant relationship provides infants with their first social experiences, forming templates of what they can expect from others and how to best meet others' expectations.... Taken together, this research suggests that networks of highly conserved hypothalamic-midbrain-limbic-paralimbic-cortical [i.e., brain] circuits act in concert to support aspects of parent response to infants, including the emotion, attention, motivation, empathy, decision-making and other thinking that are required to navigate the complexities of parenting. Specifically, infant stimuli activate basal forebrain regions, which regulate brain circuits that handle specific nurturing and caregiving responses and activate the brain's more general circuitry for handling emotions, motivation, attention and empathy – all of which are crucial for effective parenting.

In mammals such as rats and mice, just as in humans and other primates, many of the same brain centres work together to regulate mothering behaviour. In these mammals, the same neurohormones are important in producing social bonding, and also in the neurobiology of parenting behaviour. To support breastfeeding and the rearing of their immature offspring, there are some behaviours that are seen in all mammals.[26] The first of these is "nest building and maintenance – place preference."

Injuries near the medial pre-optic area in rats are found to "completely abolish all aspects of maternal behaviour." Drugs such as cocaine can disrupt mothering behaviour, as they apparently take over, or "hijack" and then alter, the brain's centres that normally reward mothering. Then the infant's appeals can bring forth no mothering response, because the distressed infant can give her mother no additional satisfaction. Such experiences may so disturb an infant's development that *when she grows up, her own capacity for mothering will be impaired. With babies of her own, the harm may be repeated in the next generation.*

Swain and co-workers describe how various psychiatric disorders, such as depression, anxiety, and obsessional states may be related to disturbances of early attachment and mothering. They conclude, "We argue that an integrated understanding of the brain-basis of parenting has profound implications for mental health."

In studies of mammals such as rats and monkeys, Professor Craig Kinsley has shown that giving birth and caring for the young result in positive changes in the structure and function of the brain. These mothers perform better on tests of learning and memory, and are less fearful in anxiety-provoking situations when compared with females who have not had babies. They are much more capable at performing a range of tasks, and in rats these benefits continued after the babies were born, up to an age that corresponds to 60 years in a human. However, it has yet to be shown to what extent similar effects occur in human mothers (Galletly, 2008).

As long ago as 1951, John Bowlby, in *Maternal Care and Mental Health*, concluded his chapter on "Causes of family failure in Western communities, with special reference to psychiatric disorders," by saying:

---

26. Some common behavioural elements of maternal care across mammalian species are: i) nest building and maintenance (place preference); ii) perceptual exploration (identification of nest and/or offspring); iii) retrieval (reciprocal calls); iv) grooming and kissing or licking; v) crouching or preferred nursing position; nursing and lactation and/or feeding; vi) prolonged physical contact/sleeping together; vii) aggressive behavior in response to perceived threats to offspring (Swain et al., 2007).

> From the foregoing, it is evident that in a society where death-rates are low, the rate of unemployment high, and social welfare schemes inadequate, it is emotional instability and the inability of parents to make effective family relationships which are the outstanding cause of children becoming deprived of a normal home life. This itself is an important conclusion, but it is perhaps even more important to note that the origin of adults being unable to make effective family relationships is not infrequently itself the result of their having been deprived of a normal home life in their own childhood. Thus the investigator is confronted with a self-perpetuating social circle in which children who are deprived of a normal home life grow up into parents unable to provide a normal home life for their children, thus leading to another generation of adults unable to do the same for theirs. Most workers in childcare regard this vicious circle as playing an important part in the total problem. It is a matter which clearly requires much further investigation (Bowlby, 1951: 82).

Along with other matters, Bowlby is, in effect, writing about a lack of normal empathy and love. Swain et al., 2007, say "Empathy, defined as appropriate perception, experience and response to another's emotion, is especially relevant to parenting, in which the infant's needs are great, yet most communication is exclusively nonverbal." Empathy is discussed further in Chapter 12.

As seen in the previous chapter, his knowledge of biology and his clinical experience over many years led Bevan-Brown to express much the same view in *The Sources of Love and Fear* in 1950 (Note 4).

5

Comparing some effects of mother-care and daycare

> I thought 'There's a disaster shaping up here, and it's the abandonment of babies, essentially, and the abandonment of mothering,' and so I made this little tale of the baby and its imagined thoughts, as mother puts it in the crèche and goes off to pursue her career – it was a female baby, you see.
> —Michael Leunig, 2007, on his cartoon, *Thoughts of a baby lying in a childcare centre*

> I sometimes feel like I am in the old Soviet Union where only certain facts are allowed to be facts and only certain news allowed to be news.
> —Jay Belsky (cited from Manne, 2005)

> When the facts change, I change my opinion. What do you do, sir?
> —John Maynard Keynes, when reproached for changing his mind

Studying the effects and risks of early non-family childcare

In the mid-20th century, there was a lack of hard evidence about the many possible ill-effects of early childcare. But *absence of evidence* was often regarded as *evidence of absence* – which is a quite different matter. Early childcare has never actually been shown to be safe.

Obtaining scientifically acceptable evidence about the short- and long-term effects of various forms of early childcare is not a simple matter. An outline of the design and interpretation of research studies may be found in Chapter 3 of *Early Child Care – Infants and Nations at Risk* (Cook, 1996).[27] It cites five general questions to be kept in mind about any proposition, including the interpretation of a research study. They are: 1. What is actually being said here? 2. Who says so? 3. How do they

---

27. A slightly revised presentation of that chapter may be seen on www.members.optusnet.com.au/pcook62.

know? 4. Does it make sense? 5. Is there a catch somewhere? These are derived from *How to Lie with Statistics* (Huff, 1973).

The first question is similar to another that is worthy of revival. It was long ago made popular by the philosopher C.E.M. Joad, through the BBC programme *The Brains Trust*. He would often begin answering a question by saying: "Well, it all depends on what you mean by...". Another valuable question was made memorable and used to devastating effect by the Roman orator and lawyer, Cicero. At strategic moments in a classic murder trial he paused, and then asked the Senate to consider: "*cui bono?*" – to whom goes the benefit? Who is gaining here? A variation sometimes used today is 'follow the money.'

In theoretically ideal studies, if the outcomes of care by mothers are to be compared with the outcomes of care by other family members or non-family carers, a number of identical twins would be separated into two groups. More realistically, the two or more groups of infants would be randomly selected, and one 'experimental' group would be exposed to the new environment being studied – for example childcare – while the other group, matched for some key variables, would be a 'control' group, remaining in maternal care with no change of situation, or else given some regime believed to have no relevant effect. It would be 'double-blind' in the sense that neither the research assessors nor the subjects would know which was the experimental group and which was the control group until the results were finalised. Much of this is impossible in research about the effects of childcare. You cannot randomly decide for a mother, or conceal from her, which form of care her baby will have. Many other questions have to be solved and 'ideal' studies are not possible, so the research becomes more complicated and various methods are used to try to compensate for these problems.

Karen (1994) has chronicled in detail the conflicts that were termed the 'daycare wars' as they developed during the 1980s. Early studies of childcare increasingly showed grounds for concern, but this evidence was dismissed by childcare advocates, who highlighted any findings showing benefits, as sometimes occurred when children from disadvantaged backgrounds were placed in the best quality childcare that could be made available. These benefits were often in the cognitive rather than the emotional aspects of the child's development, and cognition is easier to study. Sometimes the results were generalised by childcare advocates, as if they also applied to childcare of lower quality, and/or to children from less disadvantaged homes.

The fact remains that for children under three years of age, non-family childcare involves a massive experiment in raising infants and young children in institutional centres in the absence of any adults who are related or who have any continuing commitment to them. It was advocated and implemented with disregard for the implications that Bowlby's work might have for this period of their lives, and when important foundations of the emotional life are being laid (e.g., Nurcombe 1971; Note 9; Cook, 1996: 18; Cook, 1999a). Moreover, this disorganised social experiment continues to be carried out in the years when infants are learning more rapidly than at any other time in their lives. The burden of proof that it involved risks or adverse consequences was left for others to demonstrate, and if the results of such research were unwelcome, reasons were found for denying or disregarding them (Note 9).

In 1992 Professor Jay Belsky wrote: "On the basis of this developmental and social ecology of daycare in America, I conclude that we have a nation at risk" (Belsky, 1992: 90). A mass of subsequent evidence has confirmed that conclusion.

The NICHD Longitudinal Study into some effects of early childcare

To address a number of these important issues, the National Institute for Child Health and Development (NICHD) in the USA established the Early Child Care Research Network (ECCRN) with more than twenty leading American child development researchers, and they were required to reach agreement on each of their reports before results could be published. Many of those in the Network were women who had written in support of early childcare and in some cases they had depended on it to advance in their professional careers.

In 1991, the Network began a major longitudinal study designed to investigate and follow-up the effects of various types of early care on children's development. Some children were cared for by their mothers during the early years, while others were in various types of non-maternal care at various ages and for varying periods of time from birth through to school entry, around 5 years of age. From the time the infants were one month old, they and their mothers were studied, and the development and outcomes of the various groups were compared. The method and the successive findings are described in a series of NICHD ECCRN reports where the children's subsequent development has been followed up. An outline of the study design and two early reports to 1997 were summarised in *Early Child Care* (Cook, 1997). Nothing about breastfeeding was recorded in this study.

Security of infant-mother attachment

Early results showed that when the infant is 15 to 18 months of age, the security or insecurity of his attachment to his mother can be reliably assessed by the Strange Situation test, and also that attachment security is a meaningful variable. Boys having more than 30 hours a week in non-maternal childcare had a significantly increased risk of insecure attachment, *regardless of the quality of the childcare or other factors.*

For those infants whose mothers were rated in the lowest 25% on assessments of their 'sensitivity' in relating to their infants, it was found that, *regardless of the quality of childcare,* the risk of insecure attachment was increased if the infants had more than just ten hours in childcare, or either of two other risk factors – for example, low-quality care or more than one change in carer. Also, irrespective of its quality, the more time that a child spent in childcare during the first 36 months, the more insensitive the mother's mothering of her child became. Thus, having her infant in childcare had a negative effect on the sensitivity of her mothering behaviour in such time as they did have together.

Since the children will not be that age again, these results are final for this part of the Study. A preview of the possible later significance of attachment security during infancy may be seen in the Minnesota Longitudinal Studies. These followed up infants whose attachment security was assessed in the 1980s. It was found that, while peer and family experiences each make distinctive contributions to future close relationships, the quality of the early attachment experience has particular importance for the intimacy, trust and other emotional aspects of both teenage and adult relationships, and also for the capacity for successful partnerships in adult life. Children and teenagers with secure attachment histories were found to excel in social and emotional health, leadership skills, morality, social behaviour, self-reliance, self-control and resiliency – as appropriate in each stage of development (Breazeale, 2001; Cook, 2004).

Ideology masquerading as science

In an editorial in *The Wall Street Journal* of July 16, 2003, Belsky – as one of the leading scholars in the NICHD Network – summarised the results of their latest study. He said that, contrary to the expectations (and desires) of many in the field, the most comprehensive investigation into the effects of daycare on child development had now confirmed that the more time children spent in daycare arrangements up to 54 months of age, the more aggression, disobedience and conflict with adults these children showed in kindergarten at that age. These patterns remained, even after the study had controlled for many features of the children's families and the quality and type of daycare that the children had experienced. The study found that spending a lot of time in daycare predicted more truly aggressive and disobedient behaviour, not just more assertive or independent behaviour, as some had alleged (Belsky, 2003).

Belsky added, "Not that you'd know any of this from reading the NICHD's press release or listening to many of the commentators". He pointed out that the results were not politically popular, since "many have made their careers representing good childcare as a sort of social cure-all.... Because child-care is here to stay, the argument goes, only the improvement of its quality is important. Anyone highlighting disconcerting evidence is simply against child-care". He added, "One must wonder why, after the government invested tens of millions of dollars, so many are bending over backward to minimize the results". He concluded, "Ultimately, it is the tendency of all too many social scientists (and the public) to deny, dismiss or minimize findings they do not like, while embracing, if not playing up, those they do like, that gives social science a bad name – as ideology masquerading as science.... What those who deny, dismiss or minimize the latest findings continually fail to appreciate is that they hold no monopoly on wisdom or caring, nor even necessarily speak in the best interests of many American children and families. They spin developmental science in support of their political views, failing to realize the disservice they do to children and families alike, to say nothing of the scientific enterprise itself".

Wider societal effects of early non-maternal childcare

In 2001, Belsky suggested that, as more and more children were spending more and more time in non-maternal care arrangements, at younger and younger ages, even small effects, when experienced by many children, might have broad-scale implications for how classrooms, communities and even societies operate.

A large study by Dmitrieva, Steinberg, and Belsky (2007) documented such effects in the classroom. The disturbing effects of early non-maternal childcare in some children did indeed adversely influence some of those other kindergarten children who had had limited or no childcare experience. These children too, at ages averaging five to seven years showed more arguing, fighting, getting angry, acting impulsively and disruption of classroom activities when they were in classrooms with peers who had extensive childcare histories. Such behaviours presumably also increased the stresses on the teachers.

Also in 2007, the NICHD Network reported findings to age 12, saying that while "the quality of parenting that children receive is a far stronger and more consistent predictor of achievement and social functioning than children's experiences in early child-care," nevertheless "children who spent more time in center-based settings from birth through school entry have somewhat more problems with aggressive and disobedient behavior through sixth grade than children who spent less time in centers, regardless of the quality of care".

The NICHD Network now endorsed the suggestion that Belsky had made in 2001, that because large numbers of children in America are experiencing extensive and/or low quality childcare prior to school entry "there may, therefore, be collective consequences of small enduring effects of child-care – across classrooms, schools, communities, and society at large" (Belsky, 2001; NICHD ECCRN, 2007).

Inherent problems of research into early non-family childcare

As noted at the beginning of this chapter, there are many problems in conducting research into the effects of non-family childcare. Many aspects of human personality and emotional development cannot be validly measured, although they are important for long-term emotional health and family relationships, and for their impact on the wider society (Cook, 1996, 58–75).

Some of these research limitations, as well as some overall findings, were summarised in the 2006 NICHD study on the sizes of childcare effects (NICHD ECCRN, 2006). Multiple features of childcare experience were modestly to moderately predictive. The 2006 Report said, "Higher quality child care was significantly related to more advanced cognitive, language, and pre-academic outcomes at every age and better socio-emotional and peer outcomes at some ages. More hours of child care predicted more behavior problems and conflict according to the child care provider. More time in center care was related to both higher cognitive and language scores and more problem and fewer prosocial behaviors according to care providers". They concluded that while the type of childcare was an inconsistent and modest predictor, early childcare quality and quantity were constant and strong predictors of most child outcomes. But they added, "there is a great deal of error in assessment of young children, especially in measures of social and peer outcomes... there is no consensus as to what makes a finding practically important... evaluating effect sizes is not straightforward".

The Network concluded, "our results support policies that support parents and improve the quality of care by child-care providers and reduce the amount of time children spend in care". It advocated "extended welfare benefits or workplace policies that offer flexible hours and paid parental leave at any time during the child's first five years, not exclusively following the child's birth," and it described "consistent beneficial effects of warm, sensitive, stimulating parenting" (NICHD, 2006). Even if the child is in daycare, it is the parents, for good or ill, and the quality and the stability of the relationships that children have with the important adults in their lives that have the most effect on how a child turns out.

Absence of normal 'joint attention sequences' between infant and carer

Despite the difficulties of interpreting daycare research, there are some objective measures of its effects. In *Motherhood*, Anne Manne (2005) describes 'joint attention sequences.' These are moments of engagement, shared interest, with mutual enjoyment, excitement, interaction and communion, as normally occur in healthy, close relationships with babies, especially with their mothers. Three separate investigations in

Australian childcare "found that while physical needs were taken care of, there was an almost complete absence of joint attention sequences. In over 30 hours of videotape of caregivers and two infants, taken over eighteen months at two different centres, Berenice Nyland found almost none". Manne adds that Greenspan says of US centres in 2001, "Even in good centres we've seen many an eager, expectant eight-month-old baby give up and stare at the wall as his caregiver stops by his crib briefly but then hurries away to attend to a crying rival" (Nyland, 2003; Greenspan, 2001).

Raised cortisol levels due to stress during childcare are still abnormal at age 15

The research into childcare outcomes that has been discussed so far has depended largely on observations of behaviour. But there is now a relevant and objective laboratory test. As summarised in *Early Years Study 2*, part of the response to stress in mammals, including humans, is action by the brain to increase the level of cortisol in the blood so as to strengthen the body's ability to cope with this stress. In nature this would normally be a short-term event, after which the blood cortisol could return to normal levels. The normal pattern for blood cortisol is to be highest in the morning, becoming lower as the day goes on. Cortisol levels can be measured by taking a swab from the saliva in the mouth. When the child is under abnormal stress, the saliva test provides a laboratory result that can measure the effects objectively. Disturbance of normal cortisol levels during infancy can have long-term effects in 'setting' the body's response to stress.

A 2008 study by the NICHD Network cited and accepted much evidence that infants under stress in early childcare can have cortisol levels that do not fall in the afternoon but remain elevated (NICHD ECCRN, 2008). In summarising this evidence as their starting point, the Network said, "Early caregiving experiences, including those with parents and in child-care, have been shown to play a role in the regulation of the hypothalamic-pituitary-adrenocortical (HPA) axis generally and one of its primary products, the stress-related hormone cortisol, in particular".

The Study reported that over the longer term, early experiences in childcare and with parents predict HPA axis functioning (i.e., stress responses). To test the hypothesis that "early caregiving stressors ultimately result in the down-regulation of basal cortisol levels in later

Chapter 5. Comparing some effects of mother-care and daycare

life" the Network examined the cortisol levels of 15-year-old adolescents who had been studied since they were babies. They reported that "individuals who experienced: (a) higher levels of maternal insensitivity and (b) more time in childcare centres in the first three years of life had lower awakening cortisol levels at age 15. Effects were small in magnitude, but nonetheless the effects were: (a) additive in the sense that both higher levels of maternal insensitivity and more experience with centre-based care uniquely (but not interactively) predicted lower awakening cortisol levels; (b) not accounted for by later caregiving experiences measured concurrently with awakening cortisol at age 15 or by early demographic variables; and (c) not moderated by sex or by difficult temperament".

In other words, the stresses to which the children were subjected as infants – whether by childcare or by insensitive mothering, and which would have led to their having had *raised* cortisol levels when they were infants – had also adjusted their brain's continuing responses to stress in such a way that, by age 15, the adolescents' blood cortisol levels were abnormally *low* when they woke up in the morning. This is the time when these levels are normally *highest*.[28] In 2009, the NICHD Study of Early Child Care and Youth Development published another report about the follow-up to age 15 years. This presented evidence that, while some children benefited from early childcare, nevertheless "Higher hours of non-relative care predicted greater risk-taking and impulsivity at age 15" (NICHD SECCYD, 2009).[29]

---

28. As seen in Chapter 4, discussing *The Early Years Study 2*, the LHPA pathway consists of the brain's limbic system, hypothalamus and pituitary gland, together with the adrenal glands above the kidneys. When aroused by incoming stimuli, nerve impulses trigger the hypothalamus, which causes the pituitary gland to send a signal to the adrenal gland to release the hormone cortisol. This has a powerful effect on many bodily and brain functions to help cope with emergencies and stressful situations. During early childhood, levels of cortisol impact the receptors of the hippocampus and affect the abilities involved in learning, memory, and the regulation of the stress responses. The LHPA pathway is like a thermostat, in that it maintains an appropriate balance of hormones each day. Normally, cortisol levels rise in the morning when one gets up, and return to low levels at the end of the day—provided that it has not been too stressful and the LHPA pathway is functioning normally (Adapted from McCain et al., 2007, 55).
29. See Appendix 1. Do effects of childcare extend to age 15?

Such experiences disrupt brain architecture – "we can see it happening"

In February 2008, Martha Farah, PhD, presented a different study to the American Association for the Advancement of Science. It was reported that children who suffer deprivation in early life due to poor parenting and unstimulating home lives show altered patterns of brain growth by the time they are aged 15. A group of 118 African-American children from low- and middle-income American families were followed from infancy. At age 15, those who had unsatisfactory relationships with their parents were found to be likely to have an enlarged hippocampus – a structure deep in the brain that is involved in memory formation.

Dr Farrah gave reasons why the change in brain development might be a consequence of early high blood levels of stress hormones such as cortisol. Differences were also found in the prefrontal cortex, an area that governs working memory, attention, and language skills, and these were all impaired. She said, "Parental behaviour is important because it buffers against the effects of stress. We come into the world not able to dampen the stress response ourselves. If it doesn't get damped for you [by being comforted] you have these circulating stress hormones which are [toxic to the brain]". She added that children who lived in poverty were likely to suffer more adverse consequences of stress, because struggling parents were preoccupied and less able to attend to them". Jack Shonkoff, MD, director of the Center on the Developing Child at Harvard University, said, "This isn't just a hocus-pocus black box. It literally disrupts brain architecture, and we can see it happening" (Robotham, 2008).

Can high quality non-maternal childcare be harmful?

Despite the earlier findings of the NICHD Network, and those of other studies, some childcare advocates have continued to claim there is no evidence of harm from childcare if it is of "high quality". This not only denies accumulating evidence to the contrary, but also ignores the overriding fact that much childcare for infants cannot (and never will) meet standards of "high quality". Official assessments are clearly inadequate if, in many places, infant childcare can claim to be of "high quality" when it does not meet even the first two of the generally agreed and most basic criteria of good quality – an adequate ratio of staff to infants, and not more than one change of carer for each infant during the year.

Regulations in many places have allowed a staff-infant ratio of one carer for each five infants during their first two years of life. Belsky described a ratio of 1 carer to 5 children under two years of age as being "nobody's idea of quality," but rather "a license to neglect" (Belsky, 1998a; Belsky, 1998b; Lally et al., 1994).

A report on raising the childcare staff-infant ratios from 1:5 up to 1:4

That a staff-infant ratio of 1:5 is a 'license to neglect' was, effectively, endorsed in a 2006 Task Force Report: *1:4: A Report to the Minister for Community Services, New South Wales Government, on the implementation of a 1:4 staff-child ratio for children aged under two years in NSW children's services* (Cross-Sectoral Task Force, 2006). The Task Force reviewed the literature, and after studying the matter for two years said: *"The staff-child ratio is widely regarded as one of the major indicators of quality care and the research universally shows that a one-to-three ratio is desirable for children under three years of age".*[30] They recommended increasing the staff-infant ratio to provide one carer for every four infants, instead of the ratio of one carer for every five infants, as required at that time. A footnote outlining the studies that were consulted says, "These include research by Ronald Lally, a world expert on child-care matters, who calls a 1:5 ratio a 'ratio for neglect' " (Lally et al., 1994).

The Report then listed eleven significant benefits for infants that their literature review had shown would result from raising staff-child ratios up to 1 carer for every 3 babies, and 1 carer for every 4 toddlers. Clearly, these points logically mean that *the Report has also listed eleven ways in which childcare with a staff-child ratio of 1:5 for infants (as widely occurs at present) represents care that is failing to meet even these basic criteria of quality care.* So how can it be claimed to be of 'high quality'? (Note 9).

The Task Force also showed how raising the staff-child ratio up to 1:4 could be achieved without hardship to providers. However, at that time the New South Wales state government rejected this in favour of a minority report by two committee members who represented the private childcare 'industry.' They argued that staff-infant ratios of 1:4 were

---

30. Emphasis added.

"unaffordable" (Cross-Sectoral Task Force, 2006; Horin, 2007). Shortly afterwards, a major private childcare provider announced skyrocketing profits. If there are large government subsidies and economies of large scale, childcare can be a very profitable industry. After Australian stock market listing in 2001 by the founder (who was once identified as Australia's richest man under 40), it was reported in 2007 that the "world's biggest child-care company, ABC Learning Centres, had shown the benefits of global expansion by unveiling a 75% increase in profit as the first full year of benefits of its overseas acquisitions started flowing in.... Investors applauded the result.... One of the reasons for optimism within the Australian market was a 13 percent increase in government funding for child-care in 2008 to $2.1 billion" (Fraser, 2007). As it turned out, a very different scenario unfolded in 2008, following an ill-advised venture to gain control of a major section of the US childcare industry.

While higher quality childcare may sometimes predict higher vocabulary scores, the value of such gains – as against the benefits of more contact with members of the child's family – depends on factors in the family and the opportunities available from home care. The risk-benefit may be different where young children are at risk for social reasons such as a poor home environment, and especially when truly good quality daycare is available. Here it may offer intellectual and developmental benefits; but these are a special case that should not be generalised to argue for early childcare as a healthy norm for most young children, even though it is politically fashionable to do so, and even when it is demonstrably lacking in quality.

Most of the Early Child Care Network's research instruments for assessing childcare quality are not suitable for daily use by officials who rate the quality of care offered by childcare providers. Still less can they be used by parents, but a parent may be able to make some assessment of three of the NICHD's basic indicators of quality. These are: i) staff responsiveness, warmth and sensitivity to the infants; ii) the ratio of the number of staff to the numbers of infants; and iii) frequency in changes of staff – that is, the staff turnover.

Staff-infant ratios of 1 to 4 and preferably 1 to 3, with no more than one change of carer or centre per year, are considered to be preliminary requirements for infant care to be regarded as of high quality. In his book, *Raising Babies: Should under 3s go to nursery?* Steve Biddulph said that, in a nutshell, childcare has been "too much, too young and for too long" (Biddulph, 2005).

PART TWO:

WHEN THE ENVIRONMENT
DOES NOT MATCH EARLY NEEDS

6

How 'eco-genetic' mismatch can affect health

> The world is too much with us; late and soon,
> Getting and spending we lay waste our powers;
> Little we see in Nature that is ours;
> We have given our hearts away, a sordid boon!
> —William Wordsworth, 1770–1850

Mismatch between our environment and our biology

With any disorder there is a better chance of finding an effective remedy if it is based on the correct diagnosis. Some of the problems described in this book can be better understood when they are considered in the following way.

During long periods of natural selection, the genes and biology of living creatures, including humans, become as well-fitted as possible to the environmental conditions that prevail when they are alive, provided that these have been stable for long enough. But if the environmental conditions change so that they fail to adequately meet some essential need, with the result that one or more significant biological mechanisms are disrupted, then the ensuing mismatch between the environment and the genetically based 'givens' can lead to maladjustment or disorder in health and wellbeing.

In 1972 Stephen Boyden, of the Australian National University, described this as a principle of far-reaching importance for understanding patterns of health and disease in humans, but it has lacked a convenient name (Boyden, 1972; Cook, 1978). Since the mismatch is between the environment or *ecology*, and the biology based on the *genes*, it is proposed here that it may usefully be termed an 'eco-genetic mismatch.' Many of the adverse effects of non-family childcare can be better understood when seen as arising from this kind of mismatch.

For humans, eco-genetic mismatches can lead to risks at any stage in life, but they can be especially risky when they interfere with normal biological processes during pregnancy, childbirth, and infant care. Such mismatch can occur in other areas of life, and may arise from ignorance, customs, or misconceived social policies, advocated by proponents who, however well meaning, failed to understand matters that today are accepted as basic facts. Two that are considered here are still influential in Western societies, and can have ill effects on infants, families, health, and social wellbeing.

Health implications as hunter-gatherer genes meet modern environments

Good health depends on achieving an external and internal environment that, in its essential respects, is a good fit with the biology that derives from our genome. Our body's internal environment is directly affected by what we eat, drink, breathe and do. A lifestyle with an inappropriate diet and no exercise involves an eco-genetic mismatch that underlies much contemporary ill health. Examples include obesity, cardiovascular disease, diabetes and their related conditions. Human genes did not evolve in ways that allow us and our biology to stay healthy while eating large amounts of sugar, or other refined carbohydrates and saturated fats, while sitting for hours – often in front of an electronic screen.

If the environmental conditions of any living creature change gradually, then those who have some genes that better fit them for the changed environmental conditions will, by natural selection, be more likely to survive and reproduce, while those less fitted to the new conditions may become unwell or die out.

For example, an adequate amount of Vitamin D is an essential requirement for the body to make strong healthy bones, and too little vitamin D will lead to deformed bones, as seen in rickets.

Vitamin D is formed in the skin by the action of ultraviolet light from the sun, but too much of this light can cause skin cancer. Dark melanin pigmentation in the skin can screen out excessive amounts of the ultraviolet light, while still letting enough through to make healthy bones. Under the strong African sun, those humans with darker skins were protected by their melanin pigmentation, so they were selected for survival.

When humans later migrated to northern Europe, the weaker sunlight provided less ultraviolet light for the manufacture of vitamin D, but at the same time it posed less risk of skin cancer. Consequently those who possessed genes for paler skin with less melanin pigmentation were favoured and selected for, while those with genes for dark skin that screened out too much ultraviolet light were disadvantaged, and they would have died out.

Eco-genetic mismatch, pregnancy and early child development

Eco-genetic mismatch may involve risks at any stage in life, but recognising it in the early years is especially important, both for understanding disorders better and for promoting good health. Effects of eco-genetic mismatch are often seen in child psychiatry and paediatrics (Cook, 1973; 1978; Gluckman and Hanson, 2006).

Because of the rapid development of babies in the uterus and during their early years, it is vital that their environment should sufficiently match their biological needs – as in the supply of essential nutrients, stimulation and all that goes with normal mothering. Breastfeeding and experiences of sensuous satisfaction, mutual love and playful enjoyment all help to lay healthy foundations for life, and especially for the full development of infants' brains.

On the other hand, treating infants in ways that disrupt biological mechanisms can be a major source of eco-genetic mismatch. From conception onwards, deficiencies of many essential trace nutrients – for example, iodine, fluoride or folate – carry risks of lifelong handicaps, while the presence of toxic substances – such as lead, mercury, nicotine, or alcohol – can also be particularly damaging in the early years.

Thalidomide was widely marketed in the late 1950s as a safe remedy for insomnia, but its effects on the developing foetus had not been tested. It was never approved by the authorities for use in the USA, so its citizens were spared many tragedies. Unfortunately, in less well-protected countries – including Australia and New Zealand – it was released and advertised as safe, even in overdose. It produced various limb and other deformities in those who were exposed to it at critical times during their early development. In *Silent Spring* Rachael Carson (1962) drew world attention to the damaging effects of many new chemicals that were being released into the environment. A distinguished professor of child development in the USA once raised the question of whether early childcare may be 'another thalidomide'. This can remind us of the neglected fact that *absence of evidence* about ill effects is not the same as *evidence of absence*.

Boyden described how, in adapting to maladjustments and disorders due to eco-genetic mismatch, humans can resort to measures that are either corrective or symptomatic. Corrective measures aim to reverse or correct the unhealthy conditions, while symptomatic treatments ignore underlying causes, and just aim to relieve the symptoms or immediate causes of the disorder. For example, decay in teeth due to excess sugar can be prevented by appropriate changes in the diet – a corrective remedy – or treated by having a profession skilled in filling dental cavities – a symptomatic remedy. One of the problems with symptomatic remedies is that by just treating the symptoms of a deteriorating environment, the causes of the disorder may be allowed to continue or get worse.

Boyden pointed out that doctors and policemen are often agents of antidotal or symptomatic rather than corrective responses to eco-genetic mismatch. Whenever practicable, it is better to explore corrective remedies first. This approach to health is developed in *Childrearing, culture and mental health* (Cook, 1978), and also in *The Stone-Age Health Programme – Diet and Exercise as Nature Intended*, written by anthropologists who had lived with hunter-gatherers (Eaton, Shostak, and Konner, 1988).

The modern urban environment differs greatly from that to which humans have been genetically adapted. Many advantages of civilisation appear obvious, and few would forego them, but an understanding of biological processes suggests how we may evaluate the benefits and the disadvantages of any particular deviation from the evolutionary environment, whether for an infant, child or adult.

Our socio-cultural environment in a biological perspective

If we review our socio-cultural environment in a biological perspective, then areas of deviation appear that create unnecessary risks of eco-genetic mismatch without bringing much benefit. Such mismatch matters most during the development of babies and children if environmental factors interfere with needs and behavioural tendencies that are deeply rooted in our species *because* they have had important survival functions.

For example, as discussed in Chapter 2, a breastfed baby can suffer very strategic disruptions of his emotional life if his mother disappears for 40 or more hours a week (or even for 10 to 20 hours), as she leaves him in a childcare centre – even if it is officially said to be of high quality. In a nursery with other babies, he hears the distress of those who cry while he waits his turn to be bottle-fed by an unrelated carer who doesn't actually love him. Even if he has the chance to become attached to her, she may at any time move on and be replaced by someone else. Such changes frustrate any attempts by the infant to form stable secondary attachments; he may just give up trying to do so.

No such disruptions occur when a baby travels in a car with his mother, who then takes him shopping as she gathers packaged food in a supermarket. While this departs in many ways from the hunter-gatherer situation, *it does not disrupt any important aspects of the infant's biology or the mother-infant relationship.*

In any particular case, individual susceptibilities affect the outcome. Some infants are tough and resilient while others are tender and vulnerable. As Bowlby said in 1951, not all children who drink milk containing tuberculosis bacilli will get tuberculosis – but it *is* a risk. At stake here are the foundations of good physical and emotional health of the next generation. It is safest to assume the infant is tender, since prevention is easier, cheaper, and more effective than attempts at cure later on.

Eco-genetic mismatch and social settings relevant to parenting

The concept of eco-genetic mismatch can help us to understand the needs of families. Western societies, in pursuit of certain beliefs and values, have given insufficient attention to features of the social settings that are relevant to parenting behaviour. For many parents and children, the situations in which they live have been transformed, in some ways for the worse, by the industrial revolution, the motorcar, and the development of increasingly large cities, where electronic entertainment often replaces healthier activities. It is important to study what qualities in our environment and social settings can best support healthy and mutually satisfying parent-child relationships (McCain et al., 2007).

Chapter 6. How 'eco-genetic' mismatch can affect health

Inadequacies and lack of availability of resources in the following areas are common:

- support and sufficient economic freedom to allow women to mother, breastfeed, and enjoy the rearing of their infants during the early years;
- companionship and support from an extended family group, friends and neighbours;
- meaningful and sociable occupations, sometimes around homemaking, and growing and harvesting food, as used to be done by mothers while raising children;
- availability of other children or young people to assist a mother, and play with her little children;
- contact with the natural world;
- outside play areas with trees and natural features; walking and cycle tracks so that older children can travel independently, safe from traffic hazards;
- fathers, and often mothers, finding work in places and at times that allow enough contact with the family;
- adequate maternity leave or opportunities for a mother to find work where she may also be available to care for, or at least to breastfeed, her baby during early infancy;
- economic opportunities for affordable housing;
- help in the event of misfortune;
- architectural and administrative conditions that support sensitive aspects of maternal behaviour.[31]

Affluence may help to improve some of these variables, but this has not generally happened. Winston Churchill pointed out that "We shape our buildings; then they shape us". Many materially poorer and even non-literate societies have made better provision in many of these respects than most so-called affluent societies.

Even into the 20th century, infants' experiences in many societies had much in common with those of their hunter-gatherer ancestors. In 1972,

---

31. As an extreme example, a traditional Samoan hut in a natural setting, with no walls but a curtain, could be much more conducive to mothering behaviour than a small high-rise flat with no safe outside area for play or meeting others. See also Chapter 12 and Note 12.

Werner reported that in fifty pre-industrial societies that had been studied by that time, despite great cultural and geographical diversity, all of the infants shared certain common experiences during the first year. These included:

- membership of an extended family system with many caretakers;
- breastfeeding on demand, day and night;
- constant tactile stimulation by the body of a caretaker who carried the infant on her back or side, and slept with him;
- participation in all adult activities, with frequent sensory-motor stimulation;
- lack of set routines for feeding, sleeping and toileting; and lack of restrictive clothing in a tropical or semi-tropical climate.

This perspective leads to conclusions that are completely at variance with the statement: "the idea that mothering is 'both natural and a pleasure' is a 'myth'," as stated in a book for secondary school students *Children in Australian Families* (Ochiltree, 1990; cited from Duffy, 1995). This view seems to be rooted in the ideology of cultural determinism (see Chapter 10). The question then arises, 'if mothering is not natural then what, if anything, is?'

James Prescott analysed forty-nine studies of 'primitive' societies, as recorded in a different anthropological database. He showed that those societies in which the infant was not carried and provided with pleasurable body contact showed more violent characteristics in a number of ways (Prescott, 2005; Cook, 1996).

Nature's rewards and satisfactions

From evidence outlined so far it follows that:

- There is arguably no occupation available today for which a woman of child-bearing age is more specifically prepared by her genetic heritage than that of bearing, breastfeeding, nurturing and rearing her own infants, and within a supportive environment there is the potential for much in-built satisfaction and joy in doing so.

Chapter 6. How 'eco-genetic' mismatch can affect health

- There is also a genetic basis for a father to derive deep satisfactions from parenting his children and providing security for their mother.
- In humans, Nature provides pleasurable feelings associated with behaviours that are essential for the survival of the species. Of these, breastfeeding, nurturing and enjoying the young are, like mating, fundamental.

It further follows that if such satisfactions are lacking, this is a matter for diagnosis and treatment. The cause is likely to be found in the past experience or the present environment of the mother and/or father, rather than in their inherited biology. For example, in New Zealand, a survey in the late 1960s found that 40% of the mothers felt that the burden of having young children outweighed, or only just balanced, any satisfaction or enjoyment they received. This was an affluent society; what had gone wrong? The problem probably lay in both the background of the individual parents and in the childrearing tenets, culture, and social norms of that society (Ritchie and Ritchie, 1970: 43; Olssen, 1981; Cook, 1978).

> In the UK, Penelope Leach wrote, "our society is inimical to children". Describing the meaning and importance of unconditional love, she said: *"If children are to develop the self-esteem and self-respect that will maximise their fulfilment of their potential, their resilience and their ability to esteem and respect other people, they need to feel loved, respected, even celebrated, for what they are rather than for what they do. That means that they need to be as sure that extra achievement could not earn them extra love as that failure could not deprive them of the love they have. Unconditional love in infancy and early childhood, from at least one adult who is both consistently available and emotionally involved, seems a mondial prerequisite of mental health throughout life"*. (Leach, 1994: xiii; 113-4. Emphasis added.).

In chapters 8 and 9, some ideas and related practices that have often undermined the natural rewards of parenting are explored.

7

Early civilisations and environmental change

> ... but man, proud man,
> dressed in a little brief authority,
> most ignorant of what he's most assured,
> his glassy essence like an angry ape,
> plays such fantastic tricks before high heaven
> as make the angels weep.
> —Shakespeare, *Measure for Measure* II, ii.

By around 200,000 years ago, early humans were becoming *Homo sapiens* much like us. Later, they gradually spread from Africa around the hospitable lands of the earth as they hunted and gathered food. Groups of hunter-gatherers survived well into the 20th century, and theirs was more or less the physical and social environment to which all humans were genetically well adapted until the agricultural revolution began to make major environmental changes around ten to eleven thousand years ago.

In the fertile valleys of Mesopotamia, Egypt, India, China, and America, humans began to cultivate plants for their seeds. Rice, wheat and the seeds of other plants enabled them to store food. This gave them an advantage in leaner times, but to protect their stores and for defence and shelter, they had to erect walls and buildings and stay in the same place. They became more powerful than the hunter-gatherers, especially after suitable animals were domesticated and used for food. As their numbers increased, and perhaps after exhausting nearby areas of land, they could extend their influence, clearing trees if they wanted more pasture.

Males, aggression, power, psychopaths, slavery, materialism, and war

A note on the potentials for men, especially alpha males, to adopt deviant, non-parenting roles is relevant here. Chimpanzees can hunt and kill, and groups of males, perhaps with females, can organise battles if there is competition for food and territory. But the domestication of animals such as dogs, oxen, and horses, which could help with work or carry warriors, greatly increased the *power* available to men. This, together with their earlier discovery of fire and gradually improving knowledge of metals, enabled men to use faculties that they had developed through their natural selection pedigree, to exploit their fellow-creatures and control their environments in ways that were beyond the wildest dreams of their hunter-gatherer ancestors.

As early civilisations developed, leaders could manipulate gangs of cooperating, aggressive, and increasingly well-armed men, to plunder, fight, and kill – often gaining more resources and territory than they really needed. Other men, women, and children were enslaved for labour, sex, or other purposes – as continues in some places to this day. In this process, the women often became largely subservient to the dominant men who controlled the levers of power.

Some books in the Old Testament of the Bible give glimpses of life in those times, as they worshipped a male God who favoured them in warfare. We can read of the rules they were developing in their efforts to control human behaviour and 'sin,' and also their developing ideas about how and why it all went wrong. Over time, larger battles became possible, and after three or four millennia of wars, empires, and greedy competition to secure ever more resources, the industrial revolution vastly increased humans' capacity to organise destructiveness and mass killing.

In the 20th and 21st centuries, many emotionally deprived, violently reared but charismatic psychopaths have been empowered through some seductive ideology or religion. With persuasive oratory and the latest technology, they can recruit and lead like-minded thugs to garner ever more resources and power, often inflicting their totalitarianism on others, and causing vast suffering and sometimes genocide. There is a global need for the early recognition of such dangerously sociopathic demagogues and their ideologies, with measures to block the elevation of such psychopaths to totalitarian power (Grille, 2005).

Our need for well-nurtured, emotionally healthy adults, especially as leaders, has never been greater (Neill, 1962). Fraser Mustard, in his introductory words in the 2007 *Early Years Study 2* wrote: "The health, wellbeing and competence for all communities in our globalized world will determine if we can build tolerant, stable, equitable, prosperous, sustainable societies.... We now understand how early child and brain development sets trajectories in health, learning, and behavior – for life. How we apply this knowledge in our various societies will determine whether we will be successful in the 21st century.... It is now time to put the science into action for our children – and for the survival of our species".

The Tragedy of the Commons

But how is our species to survive? With the eclipse of the vision of our beautiful planet as a miracle of Nature to be cherished and cared for, our earth has been vastly injured as the world's population has more than trebled in just one lifetime. In 1968, Garret Hardin gave a presidential address before the meeting of the Pacific Division of the American Association for the Advancement of Science. It was completely ignored by the press, but published later that year in *Science,* entitled "The Tragedy of the Commons: The population problem has no technical solution; it requires a fundamental extension in morality" (Hardin, 1968; Hardin, 1972). Though seldom mentioned now, it became a classic and formed the basis for much thinking among social and environmental scientists, especially in relation to the over-exploitation of natural and economic resources, pollution of the environment, and over-population.

The 'commons' is a metaphor for any collectively owned and jointly managed asset. The tragedy unfolds when single people or groups profit greatly by exploiting this resource, while the loss is shared among so many others that for each of them individually the loss is so small that it seems negligible.

Hardin illustrated the tragedy with a parable. Imagine a pasture, traditionally known as a common or commons, on which a number of herdsmen can graze their animals. Each grazes as many as he can, and *this is sustainable so long as the number of men and animals is kept below the carrying capacity of the land*, whether by disease, poaching or war. But when these constraints are removed, numbers can increase and the logic of the commons generates tragedy unless steps are taken to prevent it.

For example, if the land can carry one hundred sheep, then ten herdsmen can have ten animals each, and this is sustainable. But then one herdsman decides to add one more animal. One hundred sheep is the sustainable limit, but there are now one hundred and one sheep – too many. By increasing his number of sheep from ten to eleven, this herdsman gains another 10%, while the effective loss in feed for each sheep is only about 1%. For each of the other herdsmen this loss of 1% seems so small that they don't object. So *the first herdsman has a much bigger incentive to increase his number of sheep than each of the others has to oppose him*. Being rational, our herdsman decides to add another animal, and so on. The other herdsmen, seeing this, each decide to do likewise. Soon, through free access to the commons, it is overgrazed and ruined.

As Hardin said, "Therein is the tragedy. Each man is locked into a system that compels him to increase his herd without limit – in a world that is limited. Ruin is the destination to which all men rush, each pursuing his own best interest in a society that believes in the freedom of the commons. Freedom in a commons brings ruin to all". Others have noted that initially this may not be exactly what happens; they point out that "Freedom in a commons only brings ruin to the commons," while those who exploit it get rich and move on. The ruin for all comes later, when there is nowhere left into which to 'move on.'

Hardin argued that in a democratic situation, restraint by "mutual coercion, mutually agreed upon" is the best way to prevent the tragedy. In 1968 Hardin foretold how – if it is not recognised and dealt with – the operation of this tragedy of the commons will inevitably lead to over-population and over-exploitation of natural and economic resources, with likely aggressive onslaughts on each other as we compete for finite resources and destroy our biosphere in the process. He discussed how the tragedy must be understood and prevented if we are to survive.

Even today, when many problems affecting the healthy survival of our planet are much more urgent than they were in 1968, our species continues to multiply, promoting unbridled materialism and behaving as if resources are infinite in a world that is finite. The operation of the tragedy of the commons is seldom recognised or acknowledged (Hardin, 1968; 1972; Cook, 2000).

In 1971, the distinguished landscape architect and planner, Ian McHarg, described in a memorable image, a view of what is happening to our earth. He pictured how it would appear to a planetary doctor out in space. Seeing ever-enlarging areas of unhealthy discoloration, the doctor comes to the conclusion that the earth must have some kind of cancer. In fact, he is looking at the destruction of the biosphere that arises from the human denial of the rules by which life, as we know it, can continue to thrive on this planet. Despite the increasing danger, there remains great enthusiasm for endlessly growing economies, as if growth were our highest good. This is mindlessly out of touch with the reality of our total dependence on this planet and its ancient and limited natural ecosystems (McHarg, 1971).[32]

---

32. A small example of being strikingly out of touch with some major and important realities about our planet was presented in the text beneath a large photograph showing a glowingly happy Iranian woman astronaut, dressed ready for blast-off in the US space shuttle. She said that "space exploration will be an important part of the future of the human race and that everyone should eventually have access to space travel." Cited from *Swinburne: The future by design*. Swinburne 1, March 9, 2008. Melbourne: Swinburne University of Technology. See also *Collapse: How societies choose to fail or survive*, by Jared Diamond.

8

Are children born as Jesus saw them, or with hereditary original sin?

> Suffer (i.e., allow) little children to come unto me, and forbid them not: for of such is the kingdom of God.
> —Jesus, Luke 18:16

> An infant's whole nature is a sort of seed of sin
> and therefore it cannot but be hateful to God.
> —John Calvin, 1559

> In fact, judged by adult social standards the normal baby is a born criminal.
> —Edward Glover, 1960

Christianity and children

During the past 2000 years, Western civilisation has been fundamentally influenced by Christianity and the status given to the earlier Hebrew Scriptures as collected in the Old Testament. Referring to childrearing, people still say "spare the rod and spoil the child", though these exact words do not appear in the Bible. They are based on an old Hebrew proverb: "He that spareth the rod hateth his son: but he that loveth him chasteneth him betimes" (Proverbs 13:24). The word 'spoil' as a verb occurs many times in the Bible, but nearly all are in the Old Testament and it is not used in connection with children.

Some ideas relating to children that have long been taught as Christian are strikingly different from the teachings of Jesus about children, as they have come down to us. The King James Authorised Version of the Bible (1611) says, "And he took a child and set him in the midst of them: and when he had taken him into his arms he said to them, whosoever shall receive one of such children in my name receiveth me" (Mark 9:36–7); and "Suffer (i.e., allow) little children to come unto me, and forbid them not: for of such is the kingdom of God" (Luke 18: 16);

"Except ye become converted and become as little children, ye shall not enter into the kingdom of Heaven" (Matthew 18:3); and "It were better for him that a millstone were hanged around his neck, and be cast into the sea, than that he should offend one of these little ones" (Luke 17:2).

In Luke 6:31 Jesus says, "As ye would that men should do to you, do ye also to them likewise". And in Matthew 22:39, "Thou shalt love thy neighbour as thyself". Yet it seems that the ancient Golden Rule commended by Jesus – "Do to others as you would that they should do to you" – was not seen as being applicable to babies and children. There seems no reason to exclude children from this, any more than women, though parents sometimes realise that they haven't thought of their children as 'people'. We could add, "Love is very patient, very kind," as in St Paul's first letter to the Corinthians (13:4), but there is little more about childrearing in the New Testament. Since they were expecting the return of the Messiah quite soon, some early Christians regarded children as an encumbrance to piety (Bailey, 1959).

Even as he was being arrested to be crucified, Jesus' last words to his disciples, as recorded in all four Gospels, commanded non-violence. Christianity was essentially a non-violent religion until it was adopted as the state religion of the Roman Empire in 392 AD.

Despite the sayings of Jesus about children, the history of violence to them in the name of God is chillingly documented up to 1990 in *Spare the Child: The Religious Roots of Punishment and the Impact of Physical Abuse* (Greven, 1990). Even in 2006, *The Australian* reported that "a Christian New Zealand group urged parents to smack their naughty children for up to 15 minutes, because 'the Bible recommends it to get rid of the problem of sin in the heart'". On this reading, why not act on Deuteronomy 21:18–21 where it commands the communal stoning to death of a stubborn and rebellious son? If that can be ignored, why should not the beating of children also be disregarded as part of the 'Old Covenant,' and superseded by the gospel of Jesus? But it has not been.

The doctrine of original sin, and misinterpreting the nature of the child

How did Christians come to such un-Christ-like views about children and their management? Although the doctrine of original sin had a

Biblical foundation in the teaching of Saint Paul (Romans 5:12–21), its clear application to the management of babies and childrearing derived from the theology of Saint Augustine (354–430 AD) who was a Bishop of Hippo, in North Africa.

Augustine had come to his Christianity with a Christian mother, a non-Christian de facto wife, a son, and a background in Manichaean dualism – a religion founded in the latter half of the third century by a Persian, Mani. This dualism held that material things, the body and its sensuous pleasures were allied to the forces of darkness and the devil. The spiritual, non-material side of humanity, and the soul were of the realm of light where God reigned.[33]

On his conversion to Christianity, Augustine discarded his wife and son and became a brilliant, charismatic, and influential theologian. After "a curious study of child psychology", he added to the gradually developing idea of original sin the concept of "guilt attaching even to the newborn child by reason of the depravation of its nature" (Lacey, 1962).

Augustine, on his interpretation of Genesis, insisted that humans were born sinful through the original sin of Adam, and he concluded that this was inherited by all Adam's descendants. Man's 'seed' must have been changed forever by Adam's fall from grace, and Eve was the temptress who had brought about this 'fall'. In those days it was thought all the hereditary contribution to a baby came from the father, while the mother was just the incubator for a man's seed.

Perhaps this is why our heritage does not sufficiently appreciate that, apart from the father's single sperm carrying just *half* of the required chromosomes, the production of a baby is *entirely the mother's creation*. She supplies the initial cell (i.e., the ovum or egg, with the other 23 chromosomes), and if her baby is exclusively breastfed for six months, she has made this child entirely from her own body – from her blood, her milk, and her mothering. Producing a well-nurtured two-year-old might well be seen as a supreme creative achievement.

However, Augustine believed (with the Manicheans) that sexual passion, like sensuousness, was of the nature of sin, and had been

---

33. sensuous: *a.* of, relating to or derived from the senses. WH: 17C. Latin *sensus* sense. The word was coined in 1641 by the English poet John Milton to avoid the erotic connotations of *sensual* (Room, 1999).

permanently corrupted by Adam's 'Fall', so that every baby born since then was conceived in sin. Before Adam's Fall, the sexual act would have been as devoid of lust as the passing of urine (Augustine, *De Civitate Dei*). Augustine was tireless in his efforts to ensure that his views prevailed over those of Pelagius, a British monk who went to Rome and more benignly argued that babies were born good, and each could later have his own 'fall'. One of his arguments was that a good God would not have created a world in which nearly all babies were pre-destined to eternal suffering in Hell, even if they died in infancy – as many did.

Augustine's views were incorporated into accepted doctrine in Western Christianity from 529 AD,[34] and some of his doctrines came across to the Protestant churches through the teachings of Martin Luther (1483–1546) and John Calvin (1509–1564). Amongst many other things, Calvin taught that infants' "whole nature is a sort of seed of sin and therefore it cannot but be hateful to God" (Calvin, 1559).

This teaching appears in various branches of Western Christianity, and by the 16th and 17th centuries Augustine's theology of original sin had been very precisely formulated in English. The final version was incorporated into the Church of England's *Thirty-Nine Articles of Religion* as they still appear in *The Book of Common Prayer* that was given legal authority by the Act of Uniformity (1662). It is still in force. By royal decree these *Thirty-Nine Articles* were to be accepted literally, and for around 350 years Anglican clergy have had to assent, affirm, or subscribe to them. These Articles have not been officially updated because there would now be too many difficulties in getting agreement about what should take their place.

Of particular concern for childrearing is Article IX – *Of Original or Birth Sin*. It reads:

> Original Sin standeth not in the following of Adam, (as the Pelagians do vainly talk;) but it is the fault and corruption of the Nature of every man, that naturally is engendered of the offspring of Adam; whereby man is very far gone from original righteousness, and is of his own nature inclined to evil, so that the flesh lusteth always contrary to the spirit; and therefore in every person born into this world, it deserveth God's wrath and

---

34. The Second Council of Orange, 529 AD.

damnation. And this infection of nature doth remain, yea in them that are regenerated; whereby the lust of the flesh, called in Greek, *phronema sarkos*, which some do expound the wisdom, some sensuality, some the affection, some the desire, of the flesh, is not subject to the Law of God. And although there is no condemnation for them that believe and are baptized, yet the Apostle doth confess, that concupiscence and lust hath of itself the nature of sin.

This meticulously worded dogma, though largely forgotten, is not an irrelevant museum piece; it is a powerful and precise declaration about the nature, inclinations, behaviour, and possible destinies of human beings from conception to eternity. It has implications for positive action from birth, when humans are most vulnerable, and it was, and is, vested with the authority of the established religion in one of the world's most influential nations for much of the past 350 years. The ramifications of its ideas continue in various guises long after its source is forgotten.

Note how easily this underwrites "The taboo on tenderness" – the title of a chapter in *The Origins of Love and Hate*, by Ian Suttie (Suttie, 1935). And what of the pleasures of breastfeeding and making love, which both release the hormone oxytocin, leading to feelings of warm sensuous satisfaction? Did the doctrine have anything to do with the psychopathology of Sigmund Freud and his patients, or with his interpretations of the clinical material he used to formulate his psychoanalytic theories, including those about the nature of human nature? Or on the prevailing Victorian view that there was no such thing as a female orgasm? And what were the consequences for childrearing of his teachings about the nature of babies and little children? The doctrine of original sin has tended to permeate ideas about childrearing in the English-speaking countries, and around the world wherever Christian churches relying on Augustinian doctrines have spread their message.

In the 18th century there was evidently some acute concern that infant souls might not go to heaven. Perhaps, as suggested in Article IX, baptism was not enough, since "this infection of nature doth remain, yea in them that are regenerated". John Wesley, an Anglican clergyman, in his sermon O*n Obedience*, quoted a letter from his mother, Susanna, who wrote to him saying:

> In order to form the minds of children the first thing to be done is to conquer their will.... Heaven or hell depends on this alone. So that the parent who studies to subdue it (self-will) in his children, works together with God in the saving of a soul: The parent who indulges it, does the devil's work.... This therefore I cannot but earnestly repeat – break their wills betimes; begin this great work before they can run alone, before they can speak plain, or perhaps speak at all. Whatever pains it cost, conquer their stubbornness; break the will, if you would not damn the child. I conjure you not to neglect, not to delay this. Therefore, (1) Let a child, from a year old, be taught to fear the rod and to cry softly. In order to do this, (2) Let him have nothing he cries for; absolutely nothing, great or small; else you undo your own work. (3) At all events, from that age, make him do as he is bid, if you whip him ten times running to effect it.... Break his will now, and his soul will live, and he will probably bless you to all eternity (Wesley, 1742).

Some 20th century versions

In the first half of the 20th century, a secular and slightly more humane version of this admonition was promulgated around the English-speaking world by Dr Truby King, whose teachings became state-sponsored orthodoxy throughout New Zealand, and he was knighted for his contribution (King, 1925; Note 5). He urged the early training of babies with strict routine from birth, ignoring their cries, four-hourly feeding, sleeping alone, and firm discipline. Yielding to maternal impulses by responding to babies' cries, or picking them up, feeding them, or otherwise 'giving-in' to them except according to his strict routine was condemned as 'spoiling', with risk of dire consequences. The *Mothercraft Manual* of 1928 was influential in England and other countries as the main vehicle for the teachings of Truby King (Note 5). It stated:

> Self-control, obedience, the recognition of authority, and, later, respect for elders are all the outcome of the first year's training.... The baby who is picked up or fed whenever he cries soon becomes a veritable tyrant, and gives his mother no peace when awake; while, on the other hand, the infant who is fed regularly, put to sleep and played with at definite times soon finds that appeals bring no response, and so learns that most useful of all

Chapter 8. Are children born as Jesus saw them, or with original sin?

> lessons, self-control, and the recognition of an authority other than his own wishes....
>
> ... the conscientious mother has to be prepared to fight and win all along the line, in matters small and great (Liddiard, 1928).

The fear that 'giving in' to a baby's wants from any time after birth would 'spoil' the child has been a potent belief in the English-speaking world for a long time, and it was almost undisputed through to the 1950s or early 1960s. A New Zealand family doctor of that time told all her young mothers, "There's going to be a battle and you've got to win it". The idea that a baby's wants are much the same as its needs was alien to much childrearing advice far into the 20th century.

Advocates of behaviour modification methods in early child rearing, while generally avoiding violence, seem in some ways to carry on the Wesley-Truby King tradition. By not responding to a baby's cries, as in 'controlled crying', it is possible to 'extinguish' this behaviour. Yet with this and other childrearing advice based on learning theory, it is appropriate to ask: "What emotional lessons is the infant really learning, and are there any other emotional effects? Could there be collateral damage? And if so, what might it be?"

In 2004, the Australian Association for Infant Mental Health issued a position paper on the controlled crying method and its associated hazards. As is often the case with behaviour modification for problem behaviours in children, the Association concluded that the message of controlled crying is: 'Do what I want you to do – or else'. In its most benign form, there is the reward of approval if the child complies and the penalty of disapproval or even the withdrawal of love if he does not. While it can sometimes resolve problem behaviours and perhaps break a vicious circle, it tends to rely on a fear of losing love, rather than on taking into account the child's point of view and possible desire to please the parent.

Psychoanalytic theory and the misreading of the normal baby

Unfortunately, in its concept of the Id, psychoanalytic theory incorporated a largely negative view about the basic nature of babies. As late as 1960 the eminent and authoritative London psychoanalyst Edward Glover wrote:

> The perfectly normal baby is almost completely egocentric, greedy, dirty, violent in temper, destructive in habits, profoundly sexual in purpose, aggrandising in attitude, without conscience or moral feeling. His attitude to society is opportunist, inconsiderate, domineering and sadistic. In fact, judged by adult social standards the normal baby is for all practical purposes a born criminal (Glover, 1960).

On the basis of this view of the nature of the normal baby, Glover based his exposition in *The Roots of Crime*, as published in the second volume of his *Selected Papers on Psychoanalysis*. It does not appear to occur to him that much of the behaviour that he perceived and interpreted in this way might be part of an infant's reactions to abnormal, culturally induced frustrations. Such ideas can, in their turn, set up a self-fulfilling vicious circle. Basic psychoanalytic theory had failed to understand that human mothers and infants evolved as social primates, with all that this implies. Some implications of such fundamental misconceptions are spelled out by Bowlby in *Psychoanalysis and Evolution Theory* – which forms the second Appendix in *Attachment and Loss, Volume 2: Separation* (Bowlby, 1973).

This mis-reading of the young child entered textbooks of child development. Professor R. Illingworth of Sheffield, in his 1957 textbook *The Normal Child*, wrote that by the ages of 12 to 36 months the child's annoying ways include behaviour that is hyperactive, irritating, clinging and destructive. By age two he is "well into the resistant stage," oppositional, aggressive, attention-seeking, frustrating his mother at every turn, made worse by smacking, refusing to go to bed, making himself sick if left alone, unreasonable, totally inconsiderate of his mother's feelings, with constant bickering, shouting, shrieking and generally making chaos and wrecking the place. He added, "This picture is not exaggerated" (Illingworth, 1957).

While many children do some of these things, this amount of perverse, angry and destructive behaviour could only ever be called 'normal' in the sense of being *common* in the (British) childrearing setting of that time. A child showing such behaviour cries out for competent diagnosis and treatment, and is very far from being normal in the sense of being *healthy*.

The Canadian film, *The Terrible Twos,* also purported to be about normal child development. Its title fell on fertile ground, and the phrase is still widely used. It appears in the American textbook of child development (Steinberg and Meyer, 1995), and it is repeated in 2007 in *Early Years Study 2*.

If two-year-olds are *perceived* to be like this, it can create a self-fulfilling prophecy. The stresses were often compounded by the parents' own emotional problems stemming from similar rearing in their own childhoods. All this led to much frustration, as parents found they were not gaining the satisfactions that Nature makes possible as compensations for the sacrifices that healthy early parenting does involve.

To offset the demands arising from their immaturity, healthy and well-nurtured two-year-olds often give moments of special delight, through little ways that soon fade, to be replaced by other rewards for parents to enjoy. I knew a father some years ago who felt under social pressure to administer 'discipline' when his little girl had a tantrum while they were out visiting. He wisely pointed out, "Look – she's a two-year-old! If you can't behave like a two-year-old when you're two – when can you?" This astonishing question was received with a stunned and thoughtful silence.

After infancy, threats of corporal punishment were called for, and many parents complained that frequent use of the ruler or strap had failed to control their children. If they could not discipline their children when they were young, how, they asked, could they hope to control them as teenagers? The consequences of such beliefs flourished in New Zealand well into the 1960s or later. As seen earlier, for many parents the burden resulting from these beliefs outweighed the natural rewards of parenting that some mothers and fathers were then learning to enjoy (Cook, 1970; 1978; Ritchie and Ritchie, 1970: 43; Greven, 1991). In the 2005 UNICEF global study of violence against children, New Zealand ranked third worst among 27 countries in the Organization for Economic Co-operation and Development. Levels of deaths due to child maltreatment were 4 to 6 times higher than the average for the leading countries (UNICEF/ Innocenti, 2005). However, in 2007, New Zealand was the first English-speaking country in the world to abolish corporal punishment both at school and home.

The negative psychoanalytic concept of the normal baby, and the focus on internal fantasy to the exclusion of real-life early traumas, may be partly why orthodox psychoanalysis has had so little to say about preventive mental health (Bowlby, 1973; Cook, 1998). Today, various applications of John Bowlby's attachment theory are sometimes valued and studied, but he was ostracised by his psychoanalytic colleagues when he was developing an evolutionary basis for the findings he described in his trilogy *Attachment and Loss* (Karen, 1994).

From his 1944 study of 'affectionless' thieves (Bowlby, 1944) and his 1951 WHO monograph *Maternal Care and Mental Health*, Bowlby came to see that his explorations of the nature of a child's tie to its mother could only be understood from an evolutionary perspective. In 1973, tucked away in Appendix II of his second Volume: *Attachment and Loss. Vol 2, Separation, Anxiety and Anger*, Bowlby wrote these remarkable words:

> On reflection it becomes clear that Freud's increasingly deep commitment to a Lamarckian perspective, to the exclusion of Darwinian ideas about differential survival rates and the distinction between causation and function, has suffused the whole structure of psychoanalytic thought and theory. With the remainder of biology resting firmly on a developed version of Darwinian principles and psychoanalysis continuing Lamarckian, the gulf between the two has steadily and inevitably grown wider. There are thus only three conceivable outcomes. The first, which is barely imaginable, is for biology to renounce its Darwinian perspective. The second, advocated here, is for psychoanalysis to be recast in terms of modern evolution theory. The third is for the present divorce to continue indefinitely with psychoanalysis remaining permanently beyond the fringe of the scientific world (Bowlby, 1973).

Eventually Bowlby's contribution could no longer be denied, and in 1980 as Freud Memorial Visiting Professor at the University of London, he gave the Freud Memorial and Inaugural Lecture *Psychoanalysis as a Science*. He said:

> I believe that all the developmental concepts of psychoanalysis will have to be re-examined and that most of them will in due course be replaced by concepts now current among those who are studying the development of affectional bonds in infants and young children by means of direct observation (Bowlby, 1980).

Bowlby died in 1990, but evidence of the value of his contribution continues to accumulate.

Two contrasting approaches to childrearing

In the 21st century, much advice about childrearing still draws from two contrasting ideas about the nature of the child. A distrustful view of the child's nature tends to support a directive or manipulative approach to achieve the desired behaviour promptly, while the contrasting view seeks a more trusting, cooperative, empathic relationship, willing to rely on the desired behaviours coming in due course through the quality of the relationship – unless, of course, urgent compliance is needed in an emergency. These two approaches are presented, both in text and a table, in *Childrearing, culture and mental health* (Cook, 1978; Note 6). William Sears, a US paediatrician, has a similar table: *Contrasting styles and results between attachment parenting and restraint parenting* (Sears, 1991).[35]

In 1974 Benjamin Spock, MD, contrasted them like this:

> There is always an argument going on, audibly or silently, between people who have two quite opposite attitudes about how children should be raised. There are those who feel that children are real human beings who are striving to become more mature, have generally good motives, are eager to learn, are perceptive of the truth and deserve kindness and respect despite their inexperience and their need for constant adult guidance. At the opposite extreme are those who believe that children are naturally lawless, lazy and uncivilized; that they can be held in line only by pressure, material rewards, threats and physical punishment administered by parents and teachers who make all the judgments and decisions. They assume that if children are not controlled with a stern hand they surely will end up incompetent or delinquent. Most people are not at the extremes in their views but lean in one direction or the other (Spock, 1974).

These two views are clearly pictured in two matching, but quite different, books published in 1979 and 1980. In *Baby Taming*, Peter Mayle portrayed the infant as a mischievous young devil, who enjoyed tormenting his mother, and sometimes showed his red, forked tail. Toilet training was "The Longest Battle of All", and another chapter offered his mother "A Cure for Combat Fatigue" (Mayle, 1979). The black humour was actually all at the infant's expense. The consequent vicious

---

35. This table by Sears is reproduced in Cook, 1996:189.

circles of mutual frustration presumably contributed to a willingness to accept non-maternal childcare as a way out.

Pyjamas Don't Matter (Or: What Your Baby Really Needs) by Trish Gibben came from the same publisher one year later. It was based on a trusting, cooperative approach to the mother-infant relationship, with consideration of how best to understand and harmonise their respective needs. It showed how well-nurtured two-year-olds can at times be amongst the planet's most delightful creatures; but its sales were much fewer than those of *Baby Taming* (Gribben, 1979; Cook, 2005a).

There is a benefit of nature's provisions that the West has been slow to recognise, though it is ancient wisdom in some countries. When a mother carries her baby, perhaps on her back, and there is close communication between them, she may be able to feel when he needs to 'go'. She can then 'hold him out' in a suitable place, so that each is more likely to stay clean. A baby can sometimes be taught by sounds to let his mother know when this needs to happen. This is sometimes known as "elimination communication". Rewarded by his mother's pleasure when they are successful, they may manage with fewer diapers and accomplish toilet training at an earlier age than is often expected. Ingrid Bauer offers a description in *Diaper Free! The gentle wisdom of natural infant hygiene* (Bauer, 2001).

9

The fateful hoaxing of Margaret Mead

> The "world images" that have been created by "ideas" have, like switchmen, determined the tracks along which action has been pushed by the dynamic of interest.[36]
> —Max Weber

> On being shown by a colleague "with chapter and verse, that a conclusion of hers was untenable, Mead's defense would always be, 'If it isn't, it ought to be,' to which she would add, 'Well, what's so bad about that?'"
> —Luther Cressman, Margaret Mead's first husband, cited by Freeman (1999: 146)

> It is in deep waters that the qualities of a canoe are tested.
> —Derek Freeman (1999), citing his favourite Samoan proverb.

Part One in this book described how five different lines of evidence converge to support the conclusion that there is a natural 'best-fit' pattern of mothering that is the norm for humans, and that it is based in our genome. In Part Two, Chapter 6 described how a mismatch between our environment and our biological 'givens' can lead to ill-health, and it referred particularly to the risks for mothers and infants. Chapter 7 outlined some changes in the lifestyles of humans over the past 12,000 years, and Chapter 8 summarised how a malign view of the baby's basic nature has sometimes led to child-rearing ideas that involved real risks for the child's mental health. Chapter 9 now describes how a seductive, but untrue, idea about human nature gave rise to powerful derivative

---

36. A switchman (or 'pointsman' in English usage) controls the switches (or points) that determine the track on which the train will travel, and therefore its destination (in other words: small things can change the course of history).

ideologies. Chapters 10 and 11 outline how these ideologies have affected mothers, their infants, and society.

Margaret Mead and her influence

Margaret Mead, who was born in Philadelphia in 1901, became an anthropologist and for much of the 20th century she was acclaimed as the world's most eminent social scientist. In her 1928 book, *Coming of Age in Samoa: a Psychological Study of Primitive Youth for Western Civilization*, she wrote that Samoans enjoyed a happy, non-violent and neurosis-free society, which she said was because their culture allowed them great sexual freedom during adolescence. Her book became an all-time bestseller, and Mead's account was used to propagate an ideology that had far-reaching consequences in Western societies.[37] These included adverse effects on the lives of many infants and their mothers, in ways that Mead herself would probably not have approved.

Mead's account and conclusions were accepted and cherished by many influential anthropologists for decades, but in 1983 Derek Freeman, a professor at the Australian National University, shocked the anthropological establishment by publishing his detailed evidence that Mead's story was seriously in error. A few colleagues applauded and were grateful to Freeman, but the anthropological establishment rejected his evidence as an attack on Margaret Mead, who had risen to the status of their celebrated "goddess".

Instead of carefully studying and appraising Freeman's detailed evidence, they rejected it, and some resorted to *ad hominem*, 'shoot-the-messenger' attacks on Freeman himself.[38] These continued even after his death in 2001 with allegations that Freeman's persistent refutation arose out of quite unworthy motives, personality defects, and so on. Consequently, despite the solid factual evidence, many people think the matter is still unsettled and that perhaps Mead was right. Yet George

---

37. ideology, noun (pl. ideologies) 1. A system of ideas and ideals forming the basis of an economic or political theory. 2. The set of beliefs characteristic of a social group or individual. (Oxford English Dictionary).
   Appell (1984) writes: "I have specifically used the term 'ideology of cultural determinism' to indicate an intellectual posture which does not permit the consideration of any contrary evidence that might modify or disprove the position."
38. *ad hominem*. Latin. 'to the man'; directed against a person rather than against his arguments; 'shooting the messenger'; 'playing the man, not the ball'.

Appell, Senior Visiting Research Associate, Department of Anthropology, Brandeis University, says: "I showed in 1984 that Margaret Mead was a pathological liar."[39]

Since Mead's book had far-reaching consequences, this important story is summarised here in some detail, drawing on five additional sources of information that are usually not cited.[40] Further details are in Note 7.

Freeman showed how Mead's misinformation and her ideas about the underlying 'pattern' of Samoan society had been used to propagate the ideology that human nature is almost wholly determined by the cultural environment – *cultural determinism*. Heredity and biology were held to play little part in the non-physical differences between men and women. Cultural determinism then led to two further persistent ideologies. *Cultural relativism* taught that all cultures are equally valid for their own people, emphasising that no culture should be judged as being any better or worse than another. *Postmodernism* took a flexible and often obfuscating approach to language and the truth. These two ideologies are still very widely influential today.[41]

Cultural Determinism – an antidote to Social Darwinism?

The publication in 1859 of Charles Darwin's book *On the Origin of Species* had begun to transform the study of life on earth, but some people misused Darwin's theory to justify racism. They said that white races were at the pinnacle of evolution, while others, such as those with

---

39. (Personal communication, 2010: on the record). Appell was referring to his 13,000-word critique that can now be seen on his website: Appell, George N. (1984). Freeman's refutation of Mead's *Coming of Age in Samoa: The implications for anthropological inquiry. The Eastern Anthropologist* 37: 183-214.
www.gnappell.org/articles/freeman.htm.
40. These sources are i) Appell , G.N. (1984); ii) The brilliant, but neglected, 1988 award-winning documentary film *Margaret Mead & Samoa*, by Frank Heimans, readily available as a DVD. iii) The complete post-production script of that film, which may be seen on this author's website. iv) The full text of Mead's 1931 contribution to a book of stories called *All True! Actual adventures that have happened to ten women of today*. A summary of this story, with a quotation of Mead's own words is in Note 7. v) Previously unpublished information about Derek Freeman's health, as in Note 7.
41. In Cook (1978), I argued that cultural relativism, as it prevailed at that time, certainly did not hold true in matters of health—especially if, in the management of mothers and infants, a society's customs led to their ill-health.

darker skins, were less highly evolved and therefore inferior – *Social Darwinism*.

In 1999 Derek Freeman, in his book *The Fateful Hoaxing of Margaret Mead: A Historical Account of her Samoan Research,* described how Franz Boas, who became Professor of Anthropology at Columbia University in New York in 1899, had worked tirelessly to oppose Social Darwinism. In 1888 Boas had written: "the data of ethnology prove that not only our knowledge but also our emotions are the result of the form of our social life and the history of the people to whom we belong". His pupils adopted his views and Freeman says that in 1917, Alfred Kroeber, Professor of Anthropology at the University of California, Berkeley, "instigated a massive intellectual schism, proclaiming that there was an abyss between cultural anthropology and evolutionary biology, 'an eternal chasm' that could not be bridged." Freeman says: "The Boasians had established their independence from biology by social fiat.[42] The breach with evolutionary biology was complete, and Boasian culturalism was poised to become one of the leading ideologies of the twentieth century" (Freeman, 1999: 23–27, 263; Kroeber, 1917).

In 1922 Margaret Mead was one of Boas' most promising students, and what she later called "the phenomenon of social pressure and its absolute determination in shaping the individuals within its bounds" was in accord with the "compelling idea" of Boas' life's work – "*the complete molding of every human expression – inner thought and external behavior – by social conditioning*". Unfortunately, there remained a serious problem: they had no evidence to support this ideology. To remedy this, Boas arranged for Mead to have a research grant for six months in 1925 for "the study of heredity and environment in relation to adolescence" in Samoa (Freeman, 1996). His hope was that she would be able to document a society where adolescents had great sexual freedom, and where the problems associated with adolescence in Western societies were absent. They (unscientifically) thought that if she could describe just one such society, this would show that human nature is determined by culture, not by biological or inherited factors. Freeman wrote that this "doctrine of the cultural

---

42. fiat. *n.* an authoritative decree, sanction, or order. Latin: let it be done. (Macquarie Dictionary).

patterning of human thought and action... was to develop into a major anthropological movement".

As a highly talented young woman, Mead seemed well-suited to this important project. However, without telling Boas, and against his explicit instructions, she arranged with the Bishop Museum in Honolulu to also carry out a quite different project in which she was much more interested. In the 1988 documentary film/DVD *Margaret Mead and Samoa*, by Frank Heimans, Mead is shown in 1971, saying: "I didn't want to study the adolescent girl, I wanted to study change. My professor wanted me to study adolescence – I wanted to come to Polynesia somewhere; he wanted me to stay in the United States. So we made an exchange: he said I could come to Polynesia if I would study the adolescent girl" (Heimans, 1998: 9 min.).[43]

The hoax, and *Coming of Age in Samoa*

What followed was eventually documented beyond reasonable doubt in 1999 by Derek Freeman. As a 23-year-old New Zealander, he had gone to Western Samoa in April 1940 as a teacher. Having read *Coming of Age in Samoa*, he looked forward to being in this South Seas paradise and confirming Mead's findings. He lived in a Samoan village and became fluent in the language; a chiefly title was conferred on him, allowing him to attend meetings of the chiefs, and in particular to see how they dealt with offences that involved aggressive and antisocial behaviours. The more he studied life in Samoa, the more he was forced to conclude that Mead's celebrated report was seriously in error (Freeman, 1999; Freeman, Orans, and Cote, 2000).

It was wartime, and after three and a half years Freeman left Samoa in November 1943 to join the Navy, but he knew by then that he would one day face the responsibility of writing a refutation of Mead's Samoan findings. After the war he studied anthropology in London and wrote his postgraduate thesis, "The social structure of a Samoan village

---

43. This 51-minute documentary film was made in 1987-8 by Frank Heimans, Sydney, who has made many award-winning documentaries. The film brings the material in this chapter vividly to life. In addition to the main filming in Samoa in 1987, it shows photographs, biographical details, archival film footage, and interviews with many academics and others who knew Mead. It is available as a DVD from Frank Heimans, and the full post-production script may be seen at www.members.optusnet.com.au/pcook62 See References and Note 7.

community". For his subsequent research in Borneo he gained a PhD from Cambridge University in 1953, and after a year in New Zealand, he moved to the Research School of Pacific Studies at the Australian National University where he became known as a Southeast Asian specialist.

In December 1965, Freeman went back to Samoa with his wife and two daughters to continue his Samoan studies. He sought to understand the gross discrepancies between what Mead had reported in 1926 in American Samoa and what he had witnessed only 15 years later in Western Samoa, an essentially identical culture. [44] But when he left in January 1968, and even after a further visit in 1981, he still did not know how Mead could have reported this as an idyllic society, free of the many social problems and aggressive behaviours that he had seen at firsthand.

In 1964, Mead had a long meeting with Freeman in Canberra, and Heimans' film shows him saying: "I laid before her all the evidence I had, and indicated that her conclusions were not empirically justified." We later see Mead's close companion Lola Romanucci-Ross saying "She told me that she had met with Derek Freeman and that he had told her about his research in Samoa, and what he thought of her work and that he was going to publish this. And I gave her a 'So what?' look and she said: 'You don't understand, he has proven me wrong'. And she looked very sad and puzzled and I thought it was very odd that I was here feeling sorry for Margaret Mead, and even stranger that I was going to have to tell her that this was not important. But I did, I said: 'What you have done in anthropology and for the world is not Samoa-dependant; it really doesn't matter whether you were right or wrong about Samoa'. And she said: 'Oh, what do you think I ought to do about it?' I just said: 'Nothing'" (Heimans, 1988: 48 min.).

Freeman realised that attempting to undo what had become established doctrine in universities throughout America was a very formidable task indeed, and he had to go about it most thoroughly. It was not until

---

44. Tim O'Meara, then Assistant Professor of Anthropology University of North Carolina, said "From what I have seen in Western Samoa and the people that I've talked to and what I've read about the debate I don't see any significant difference in the society, in the people's behaviour in 1928 and between Western Samoa and Ta'u" (as spoken in Heimans, 1988: 36 min.).

March 1978 that he was able to send Mead a draft of his first book. Unfortunately she never replied, as she was ill and died of cancer in November 1978. Freeman then felt "there must be a decent pause between her death and the publication of the refutation", so it was not until 1983 that it was published as *Margaret Mead and Samoa: The Making and Unmaking of an Anthropological Myth* [45] (Heimans, 1988: 28 min.).

Some colleagues expressed profound appreciation that his evidence had at last set the record straight, but a majority of influential American anthropologists received his evidence with anger and denial. To this he responded cogently and vigorously, but for his persistence he received much personal denigration (Appell, 1984; Heimans, 1988: 24 min.).

Freeman (1983) noted that "the explanation most consistently advanced by Samoans themselves for the magnitude of the error in Mead's depiction of their sexual morality was that, as Eleanor Gerber had reported in 1975, 'Mead's informants must have been telling lies in order to tease her.'" But it was not until four years later, in 1987, that Freeman had a totally unexpected introduction to one of Mead's original companions. It was after this event that he decided that *he must discover and document exactly what had happened during Mead's eight months stay in Samoa.* Her extensive records and letters were all available for research.

When she reached Samoa on August 31, 1925, Mead stayed in Pago Pago, where American naval personnel provided her with a nurse to help her learn the difficult language. Hoping to escape Western influences, she decided to locate her study on the small and remote island of Ta'u one of three islands in the Manu'a group, seventy miles to the east. However, by 1925, the Manu'ans had been governed by the United States for 21 years, and "had been converts to protestant Christianity for some eighty years" (Freeman, 1983). Virginity was highly valued and sometimes formally checked before marriage. Mead arrived there on

---

45. In 1996, to mark the opening of David Williamson's play, *The Heretic*, Freeman's 1983 book was reissued as *Margaret Mead and the Heretic*, with a new five-page preface.
This is an excellent summary of Freeman's position to that date and it includes a lengthy excerpt from the filmed interview with Fa'apua'a, as described in this present chapter. In the preface to the 1983 edition Freeman reiterated that "the supposition that my book is a personal attack on Margaret Mead... is without foundation."

November 9, and rather than live in a Samoan village, she decided to live with the American family who ran the US naval dispensary.

She selected girls from three villages on Ta'u for her study, but this work was completely halted when a major hurricane caused extensive destruction on January 1, 1926. So on January 5 she wrote to Boas and asked: "If I simply write conclusions and use my cases as illustrative material will it be acceptable?"

She then took two opportunities to join expeditions to further her project for the Bishop Museum, although she still had not made any proper study of the sexual behaviour of her sample of adolescent girls. Yet this was the sole purpose for which she had been given the fellowship.

Freeman says that by March 13, "60 percent of the time that Mead had allowed for the collection of the mass of information listed in her letter to Boas of February 15 had passed without her making any progress at all.... There was an immense amount still to be done and very little time left in which to do it. Thus by March 13, 1926, 'the investigation of the adolescent girl' as 'a study in heredity and environment'... was in a state of crisis. It was a crisis that had been created because, in Mead's own words, she had 'abandoned' her interest in 'socially unimportant adolescents' for almost a month in order to do quite unrelated research for her projected monograph on the ethnology of Manu'a" (Freeman, 1999).

It was vital for Mead that her study for Boas should succeed. After studying her many detailed records and letters, Freeman eventually concluded that on March 13, 1926, Mead must have taken a shortcut. She had two regular companions, Fa'apua'a Fa'amo of Ta'o and Fofoa, and on a outing with these two "girls" on a visit to the neighbouring island of Ofu, she had evidently seized an opportunity to ask for the information she urgently wanted to hear. Feeling she had their confidence, she had resorted to direct and suggestive questioning about their sexual activities, and those of other Samoan girls (Freeman, 1999: 138). Without realising it, she was now breaking Samoan cultural taboos, and she also did not know about their custom of playful joking by lying. Freeman wrote: "the stage was set for an extraordinary happening: a prank that was to completely hoax the twenty-four-year-old Margaret Mead and that was, through her, to mislead virtually the entire anthropological profession, as well as countless others in the educated Western world" (ibid. 131).

Mead suggested to her companions that it was really the Samoan custom for adolescents and young lovers to enjoy carefree nights in what she described as "trysts beneath the palm trees," and with free love sometimes occurring even after marriage (Mead, 1928: Ch.2). These two "girls" were actually young women a little older than Mead herself, and one of them was a ceremonial virgin. Being embarrassed by her culturally inappropriate questioning, and after pinching each other to signal they would respond by joking, they agreed with, and even embellished, everything Mead suggested. She did not know that such recreational lying was a Samoan custom, and they never imagined she would tell it to the world as a true account.

Mead was evidently delighted to think that, through being a young woman, she had discovered what had eluded other scientists – that the underlying "pattern" of the culture was just as she and Boas had hoped it would be. On March 14 she wrote to tell Boas the results of her study, and on March 18th she got a cable from him, agreeing to the proposal she had put to him in her letter on January 5 (i.e., "If I simply write conclusions and use my cases as illustrative material will it be acceptable?").

So now, on March 19 – the very next day – she wrote to tell Boas that she had decided to finish her research a month earlier than she had planned. Freeman says: "Cutting short the fieldwork on her Boas assignment in this abrupt way, and her involvement in even further ethnological inquiry, meant that *no systematic, firsthand investigation of the sexual behaviour of her sample of adolescent girls was ever to be undertaken*. Instead, Margaret Mead's account of adolescent sexual behaviour in *Coming of Age in Samoa*... was based on what she had been told by Fa'apua'a Fa'amo and Fofoa, supplemented by other such inquiries that she had previously made." Having heard what she so much wanted to hear, and ignoring the contrary information that she had received from her American hosts, she decided to leave Samoa. After ceremonial farewells, and "with 'so little left to do', she even found time to write to her grandmother on April 7, 1926, making up a short story about the faraway valley in rural Pennsylvania where she herself had come of age. She called it '*The Conscientious Myth-Maker*'". This gives another glimpse into how her mind could play with the truth, as she presumably was not conscious of how well this described what she herself was now doing (Freeman, 1999 [paperback 2nd edition]: 146-8; 264-5, Freeman's italicisation).[46]

She returned to Pago Pago on April 16, and on the first available ship she sailed away to holiday in Europe and write up her report. When she submitted it to Boas, he and others evidently did not check her field records as they should have done, so the deficiencies and inconsistencies were not then detected. Instead, it was acclaimed as quality research and they actively used it to propagate Boas' ideology of cultural determinism.

In 1928 Mead published *Coming of Age in Samoa: a Study of Adolescence and Sex in Primitive Societies* and it became a classic. Freeman described it as a captivating but untrue account of free love in "far-off Samoa", adding "there could not have been a more mentally seductive concoction." It was a continuing bestseller and on the reading lists in most universities. Freeman described how "the mythic process" took off, as the book was soon accepted as a "careful scientific work". Mead had it endorsed by some eminent people, including Havelock Ellis – the most famous authority on sexual matters at that time. He declared (quite erroneously) that "a whole field of neurotic possibility had been legislated out of existence", since Samoa had "no neurosis, no frigidity, no impotence". On the basis of Mead's "enlightening study" he advocated the adoption of sexual promiscuity by Americans (Freeman, 1999: 146-8, 195).

Thus Mead, read by millions of avid young intellectuals, redefined the tone and scope of the human sciences, and established in the Western imagination an idyllic image of harmonious primitive societies. She later described it as her "classical research", and it launched her career as one of the most acclaimed and influential women of her time, great pathfinder of personal sexual liberty and, according to *Time* magazine, "Mother to the World". In 1976 she became the President of the American Association for the Advancement of Science, and her fame

---

46. For those who doubt Freeman's documentation of this, note that he cites details of the crucial Mead-Boas communications at this time in the new material that the publisher squeezed into pages 146 and 148 of the paperback 2nd edition of *The Fateful Hoaxing of Margaret Mead* (that did not appear until late 1999), but gave no indication that this new evidence was additional to that in the earlier 1999 hardback edition (see References).

reached the heavens when a large impact crater on Venus was named after her.[47]

Having achieved her scoop, Mead made no further inquiries into Samoan society, although in anthropological parlance she regarded it as "her country". She wrote many books and re-visited other societies that she had studied; but she returned to Samoa only once – on a "sentimental" five-day visit in 1971 (as shown in Heimans, 1988: 47 min.).

Freeman emphatically denied that Mead was guilty of scientific fraud, but rather that, on hearing what she very much wanted to hear, she eagerly believed it (Freeman, 1999: 146). He cited Luther Cressman, a newly ordained clergyman whom Mead had married in 1923. The marriage did not go well, and after leaving Samoa she told him she wanted a divorce. Cressman, who later became a professor of sociology, recorded how as a graduate student of anthropology at Columbia University, even when she was shown "with chapter and verse, that a conclusion of hers was untenable, Mead's defense would always be, 'If it isn't, it ought to be,' to which she would add, 'Well, what's so bad about that?'"

Mead tells of her lies, in a book called *All True!*

In November 1987, Freeman's conclusion that she must have been misled by her Samoan companions was confirmed quite unexpectedly. He had accepted an invitation to accompany the award-winning Australian filmmaker Frank Heimans on his visit to film on the island of Ta'u to make the Samoan scenes of his film, *Margaret Mead and Samoa*. When they arrived to film on Ta'u Island, they did not know that High Chief Galea'I Poumele, the Secretary of Samoan Affairs, had a surprise for them. He introduced them to a lady aged 86. She had agreed to take part in the film, and Freeman was astonished to find that she was Fa'apua'a Fa'amo, who had been one of Mead's two close companions in 1926. After living in Hawaii for many years, she had returned to Samoa to live in one of the villages where Mead had worked 60 years earlier. She was still mentally alert and active. Wishing to set the record straight, she had asked for the occasion to be recorded on film, and so, before a distinguished gathering, she took a solemn oath on the Bible

---

47. For a more detailed summary of Mead's fame and reputation see Cook, 1999c.

that she would speak only the truth. She then gave detailed testimony that included her memories about the events that had taken place when she was aged 24, during the trip with Margaret Mead to the island of Ofu in March 1926.[48]

Freeman published all this in early 1999, in the hardback edition of *The Fateful Hoaxing of Margaret Mead*, but unfortunately it was not until *after* this, when clearing his records to be archived, that he belatedly unearthed a reference to a story that Mead herself had written in 1931. She had contributed to a collection of stories in a book called *All True! The Record of Actual Adventures that Have Happened to Ten Women of Today*. When Freeman got a copy of this rare book, he was astonished to read Mead's own story. In *Life as a Samoan Girl* she wrote: "In all things I had behaved as a Samoan, for only so, only by losing my identity, as far as possible, had I been able to become acquainted with the Samoan girls, receive their whispered confidences, and learn at the same time the answer to the scientists' questions" (Mead, 1931). [49]

Was Mead's *Coming of Age in Samoa* "just plain rubbish"?

Fifteen years before Freeman discovered the circumstances of Mead's hoaxing, a scholarly 13,000-word analysis of his 1983 book, *Margaret Mead and Samoa*, was published in 1984 in *The Eastern Anthropologist*

---

48. In Heimans' film, Fa'apua'a Fa'amo describes the circumstances of Mead's questioning, and how, before answering her questions, she and her friend had pinched each other in silent agreement that they would respond by 'joking.' The chief asked Fa'apua'a: "Was there ever a day or a night when the woman [i.e. Margaret Mead] questioned you about what you did at nights, and did you ever joke about this?" She replied: "Yes, we did, we said that we were out at night with boys; she failed to realize that we were just joking and must have been taken in by our pretences. Yes, she asked: 'Where do you go?' And we replied 'We go out at nights!' 'With whom?' she asked. Then Fofoa and I would pinch one another and say 'We spend the nights with boys, yes, with boys!' She must have taken us seriously, but I was only joking. As you know, Samoan girls are terrific liars when it comes to joking. But Margaret Mead accepted our trumped-up stories as though they were true... we just fibbed and fibbed to her."
In 1993, after Freeman had done more investigation into some relevant archives, the old lady's memory was tested by a Samoan scholar who knew the correct answers, as he asked her about various early details. At age 92 she was found to be "lucid" and "still able to remember well." Some of her replies were confirmed by notes that Mead had made in 1926 (Freeman, 1999: 2–8, 13; Freeman et al., 2000).
49. See Note 7 for a longer quotation, as Mead describes how her elaborate lying helped her out of a threatening situation that arose from her earlier misrepresentations.

by George Appell, who was then Senior Research Associate at Brandeis University, Massachusetts. He emphasised that Freeman's refutation of Mead's account was based on six years of study in Samoa, over a period of 40 years between 1941 and 1981, as well as on detailed research in archives and libraries (Appell, 1984).

Appell analysed and acknowledged the profound significance of Freeman's work for anthropology and the social sciences, saying: "Freeman's history of these disputes and how they provided the background for Mead's Samoan researches is one of the most fascinating and enlightening accounts of our intellectual history that I have ever read." His paper then brought together and classified the many reasons for concluding that Mead's *Coming of Age in Samoa* was really an imaginative account of what she had wanted to see there.

Appell also emphasised that Freeman's refutation was not about Mead's *interpretation* of Samoan culture, but was entirely concerned with showing that *she had got the actual facts wrong*. He concluded: "Anyone who can read with a discerning mind would have seen that Mead's *Coming of Age in Samoa* was just plain rubbish." As a concrete example he wrote:

The Smoking Gun

In detective fiction the critical piece of evidence is referred to as the 'smoking gun.' Is there a smoking gun in Mead's publications? Did she 'cook up' her data like Cyril Burt? I think not; she left a trail of too many ambiguities.

But much of the evidence Freeman uses to make his point was also available to Mead (see bibliography in Mead, 1930). How did she reconcile these contradictions with her own data? Was she simply a poor scholar? Perhaps, but I also think it is clear that personal and ideological bias has crept in to distort her account. This has of course been disputed. Social facts are frequently ambiguous in their meaning and interpretation. But certainly not physical facts. What did Mead say about the environment? 'Neither poverty nor great disasters threaten the people to make them hold their lives dearly and tremble for continued existence' (1973: 110, orig. 1928).

Freeman points out that this statement is "scarcely true, for the Samoan islands are regularly stricken by severe hurricanes. In the hurricane of 10 January 1915 [ten years prior to Mead's arrival]... the churches, schoolhouses, stores, and most of the houses of Manu'a were blown down and the greater part of the crops destroyed. Indeed so severe were the food shortages following this hurricane that over half the population of Manu'a had to be transported to Tutuila and maintained there for several months. Again on 1 January 1926, during the course of Mead's stay in Manu'a, there was a severe hurricane which, so she states... 'destroyed every house in the village and ruined the crops'" (Freeman, 1983: 320).

Freeman also quotes Mead (1983: 70-71) to the effect that, for several weeks, informants were 'not to be had for love or money' because of the damage that everyone was busy repairing; and 'adult energies were devoted almost exclusively to house-building' so that she had 'very little opportunity to witness social ceremonies of any kind.'

In his conclusion about Mead's cultural influence up to that date, Appell added that "Mead's monumental error was largely the result of her attempt to prove the doctrine of cultural determinism". He argued that the ideology of cultural determinism has "so addled the anthropological mind, has so consumed it, that no one has come to realize that Mead's research design and her findings could be used to argue the exact opposite of what she claimed".[50] Appell said he "specifically used the term 'ideology of cultural determinism' to indicate an intellectual posture which does not permit the consideration of any contrary evidence that might modify or disprove the position".

On being a heretic – follow the facts

As a heretic, Galileo knew that whether he recanted or not, the moons of Jupiter would still be there for others to see, and thereby show that the earth goes round the sun, and not the other way round.

Freeman's situation was different. He knew that if *he* did not do it, then no one else would ever be better able to unearth *the facts* about what

---

50. Appell (1984) wrote: "Let us try a thought experiment. Let us assume that Mead's conclusions on Samoan culture are correct and that coming of age in Samoa is without stress and strain. Her explanation for this difference in behavior between Western society and Samoa was that of cultural determinism.... But Mead's 'experiment' was flawed. For Mead did not hold the racial variable constant. As behavior varied with race in her 'experiment', one explanation for her findings would be racial. That is, the Samoans behave differently because they have a different genetic constitution."

really happened when Mead was in Samoa in 1925, nor demonstrate the erroneous basis of the ideology that she and others had promulgated on the basis of her story. That he was carefully presenting *evidence about the independently verifiable historical facts* is shown by the subtitle of his 1999 book: *The Fateful Hoaxing of Margaret Mead: A Historical Account of her Samoan Research.*

The conclusion of Heimans' film shows Freeman in 1988 saying:

> My passion in life is that we will develop a genuine science of the human species. Nothing is more important for humans than that we succeed in this. Now I have said that the question that Boas gave Margaret Mead to answer was a profoundly important anthropological question, and I think that now, in the late 1980s, we have resolved that problem. It is apparent to all knowledgeable behavioural scientists that we must operate within a framework in which we simultaneously take into account our evolutionary history and our cultures. And it is only when these two things are combined within an interactionist paradigm that you have the imperative precondition for a genuine science of our species. I think being a heretic is a most beautiful thing... a heretic is someone who thinks for himself and doesn't run with the mob and I have always found great joy in it. But what you've got to be in science is a heretic who gets it right. It's no good being a heretic who gets it wrong... but if you are a heretic who gets it right, you can't do better".

Freeman's "sweeping clear the faulty foundations of his discipline"

In March 2000, Professor James J. Fox, director of the Research School of Pacific and Asian Studies at The Australian National University, supported the nomination of Freeman for an Australian honours award. Urging special recognition for Freeman's distinguished contribution as a scholar, he wrote:

> Derek Freeman, Emeritus Professor of Anthropology at the Australian National University... has contributed significantly to the formulation of a new paradigm for anthropology by his

> uncompromising opposition to, and eventual refutation of, the views of Margaret Mead, one of the 20th century's most celebrated social scientists... By sweeping clear the faulty foundations of his discipline, Professor Freeman... has prepared the basis for a more biologically attuned human science for the 21st century. His efforts in advancing his arguments against notable opposition have been recognised and acclaimed throughout the world (Fox, 2000).

Freeman died on July 6, 2001 at the age of 84, believing that his work was done. The honour was not awarded, and *ad hominem* attacks continued after his death.

Freeman had shown that, however worthy the intentions, the ideology of cultural determinism was founded on untruths and hence, so were the derivative ideologies of cultural relativism and postmodernism. Yet these ideologies have had far-reaching influences on many aspects of Western culture, with continuing harmful effects for infants, women and society, as shown in the next three chapters.

10

Social sciences detach from biology

> Sociology is a mess.
> —Theile, 2005

Is sociology "a mess"?

In his book *Consilience: the Unity of Knowledge*, E.O. Wilson described some effects of the ideology of cultural determinism on the social sciences. He says social scientists as a whole have paid little attention to the foundations of human nature, and they have shown almost no interest in its deep origins. Ignorance of the natural sciences was a strategy fashioned by the founders – in particular Emile Durkheim, Karl Marx, Franz Boas, Sigmund Freud, and their immediate followers. He continues:

> The theorists were inhibited from probing by another problem endemic to social sciences: political ideology. Its effects have been especially clear in American anthropology. Franz Boas, aided by his famous students Ruth Benedict and Margaret Mead, led a crusade against what they perceived (correctly) to be the eugenics and racism implicit in social Darwinism. With caution swept aside by moral zeal, they turned opposition into the new ideology of cultural relativism.... Believing it a virtue to declare that all cultures are equal but in different ways, Boas and other influential anthropologists nailed their flag of cultural relativism to the mast. During the 1960s and 1970s this scientific belief lent strength in the United States and other Western societies to political multiculturalism.... Many anthropologists, their instincts fortified by humanitarian purpose, grew stronger in their belief in cultural relativism, while stiffening their opposition to biology in any guise.
>
> So, no biology. The reasoning then came full circle with a twist that must have brought a smile to the little gods of irony. Where cultural relativism had been initiated to negate belief in hereditary behavioral differences among ethnic groups – undeniably an

unproven and ideologically dangerous conception – it was then turned against the idea of a unified human nature grounded in heredity. A great conundrum of the human condition was created: If neither culture nor a hereditary human nature, what unites humanity? The question cannot be just left hanging, for if ethical standards are molded by culture, and cultures are endlessly diverse and equivalent, what disqualifies theocracy, for example, or colonialism? Or child labor, torture, and slavery? (Wilson 1998: 204–3).

Describing the ensuing schism in anthropology, Wilson says that some adopted "the extreme postmodernist view that science is just another way of thinking, one respectable intellectual subculture in the company of many." Despite some exceptions, "academic sociologists have remained clustered near the nonbiological end of the cultural studies spectrum. Many are... biophobic – fearful of biology and determined to avoid it." Thus the reasoning of the American Standard Social Science Model is "based on the slighting or outright denial of biologically based human nature" (Wilson, 1998).

David Theile, an Australian sociologist and academic, wrote that, although sociology has been well represented in universities across the Western world for about one hundred years, "sociologists have produced little disciplinary knowledge; they agree on almost nothing, not even on the nature and extent of their disagreements. Sociology is a mess. Yet few sociologists, at least in their more public pronouncements, acknowledge this, preferring instead to present their work as an organised discipline producing knowledge that contributes to the wellbeing of humanity" (Theile, 2005).

How the 'blank slate' theory of the child, and behaviourism, influenced childrearing

From the theory of cultural determinism, it followed that the newborn baby was simply raw material, ready to be moulded to any pattern – like a blank slate or *tabula rasa*. This resurrected an idea that John Locke had presented in his 1689 essay *Concerning Human Understanding*.

So another misconceived notion joined the stream of influences on Western childrearing advice. Mead's theory was used to support the behaviourist school of childrearing, as advocated by American psychologist J.B. Watson. His influential *Psychological Care of the*

Infant and Child also appeared in 1928. He advocated relentless conditioning of the infant from birth, and likened the parents' task to that of a blacksmith shaping hot metal with hammers. He warned that "the blacksmith has all the advantage" because after a mistake he can begin again. But with a child "every stroke, be it true or false, has its effect. The best we can do is to conceal, as skillfully as we can, the defects of our shaping." He taught that children should be treated as young adults: "Let your behavior always be objective, and kindly firm. Never hug and kiss them, never let them sit on your lap. If you must, kiss them once on the forehead when they say goodnight. Shake hands with them in the morning. Give them a pat on the head if they have made an extraordinary good job of a difficult task" (Watson, 1928).

Marxist utopians were likewise supported in their belief that, with no basic human nature to stand in their way, the new communist man and woman would be produced by social conditioning. After all, the early seeds of behaviourism were laid in Russia, where Pavlov carried out his influential experiments to control the behaviour of his dogs by conditioning.

These views also supported the idea that women were in no way more able than men to raise their children, thus inviting the devaluing of mothering.

11

Equality feminism – and mothering denied

> As I look back, wondering, on the credulous adolescent that I was, I am astonished when I realise how thoroughly I have been cheated.
> —Simone de Beauvoir, at the age of 54

> The equality we fought for isn't liveable, isn't workable, isn't comfortable in the terms that structured our battle.
> —Betty Friedan, 1981

> In *The Female Eunuch* I argued that motherhood should not be treated as a substitute career; now I would argue that motherhood should be regarded as a genuine career option, that is to say, as paid work and as an alternative to other paid work. Dignified motherhood is a feminist priority.... The immense rewardingness of children is the best-kept secret in the Western world.
> —Germaine Greer, 1999

> Motherhood has almost been erased from the lexicon of family policy. Instead, mothers and fathers have been subsumed into one: the gender-neutral parent... motherhood consists of a number of narratives.
> —Yvonne Roberts, 2008

In the Victorian era – despite the insights of Mary Wollstonecraft, Mary Ann Evans (George Eliot) and others – women's capacities were regarded as necessarily arrested by their reproductive duties. Even Charles Darwin was led astray by this view. Sarah Hrdy cites his opinion that "whether requiring deep thought, reason, or imagination, or merely the use of the senses and hands, [man will attain] a higher eminence... than can woman" (Darwin, 1874). She comments, "It did not occur to his Victorian imagination... just how resourceful and strategic a woman [in a hunter-gatherer society] would have to be to keep children alive and survive herself." She added, "No wonder women turned away from biology" (Hrdy, 1999: 18–19).

Chapter 11: Equality feminism—and mothering denied

Yet by 1893, Alfred Russel Wallace, the co-discoverer of evolution, expressed a quite different view. When asked about the effect on human progress of the social revolution occurring in the education and general development of women, he said, "the effect will be entirely beneficial to the race. Women at the present time, in all civilised countries, are showing a determination to secure their personal, social, and political freedom... the hope of the future lies with women" (Wallace, 1893). But his views made little impact.

Women continued to seek reform of the injustices and inequalities that they suffered in patriarchal societies, but as Boasian cultural determinism became widely accepted in academia, and adopted by thinkers like Sartre, it became the basis for the prescriptions by Simone de Beauvoir (1908–1986) in her feminist classic *The Second Sex* (1949). She said "A woman is not born but made." Lorna Sage comments that "Her whole life's work, and *The Second Sex* in particular, depends on the conviction that people are constructs: we come from the matrix of the culture at large, not from God, or nature, or (even) Mother." On the basis of this ideology, de Beauvoir argued that woman's nature and behaviour, being environmentally determined, can and must be changed (Sage, 2001).

Inspired by de Beauvoir, and fortified by their adoption of the ideology of cultural determinism, feminists insisted that all, or nearly all, the differences between men and women were determined by cultural influences, and not through biology, and the movement for women's liberation gave priority to seeking equality with men legally and in the workplace. During the Second World War many women enjoyed working together with a common purpose, but even in Britain's darkest days, mothers were officially seen as doing a more important job in caring for their young families than if they were conscripted into the workforce.

In *The Feminine Mystique* of 1963, Betty Friedan had portrayed mothers as trapped in "the concentration camps of their own homes," and she encouraged women on the path to careers and equality, while avoiding motherhood. She was later reproached by her disillusioned followers who pointed out that, unlike them, she already had a husband and children when she urged this life pattern. Anne Manne described Friedan's book as a "paean in praise of the rat-race – she just wanted women to join it". Thus feminism was "abducted by the hedonism of a service-oriented society". Manne quotes Don Edgar – who had been in a position to influence the direction of much family research in Australia – as saying, "We have to work to make us fully human." Yet Winston Churchill was probably more realistic when he observed that the world was divided into two classes of people: a minority who work at jobs they like – and the rest (Manne, 2008: 17, 20).

"Women should not have that choice"

When Friedan later told Simone de Beauvoir that she now believed women should have the choice of staying at home and raising their own children if that was their wish, de Beauvoir replied, "No, we don't believe that any woman should have that choice. No woman should be authorised to stay home to raise her children. Society should be totally different. Women should not have that choice, precisely because if there is such a choice, too many women will make that one" (Manne, 2005, citing Somers, 1994). Manne appropriately asks, "Just who is the 'we' here? And what do women want?" (Manne, 2008: 26). James Tooley, Professor of Education Policy in Newcastle, UK, cites de Beauvoir as adding: "It is a way of forcing women in a certain direction."[51] De Beauvoir is here using the formula underlying so much utopian inhumanity down the ages: "I know what is good for you, and I shall see that you get it" (Note 8).

Feminist icons recant

De Beauvoir was, in fact, well aware of the satisfactions and joys of mothering and family life. She described them with tenderness and insight in lesser-known passages of *The Second Sex*, sometimes showing feelings of deep envy (Tooley, 2002: 65–70). It seems that this brilliant woman – so widely regarded as an icon and pioneer of equality feminism – was grievously misled in many ways by her adoption, with Sartre, of a misconceived ideology and philosophy.

In *The Miseducation of Women*, Tooley, in Chapter 3, *Romantic Illusions*, presents some less well-remembered writings of influential feminists, especially those of de Beauvoir. Summarising what led to the following *cri de coeur* by de Beauvoir, he wrote: "At the age of 54 – hardly old age in many people's view – she wrote a 'devastating' picture

---

51. Tooley (2002) cites this as from Graglia, 1975.

Chapter 11: Equality feminism—and mothering denied

of her life." [52] Describing how she felt she had been misled and selfishly exploited, she wrote: "as I look back, wondering, on the credulous adolescent that I was, I am astonished when I realise how thoroughly I have been cheated" (de Beauvoir, cited by Tooley, 2002: 71; also see Note 8).

Betty Freidan, too, had second thoughts. By 1981, in *The Second Stage*, she wrote, "The equality we fought for isn't liveable, isn't workable, isn't comfortable in the terms that structured our battle." But equality feminists continued to implement her earlier prescriptions, and her recantations were ignored. The National Organization of Women, which she founded, was soon taken over by zealots, and Friedan resigned (Friedan, 1981).

Germaine Greer, too, had a belated and poignant rethink. After her 1972 best-seller, *The Female Eunuch*, had inspired a generation of women to forego motherhood, she later admitted that she "mourns for her unborn babies," confessing, "I still have pregnancy dreams, waiting with vast joy and confidence for something that will never happen". This was published under the tabloid headline: "I was desperate for a baby and have the medical bills to prove it!" (Krauthammer, 2000). By 1999, in *The Whole Woman* – having greatly widened her knowledge and understanding of women and their ways of life – she wrote: "In *The Female Eunuch* I argued that motherhood should not be treated as a substitute career: now I would argue that motherhood should be regarded as a genuine career option, that is to say, as paid work and as such an alternative to other paid work." She also declared that "the immense rewardingness of children is the best kept secret in the western world" (Greer, 1999: 260, 415).

While women had been 'liberated' in some ways, many were also caught in a web of dilemmas and over-work. Equality feminists achieved power and worked for social policies that did, in effect, implement de Beauvoir's program of denying choice for millions of mothers of young children.

This agenda turned a very blind eye to evidence about its possible repercussions on the emotional development of the next generation of

---

52. *cri de coeur*. n. 'cry of heart'; deeply-felt, passionate request or complaint.

'sisters' – let alone on that of the little boys who would become their future partners (cf. Nurcombe, 1971; see also Note 10).

Mothering denied

It is perverse that, in their efforts to raise the status of women, the movement for women's liberation – often called 'women's lib' in the 1970s – was directed down the path of rejecting and undermining a more maternal feminism that supported those women who wished to mother their own babies. Instead, the devaluation of mothering that pervaded early writings of Simone de Beauvoir, Betty Friedan, and Germaine Greer, became the entrenched orthodoxy of equality feminism. Then the very word 'mothering' became politically incorrect – but as Greer says in 1999, "What none of us noticed was that the ideal of liberation was fading out with the word. We were settling for equality. Liberation struggles are not about assimilation but about asserting difference, endowing that difference with dignity and prestige, and insisting on it as condition of self-definition and self-determination... even if it had been real, equality would have been a poor substitute for liberation...." (Greer, 1999: 2–3).

How all this developed, and the dire effects of equality feminist ideologies in the UK, through the required curriculum for the education of girls and women, is described in *The Miseducation of Women*. In a revealing chapter, "Romantic Illusions," Tooley documents the extraordinarily far-reaching influence of de Beauvoir and her life choices (Note 8). He adopts the distinction made by Greer in 1999, when she described how equality feminism had failed to meet the needs of so many women, and called instead for a Liberation Feminism that includes freedom and support for those women who, at some stage in their lives, choose the path of a maternal feminism that supports creative experiences in mothering their infants and children. Greer wrote, "every woman who decides to have a child would be paid enough money to raise that child in decent circumstances... the choice should be hers.... The sooner we decide that mothers are entitled to state support to use as they wish, the less it will cost us in the long run.... Dignified motherhood is a feminist priority" (Tooley, 1999: 40–41; Greer, 1999: 260; 412–25).

The eclipse of mothering, and its removal from the lexicon of family policy

In 2008, Yvonne Roberts, in *The Guardian*, wrote: "motherhood has almost been erased from the lexicon of family policy. Instead, mothers and fathers have been subsumed into one: the gender-neutral parent. Feminists in the 1960s saw motherhood as house-arrest. Then, mothers were at the cradle, while fathers brought home the bacon. Now motherhood consists of a number of narratives."

The word 'mothering' rarely appears in relevant books, and the terms 'parenting' and 'caregiver' are almost universally required instead. Yet each of these words has a different meaning. Although *Mother Nature*, by Sarah Hrdy, is mostly about mothering, that word does not appear in the index, although there are many references to 'parents,' and even more to 'parental investment' (Hrdy, 1999).

In the 1999 Canadian report, *Reversing the Real Brain Drain: The Early Years Study*, the word 'mothering' *is* used, though it appears just once – in quote marks at the end of the summary:

> The new evidence is a celebration of what good "mothering" has done for centuries. Parents have always known that babies and young children need good nutrition, stimulation, love and responsive care. What is fascinating about the new understanding of brain development is what it tells us about how good nurturing creates the foundation of brain development and what this foundation means for later stages of life.

But by 2007, in the updated report, *Early Years Study 2,* the word 'mothering' does not appear – except for one mention, where it is equated with 'peer-rearing' in disturbed monkeys:

> High-reactive monkeys who experienced poor mothering (or peer-rearing) during their first six months showed disrupted sleeping patterns as infants, high cortisol levels in the face of mild challenges throughout the lifespan, excessive adrenalin following challenges, increased risk of anxiety and depression, excessive alcohol consumption, aggressive behaviour, and for females, risk for poor maternal behaviour when they became mothers themselves.

On the other hand, the word 'parenting' appears in the Report at least 80 times (McCain et al., 1999; 2007).

The juggernaut of the childcare 'industry'

The breakup of the extended family, urbanisation, and the stresses of childrearing, burdened by teachings like those described earlier, had undermined many women's natural satisfactions in mothering. This lent force to the idea that they should go out to work and let 'experts' rear their little children.

Finding a place to 'nest' before having a baby is the first of the mothering behaviours common to all mammals. Yet a situation was created that encouraged dual-income couples to outbid single-income families in securing a home. Potential mothers and mothers with young families were increasingly pressured into the workplace, where they were of more value to 'the economy'; meanwhile they were assured that their infants and young children could safely be reared in childcare for 40 or 50 hours a week.

This whole agenda of equality feminism denies the importance of mothering, and it ignores the precautionary principle. In other words, it reverses the normal burden of proof that it is the responsibility of the proponent of a massive environmental change to establish that it will not – or is very unlikely to – result in significant harm to those most likely to be affected, especially when they are young human beings at the most vulnerable time in their lives. It was noted in Chapter 5 that this disorganised social 'experiment' is still being carried out in the years when infants are learning more rapidly than at any other time in their lives, and institutional daycare entails a drastic reduction in the possibilities of meeting the infant's primal birthright – mothering.

Part One of this book outlined evidence that mothering includes breastfeeding, extensive carrying, and personal sensuous contact, in a loving relationship that offers mother-infant attunement and mutual enjoyment. Realistically, these cannot be provided in institutional childcare. *It cannot be a job requirement, and it may seldom even be possible, for an unrelated woman who works in the average childcare nursery to love – let alone delight in – your baby or child.* Most carers have little time to enjoy even joint attention sequences. If a willing relative is not available, a motherly woman who is willing to be a supplementary mother until the child is at least 4 or 5 years old is likely to be the best alternative, as some privileged women can attest (e.g., Hrdy, 1999).[53]

In Australia, the National Childcare Accreditation Council pointed out in 1993 that children could be in childcare for nearly as many hours by the age of five as they would spend in school over the next thirteen years of their schooling.[54] Far from sensing that something was wrong with this childcare agenda, the Council unashamedly used this fact to argue for ever more money and staff – so that childcare could really be of "high quality".

Although vast sums of money have been made available, an authoritative account of the lamentable situation that still prevailed thirteen years later was provided in the *Report on the implementation of a 1:4 staff-child ratio for children aged under two years in New South Wales children's services* (Cross-Sectoral Task Force, 2006, summarised in Note 9).

In a 1996 review for the Institute of Economic Affairs in London, Patricia Morgan analysed the effects of early childcare and demonstrated what had long been almost self-evident. In her report, *Who Needs Parents? The effects of childcare and early education on children in Britain and the USA*, she wrote:

> The singular difficulties and cost of providing good quality care, with its highly involved and trained staff, small group size, caregiver stability, and low infant to caregiver ratios, should surely demonstrate how 'affordable, universally available, good-quality, easily accessible childcare' (to use the popular mantra) is a chimaera, unrealisable in the real world. Affordable care is *low-quality* care. Universally available *high-quality* care is achievable nowhere on earth" (Morgan, 1996; also see Note 9).

Yet, more and ever more subsidised early childcare is widely advocated and created, while all the evidence, inconsistencies, and contra-indications that this involves continue to be ignored.

---

53. When childcare is unavoidable, a list of alternatives in order of preference, as listed by Burton White, may be found in Chapter 2, of *Early Child Care* (Cook, 1996). www.naturalchild.com/peter_cook/ecc_ch1.html.
54. The National Childcare Accreditation Council [of Australia] (1993), cited above, calculated that childcare can be 50 weeks x 50 hours x 5 years = 12,500 hours, while schooling takes: 40 weeks x 25 hours x 13 years = 13,000 hours. Clearly, there may be local differences, but these are still remarkable figures.

What would Betty Friedan have thought if she had realised that she had effectively promoted a situation where many of tomorrow's 'sisters' are "trapped in the concentration camps" of their childcare institutions, while their mothers are financially locked into unsatisfying jobs? This social engineering was put in place despite the fact that most infant care professionals privately believed this was not in the best interests of the infant (Leach, 1997). Moreover, surveys in many countries showed that most mothers would rather be able to care for their young children themselves (Evans and Kelly, 2001; 2002).

Some childcare advocates argue that infants are being properly returned to group care with multiple carers, as in a tribe; but they ignore the fact that, uniquely in the history of our species, this policy raises infants in institutions that do not include their mothers or anyone having an enduring bond with the child, let alone any real love for these very young children. By 1999, 9.8 million American children under the age of five years were in childcare for 40 or more hours a week, with many beginning in the first year, and by 2007 over 25% of babies in Australia were in childcare before they were 12 months old.

Despite many warnings, our brave new world still supports a vicious circle, as the increasingly powerful and wealthy childcare industry profits from centre-based daycare. The influential gatekeepers promote its growth, and the early education industry, also, has cherry-picked the Canadian *Early Years Studies* of 1999 and 2007. These reports are used to promote 'education' from early infancy, while ignoring the studies' evidence about the value of breastfeeding, and the developmental value of mutual experiences while the infant is in his mother's arms, and as she suckles, enjoys, and plays with him.

Our provision for many young humans aims to meet the impersonal demands of industry and a materialistic ideology at the expense of the basic needs of babies and very young children, as witnessed by Belsky's intended title, *The Politicized Science of Childcare*, for his editorial, that was printed as *The Dangers of Day Care* in *The Wall Street Journal*, July 16, 2003 (see chapter 5).

It is a curious irony, that while feminism campaigned for men to take a more equal share in parenting, institutional childcare is staffed almost exclusively by women, since fears of paedophilia deny children any experience of father-figures while they are in childcare. A further anomaly is that the childcare industry is staffed by women who have been generally among the lowest-paid in our society.

Is the term 'childcare' for infants often a euphemism?

So far as infants are concerned, the terms 'daycare' and 'childcare' are often euphemisms for what might be more accurately described as early institutional childcare (see footnote 1 in the Introduction).

The noun 'euphemism' is defined in *The Cassell Dictionary of Word Histories* (1999) as "the use of a soft or pleasing term or phrase for one that is harsh or offensive." The words 'high quality childcare' imply that, so far as possible, a child placed there will have a 'soft and pleasing' experience – but we have much reason to think that this is not at all how it feels to the infant.

As seen in Chapter 5, The Task Force Report to the New South Wales Government said, "the research universally shows that a one-to-three ratio is desirable for children under three years of age," and referred to a "world expert on childcare matters, who calls a 1:5 [staff-infant] ratio a 'ratio for neglect'". Yet a staff-infant ratio of 1:5 has been in no way unusual. From the viewpoint of a baby, or indeed any two- or three-year-old child, the evidence suggests that the experience, month after month, of what is more accurately termed institutional, long-day care, could indeed be 'harsh and offensive.' Harsman's observations outlined in Chapter 3 suggest that Leunig's cartoon *Thoughts of a baby lying in a child care centre* are all too often an accurate representation of a baby's experience and point of view.

Clearly, the term 'childcare,' when used in connection with infants, can fairly be regarded as a politically correct euphemism.

PART THREE:

CONCLUSIONS

AND WHAT CAN BE DONE?

12

What conclusions may we draw?

Intimate attachments to other human beings are the hub around which a person's life revolves, not only when he is an infant or a toddler or a schoolchild but throughout his adolescence and his years of maturity as well, and on into old age. From these intimate attachments a person draws his strength and enjoyment of life and, through what he contributes, he gives strength and enjoyment to others. These are matters about which current science and traditional wisdom are at one.
 —John Bowlby, 1981, concluding words in his trilogy.
 Attachment and Loss

Our gross national product... counts air pollution and cigarette advertising, and ambulances to clear our highways of carnage. It counts special locks for our doors and the jails for the people who break them. It counts the destruction of the redwoods and the loss of our natural wonder in chaotic sprawl. It counts... armored cars for the police who fight riots in our streets.... Yet the gross national product does not allow for the health of our children, the quality of their education, or the joy of their play – it measures everything, in short, except that which makes life worthwhile.
 —Robert F. Kennedy, 1968

Not feeling 'loved a lot' was the best predictor of marihuana use in 13-year-old boys in Sydney.
 —Marilyn Rob et al., 1990

Was women's liberation misled by misconceived dogma and ideology?

In the West, the natural satisfactions and rewards of the early mother-infant relationship were undermined, and sometimes poisoned, by childrearing ideas deriving from ancient misconceptions about the nature of the child. In this setting, normal infant reactions often led to much frustration, and sometimes to violence. Societal changes, with the loss of social supports that had been available through the extended family and social networks, prepared the way for a further set of problems.

As the movement for women's liberation adopted the misconceived ideology of cultural determinism, with its 'blank slate' view of the child, feminism – in its quest for equality with men – regarded mothers and fathers as interchangeable. It rejected a more maternal feminism that could have worked for equal rights between men and women, while also emphasising the special role that women play in mothering babies and very young children, and their need for ample maternity leave (Cook, 2002; 2004).

Instead, in some Western countries the equality feminists' objective became that mothers should return to work soon after delivery, while infants were provided with institutional group care, stimulation and education by experts. The core values of mothering were ignored, as were the high costs of training and employing qualified early childcare professionals. As career equality feminists moved into positions of power and influence, they engineered social policies that made it increasingly difficult for women to mother and breastfeed their infants. In his important, but neglected, book, *The Miseducation of Women*, Professor James Tooley says, "it is the ideas of equality feminists that hold sway over government and education reform, in America, Australia, and Britain as well as elsewhere.... The important point is that reforms for 'gender-neutral' curricula and school organisation fit in with the ideas of the equality feminists. And it is the equality feminists who dominate the debates about overcoming gender stereotyping, who argue for vigilance and struggle in order to climb the lofty heights of gender equity" (Tooley, 2002: 42).

Management of childbirth – "Like a snowball rolling downhill..."

The successful working of our physiology depends on a facilitating environment, especially for childbirth and for initiating breastfeeding and early mothering. Strategic disruptions can cascade, as described by Haire in 1972 in *The Cultural Warping of Childbirth*. Of maternity hospital practices that sometimes prevailed at that time, she wrote:

> Most of the practices... have developed not from a lack of concern for the wellbeing of the mother and baby but from a lack of

awareness as to the problems which can arise from each progressive digression from the normal childbearing experience. Like a snowball rolling downhill, as one unphysiological practice is employed, for one reason or another, another frequently becomes necessary to counteract some of the disadvantages, large or small, inherent in the previous procedure.

Such disruptions can cut across the fabric of hormonal and other biological mechanisms that evolved to promote healthy mother-infant relationships.

Can we evolve new humans to fit the childcare environment?

The ideological detachment of some social sciences from their scientific bases in biology can lead to extraordinary claims that we can re-arrange the basic patterns of mother-infant relationships with impunity. For example, in a review of the effects of childcare, it was suggested that the nature of the infant may have to evolve to suit modern childcare conditions: "In this version it is accepted that humans are still evolving and different attachment patterns will emerge adapted to the new pressures in the environment." This may sound acceptable to some people, until they think about it enough to realise that for this to occur, all those who are less well-adapted must be selected out – that is to say, they must die without having reproduced. It also assumes that fundamental aspects of human biology that are deeply built into the mammalian-primate brain, can and will be re-arranged to suit the "new pressures in the environment" that are being created by childcare policies. This glimpse into a brave new world was in a seemingly authoritative review of childcare, published by a large, government-funded family studies institution in Australia (Ochiltree, 1994; Cook, 1996).

Love, alloparents, and the comparative costs of childcare and mothercare

Love appears to have originated early in our mammalian and primate past. Jane Goodall had the privilege of studying chimpanzees at close quarters, beginning in 1960 when little was known about their life in the wild, and before humans had greatly reduced their numbers and ravaged their habitat. She wrote a short book with pictures, suitable for children, and called it *With Love: Ten Heart-warming Stories of Chimpanzees in the Wild*.

One definition of love is the emotions and behaviours in a relationship that contribute to the mutual wellbeing of those involved. It appears that such love – which includes empathy and compassion – developed on earth only in the context of mothering offspring who were dependent and slow to reach maturity. To a lesser but important extent, the same applies to fathering, when a father can support the nurturing of the young. Likewise, in the human child, the capacities for empathy and love develop best in the context of such parenting.

Since a mother and her infant can better survive with help from the father, love between mother, father, and child has additional survival value. Hrdy says that "In many species... infant survival depends on the mother being assisted by others – the father and/or various individuals other than parents – alloparents.... Among humans living in foraging societies, a helpful mate, and/or alloparents, were usually essential for a mother to rear an infant at all. In a surprisingly broad range of creatures, indispensable alloparents provide many of the same forms of care a mother might, protecting and provisioning, even suckling another female's infant in cases where the alloparent is lactating" (Hrdy, 1999:90-1).

Such alloparents would be unlikely to sustain such care in the absence of some rewarding love for the child. Hrdy describes how she was fortunate in securing a reliable and enduring allomother who helped in mothering her children, while she was partly freed to pursue her studies. But this is quite different from the situation in a childcare nursery. Such carers are under a number of pressures, and it can hardly be job requirement for a daycare employee to love your infant – as in an allomother relationship. However much a parent may go on loving a child, an infant cannot experience this if the parent is not there. The baby's feelings and imaginings may well be more accurately represented in the Leunig cartoon at the front of this book.

Yet even in economic terms alone, does early institutional childcare really make good sense? After reviewing the evidence available by 2001, Belsky raised the question of whether such parental leaves would actually prove less costly than the consequences of their absence. He said:

It seems to me that the data considered in this paper should encourage the expansion of parental leaves, preferably paid, ideally as lengthy as they are in some Scandinavian countries, or other strategies for reducing the time children spend in nonmaternal care across the infant, toddler, and preschool years (e.g., part-time employment). One of the interesting questions that only history will answer is whether the cost of such leaves will prove less than the consequences of their absence. Relatedly, tax policies should support families rearing infants and young children in ways that afford parents the freedom to make childrearing arrangements which they deem best for their child, thereby reducing the economic coercion that necessitates many to leave the care of their children to others when they would rather not. Finally, given the clear benefits of high quality child care, its expansion seems called for as well. Of significance is that all of these conclusions could be justified on humanitarian grounds alone.

At the Institute for the Study of Children, Families and Social Issues, in London, Professor Ted Melhuish joined Professor Jay Belsky in saying that with no compromise on quality, the cost of subsidising childcare for the under-twos is broadly comparable to the cost of generous parental leave for 2 years. Melhuish pointed to the case of Sweden as evidence of what parents might want if they had a real choice, "The Swedish case is very revealing – there was high-quality infant care available to all and heavily subsidised. It was widely used in the 70s and 80s, but in the early 90s, parental leave was increased and now there is remarkably little use of childcare under 18 months. Parents voted with their feet" (Bunting, 2004).

Manne (2008) outlined the opportunities then available to Scandinavian parents of children under three: "either parent can take up to three years' parental leave, much of it paid. They have the right to return to their previous job. They have the choice of a high quality child-care place or taking a home-care allowance. Where it has been introduced, the home care allowance has been extremely popular. Very few babies are in childcare…. Breastfeeding rates are high. The Swedes also offer the right to work six-hour days on reduced salary until the child is eight. All these measures are regarded as parents' and children's rights."

Potential costs of total 'collateral damage' in early childcare policies

Yet Belsky's further question as to whether lengthy parental leave and support would *actually cost less than the consequences of their absence* has not yet been honestly faced. Melhuish appears to be suggesting that the *immediate* costs of supporting mothers to care for their own infants may be no higher than the costs of providing quality childcare. Belsky's use of the word *consequences* suggests that the costs of any adverse impacts of childcare on the developing child should also be included. At present, *these are never taken into account.*

Since economic arguments and pressures are so often used to get mothers back into the 'workforce' and infants into early childcare, this policy is overdue for a full economic analysis that takes account of all the 'externalities' and 'collateral damage' that economists find it so easy to ignore and so hard to evaluate. If they think that this collateral damage matters, but they cannot put a price on it, they should say so.

Evidence already available, and outlined in earlier chapters, shows that the full costs of subsidising childcare, so that the 'economy' may benefit from 'getting mothers into the workforce', may be very great. Consider the potential costing in just five areas.

a. Breastfeeding. The health benefits of breastfeeding are well documented, as seen in Chapter 2, but they have not been clearly costed. In this area alone, departures from normal breastfeeding over a large proportion of a total population must increase health costs very greatly. The relevant evidence was scrutinised by the Australian Productivity Commission (2008) in its Inquiry into Paid Parental Leave and its Draft Report summarised:

> Breastfeeding is considered the optimal form of infant feeding and a key determinant of infant health. The evidence indicates breastfeeding reduces the incidence and severity of a number of infectious diseases in infants, including gastrointestinal illnesses, respiratory tract infections and middle ear infections. More exclusive and longer periods of breastfeeding are also associated with lower rates of infant illnesses (particularly gastrointestinal illnesses). Possible protective effects from breastfeeding against SIDS [sudden infant death syndrome] in the first year of life, the incidence of insulin-dependent (Type 1) diabetes and some

childhood cancers have also been found, although more research is required.

There is also increasing evidence that breastfeeding may have longer term effects, including the reduced incidence of obesity, diabetes, blood pressure and high cholesterol in later life. And some (but not all) studies find an impact on later intelligence.

For mothers, the evidence suggests that benefits include promotion of maternal recovery, reduced risks of breast cancer and ovarian cancer and possible reduced risk of post-menopausal hip fractures.

So some estimate should be made of the added costs for health services to treat all these disorders. Without this, the so-called 'benefits to the economy' of mothers' early return to the workforce are seriously in error – if not meaningless. For example, see Appendix 2: The Dollar Costs of Suboptimal Breastfeeding in the US.

b. School classrooms. The overall negative impact of too much early childcare on the quality of school education must also be serious. As outlined in Chapter 5, the studies of the NICHD ECCRN show that childcare of enough quantity or low enough quality to impair attachment is associated with behaviour problems, such as increased arguing, and more disobedience, fighting, and aggressiveness at school. Then, to make matters worse, non-childcare children copy these behaviours – as if such behaviour is contagious. This must have educational costs for the pupils, and also for the recruitment of good teachers and for their work satisfaction, and the stresses that they experience.

c. Societal effects. The NICHD Network already acknowledges that, even when the adverse effects due to early childcare are small, when large numbers of people are affected, there are likely to be subsequent adverse effects on society as a whole. Even if only a few of the children who show increased aggression and problem behaviours in school then continue to show such behaviour in adolescence and into adult life, the costs could be very high. For example, do such behaviours carry over into how young people drive, drink alcohol, or take drugs? As noted in Chapter 5, in 2008 the NICHD Early Child Care and Youth Network reported that, amongst other findings at age 15, "higher hours of non-relative care predicted greater risk-taking and impulsivity..." (NICHD ECCYN, 2009. For abstract see Appendix 1).

d. Quality of relationships in adolescence and adult life. The Minnesota longitudinal studies indicated that infants who had insecure early attachments had increased risks of impaired emotional relationships in adolescence and early adult life. Such emotional disturbances may turn out to be very costly for society. Increasing numbers of therapists of various disciplines and skills are called upon – at considerable public and private expense – to counsel and heal such suffering, although healing is often difficult and not always possible (Breazeale, 2001; Karen, 1994: 181-194).

e. Increased stress. Post-traumatic stress disorder is becoming more commonly diagnosed in adults, and it sometimes leads to litigation. If stress in early childcare can cause abnormal cortisol levels during infancy (and it can), and it can lead to abnormal stress responses in teenagers (as it evidently does), then it is not fanciful to suggest that verifiable stress in early childcare has a causal relationship to a verifiable post-traumatic stress disorder in adolescence and perhaps later in life. The overall cost implications are unlikely to be zero. This could arouse legal interest.

Certainly, home-care and mothering, and the environment in which it occurs, can be problematic and need improvement, especially in an urban environment. But the 'stitch in time saves nine' principle suggests that early professional follow-up can help support healthy mothering, and see that things are going well in the early period after the baby's birth, and at least through the first year. In addition, supporting the involvement of the father, and the provision of parent and child centres and open pre-schools, is likely to be much more cost-effective and good for 'the economy' than the present goal of getting infants into childcare and hurrying mothers back into the 'workforce'.

Universal, affordable, high quality childcare is an 'abstraction'

Most of the material in my 1996 book, *Early Child Care – Infants and Nations at Risk,* continues to be valid and relevant. In many ways the situation has become worse. For example, it is still important to take account of what Anne Manne wrote in 1996:

> Few of those proposing quality of care arguments really face the reality of the likely pressures on the welfare state in the foreseeable future. This

means we are in a sense talking about an abstraction, for the very things which improve the possibility of high quality care – decent wages and conditions, good staff-child ratios, incentives for stability of tenure – cost money, and a great deal of it. If we are to increase funding, why fund centres and not parental leave? (Manne, 1996: 12; cited in Cook, 1996, 121).

Professionals privately think mother-care is best in the early years

A large, anonymous, and strictly confidential survey by Penelope Leach found that most infant mental health professionals privately considered that care by mother is generally best for the child. When asked for how long, if at all, they considered it "very important" for infants to have their mothers available to them "through most of each 24 hours", most replied "more than a year," with a mean of 15 months. When asked whether there is a further period during which it is "ideal" for infants to be cared for "principally by mothers," most said "more than 2 years" – the mean being 27 months.

Leach concluded, "There are many professionals in infant mental health who believe that children's best interests would be served by patterns of childcare diametrically opposed to those politicians promise, policy-makers aspire to provide and parents strive to find" (Leach, 1994; 1997). Yet it seems that it would entail too great a risk to their careers if these professionals were to speak out publicly, for they have not done so. Belsky had been subjected to much denunciation and ostracism after tentatively pointing out in 1987 that accumulating evidence suggested that early childcare could have adverse consequences (Karen, 1994: 319-346).

Mothering needs maternity leave and support

Our economists value the Gross National Product as an indicator of societal wellbeing, while neglecting environmental damage, and some of the most important aspects of human life.

In 1968 Senator Robert F. Kennedy said: "Too much, and for too long, we seem to have surrendered personal excellence and community values in the mere accumulation of material things. Our gross national product, if we judge the United States of America by that... counts air pollution and cigarette advertising, and ambulances to clear our highways of carnage. It counts special locks for our doors and the jails for the people who break them. It counts the destruction of the redwoods and the loss of our natural wonder in chaotic sprawl. It counts... nuclear warheads, and armored cars for the police who fight riots in our streets.... Yet the gross national product does not allow for the health of our children, the quality of their education, or the joy of their play... it measures everything, in short, except that which makes life worthwhile."

Surveys from 24 countries showed that the great majority of mothers think that mothers should not undertake paid work that requires them to leave their children while they are of pre-school age. In Australia this majority was 71 percent, while 27 percent thought that employment with young children should just be part-time; only a tiny minority favoured full-time work (Evans and Kelly, 2001; 2002). As seen earlier, even part-time work can have a very negative effect on breastfeeding rates (Cooklin, 2008).

If the community is to pay a lot of money for infant care, then why not offer this to mothers and help them to care for their infants, if that is their wish? We now have robust evidence that the breastfeeding of infants, and all the experiences that naturally go with it, can be of far-reaching importance for health and wellbeing.

If a nation can support what is agreed to be the best practice of mothers' breastfeeding, and for the recommended duration, then it is likely that other reforms in the care of infants and young children could be more readily achieved. Mutually desired breastfeeding for up to two years (or more) carries with it a requirement for social conditions that bring many other benefits to families with young children, and hence to society. Adequately supported maternity leave of at least one year, and preferably up to three, as has been available in Sweden, is a prerequisite for a generally healthier alternative to childcare.

It is a lamentable failure of social policy when many women in some of the world's most affluent societies can no longer afford to breastfeed and mother their own babies, however much they may wish to do so. No one makes *money* out of mothering, and we have seen that it does not count in the gross 'domestic' product, that we are told must increase. 'The economy' is said to require mothers' labour. But who has a greater claim on a mother's presence than her own baby? Money cannot buy love, or breastfeeding, or all the other nurturing that normally occurs in healthy mothering and fathering.

Mothering needs appropriate environments

Opportunities for mothers, with their infants and young children, to meet in suitable centres or playgroups can more nearly provide some features of our traditional social environment. Childcare centres could change to offer services like those of Swedish "open preschools" or "child places" (Leach, 1994; Cook, 1997). These offer support and companionship for home-caring parents and family daycare providers. They could also help parents to learn non-violent, empathic approaches to childrearing, and promote trusting, co-operative relationships.

Manne summarises: "Establish early childhood centres. Transcend the current narrow emphasis. The idea is to surround *all* parents and *all* children with support from birth onwards. The centres would be focal points for parents to create their own community networks as well as the contact point for referral to professional services: pre-natal visits, maternal nurses, mothers' playgroups, babysitting co-ops, toy libraries, playgroups, as well as professional outreach services" (Manne, 2008: 77).

This could offer a much healthier and more satisfying set-up for children, parents and staff than institutional childcare. Help in re-entering the workforce could come later, if desired. Retirement provisions should recognise the social value of the time taken by mothers or fathers in early child nurture. The benefits of older people having freedom to be involved in helping with young children could be encouraged. Of what value are the ever-faster and cheaper means of producing short-life products, with ever-increasing pollution and destruction of our biosphere's diversity, if we have no time to enjoy our children? (Cook, 1995; 2000).

Fathers' natural roles

Fathers are certainly important and can share with mothers as partners, playmates, parents, protectors and providers. But, as in all other mammals, the roles of the two parents are different. Only mothers can breastfeed. We have seen how in primates this is associated with the carrying and co-sleeping that promote secure attachment, and in which fathers can participate. While breastfeeding gives the mother a unique role during early infancy, we need to value the development of involved fathering at each stage. As the child grows and is weaned, many roles of mothers and fathers become increasingly interchangeable, according to individual personalities and circumstances.

Nurturing the natural child in the 21st century

A higher quality relationship is implicit in cooperative childrearing approaches that involve empathy and mutual love. Elliott Barker, MD, a Canadian forensic psychiatrist who has had extensive experience with murderers, has stressed the importance of "two-part empathy," in which a person not only knows, or perceives, what another person is feeling, but also actually *feels* appropriately moved and compassionate about another person's suffering. He finds psychopathic criminals may be expert at the first, but they do not, and cannot, emotionally empathise with the other person's situation. He concluded that these personality disorders arise from early emotional damage that cannot be remedied, so he founded the Canadian Society for the Prevention of Cruelty to Children to promote the early primary prevention of these and similar emotional disorders. He created a valuable and freely available on-line parenting course, appropriate for adolescents in school, as well as for others, to teach emotionally healthy infant nurturing. It shows how empathic parenting involves being willing and able to put yourself in your infant's place, so as to better understand and take into account his or her feelings. It is freely available at www.parentingcourse.net. A fuller account of two-part empathy as described by Barker is in *Early Child Care* (Cook, 1997: 148–9).

Another appealing and practical guide showing how some principles of natural parenting can be achieved in the contemporary situation is *The Natural Child: Parenting from the heart* by Jan Hunt – a parent, psychologist, and educator (Hunt, 2001). A useful account of mother-care at home is *Being There: The benefits of a stay-at-home parent* by Isabelle Fox (1996). Steve Biddulph has a series of books about raising children. These include: *The secret of happy children; Raising Boys: Why boys are different – and how to help them become happy and well-balanced men*, and *Raising Babies: Should under 3s go to nursery?* There is also *Raising Girls: Why girls are different and how to help them grow up happy and confident*, by Gisela Preuschoff with a foreword by Steve Biddulph. There are many other such accounts. Some essentials are summarised in *Simplified parenting for mental health – a framework* (Cook, 2005a; Also Cook, 1970). A program to help parents communicate more sensitively with their children after infancy is taught in *PET – Parent Effectiveness Training*. It is based on 'active listening' to understand the real message and underlying feelings, and avoiding 'roadblocks' that impair communication. It describes how a parent can communicate his or her wishes to the child in a way that is more likely to be followed, without undermining the relationship (Gordon, 1970).

It takes a child to raise a village

Early Years Study 2 cites the proverb "It takes a village to raise a child." This recognises that children live in families, and families live in communities; but the authors reverse this and say "It takes a child to raise a village", highlighting how taking the needs of children into account in planning an environment also leads to better design for the whole community.

Many years earlier, Paul Ritter, an architect and town-planner, aimed to design such an environment in a 500-dwelling development in Perth, Western Australia. In 1959, he and his wife, Jean Ritter, wrote *The Free Family – a Creative Experience in Self-regulation for Children* (Note 12).

The power of the case comes from the evidence presented in the *Early Years* studies, as they show "how child development and experience-based brain development in the earliest years of life set biological pathways that affect cognition, behavior, the capacity to learn, memory, and physical and mental health throughout the life cycle." The authors add: "How societies understand and apply their knowledge of human development will determine the kind of cultures, societies, and civilizations created.... The early years are a period of heightened opportunity and risk" (McCain et al. 2007: 54).

As our world becomes ever more urbanised, there is a great need to think about how we can create environments or centres that are mothering-friendly, especially for those with infants. How can we bring into modern life some of the key ingredients of traditional societies, as well as supply the facilitating environment that is so widely lacking in most centres of population today?

Normal infancy involves a love affair – infancy cannot be re-run later

One of the most beneficial experiences for a child is to feel that he or she is *enjoyed*. Our genes for healthy nurture are still present and active, sometimes offering us their ancient, pre-cultural promptings, if we can respect and 'listen' to them. We can experience these as maternal and paternal feelings and intuition. They encourage us toward the basic activities involved in producing a healthy succeeding generation. Unfortunately, their message is quite vulnerable to distortion by unhealthy patterns of culture that can generate psychopathology and pass on disturbances to succeeding generations.

While other groups in society can campaign for their needs and rights, babies depend on parents and other adults to do it for them. It is urgent to bring our culture into better harmony with our hard-won biological givens. One of our best hopes for the future lies in supporting women when they are mothers of very young children.

There has been an explosion of interest in 'early education,' but it remains most important to distinguish the needs of children approaching school age from those of infants in their first two to three years, when their primary needs revolve around empathic early mothering and fathering, within a sociable environment. Since mothering cannot so readily become an academic or government concern, nor a profit-making industry, it has received much less attention.

There is much we might do. We could aim to bring our culture and society – that we *can* change – into better harmony with our biological 'givens' that we *cannot* change and would therefore do well to accept. This involves encouraging maternity leave for up to three years and supporting healthy mothering, breastfeeding and attachment. The natural patterns of mothering work best if help is available through an extended family and/or social group in a suitable environment.

Various steps were outlined in *Early Child Care* (Cook, 1996), including: recognition of the special needs of families with children in the first three to five years; respect and social status for home-caring parents; affirmative action to support early mothering; encouraging the carrying of babies; support for open pre-schools, as in Sweden; ensuring enough economic support in the early years; assistance to mothers in updating their skills and returning to work if they wish to do so when children are of school age; retirement provisions that recognise the value of their time devoted to early mothering.

In 2008 Manne outlined some things we should do, as summarised below:

1. Adopt active neutrality as the guiding principle of family policy, without trying to engineer choices about the balance struck between family life and paid employment.
2. Bring in maternal equity policies based on choice. The state should be neutral on women's different choices – as between a child-care place and an equivalent cash benefit as a home-care allowance.
3. Extend parental leave – up to three years.
4. Establish early-childhood centres to support parents and children from birth onwards.
5. Introduce the right to request part-time work and flexible work for family reasons.
6. Improve the quality of childcare, in line with overseas best practices.
7. Integrate new understandings about attachment principles, and the importance of sensitivity and responsiveness in the child's relationships, and – in childcare settings – the importance of the primary carer staying with children until they are at least three years old.
8. Reduce the number of hours each day in childcare, allowing parents shorter working hours after children's entry to childcare.
9. Keep centres small and the overall number of children low.
10. Pay childcare workers respectable wages.
11. Establish pre-school that is voluntary, free, and universal.
12. Strengthen accreditation standards. (Manne, 2008: 76-8).

Manne concludes:

> We need to go beyond band-aid solutions, such as short maternity leave, to create a radical new social imagination around care. Instead of advocating self-sufficiency for all, we should recognise our interdependence. Devaluing parenting and care as a "lesser life" helps no one. All of us, deep down, know that in small and

large acts, men and women must take responsibility for each other. Together, we must knit the fabric of care for those who depend on us. All that takes time.

And equality? We will truly have equality when women no longer have to make impossible choices. When they are everywhere in public life and when both men and women are respected for their contribution to love's never-ending labour. It is only then that being female will be felt as a presence and not an absence (Manne, 2008: 75–79).

It is necessary to work with Nature and not against her if we are to promote health and wellbeing in young children, their mothers, and society. We were all babies once, and the fruits of good mothering and early nurture are among the greatest blessings a person can have in life. In offering these to their babies, mothers and fathers are setting the pattern of relationships that can be creative, mutually rewarding, and last for the rest of their lives. This may be achieved with joy and satisfaction. For parents who wish the best for their children and themselves, few things are more important for their healthy future – and for the quality of life on our planet.

A normal mother-child relationship is a love affair that needs the right conditions to flourish. Infancy cannot be re-run later.

Summary

Part 1: Five lines of evidence for natural, 'best-fit' mothering

Although the American Psychological Association has long declared that the word 'mothering' should generally be avoided, the facts of life remain unchanged. It seems that there is a natural, biologically based, best-fit pattern of human mothering that includes breastfeeding, carrying, secure attachment, mutual rewards, enjoyment, and empathy – that is, a mother's sensitivity to her baby's feelings and her appropriate response. Mutual playfulness and joy help to sustain healthy development if the environment is supportive and meets basic human needs.

Five different lines of evidence now converge and complement each other to support this biologically based understanding of healthy mothering and the management of infancy. This is an example of 'triangulation,' where greater validity is achieved when multiple streams of evidence come from different directions to support the same conclusion (see footnote 4).

1. Some facts that can be deduced from the pedigrees of our maternal ancestors

Every person alive today has a personal line of direct maternal ancestors, and over many generations each ancestor contributed to that person's genetic inheritance. By considering what must have been achieved by each of these mothers – whether as a woman, as a little girl, or as a baby – deductions can be made about human mothering, infancy, health, and some aspects of human nature. The word 'infancy' is often used to cover just the first year, but it is used here to include the whole of the pre-verbal period of life – the original developmental meaning of the word.

Each of our female ancestors must have been healthy enough to bear a baby girl who grew up to do likewise. In the 18 months following conception, the brains of young humans grow to become proportionately larger than those of any other creature. To avoid major problems at birth they must leave the uterus at a much earlier and more helpless stage of development than the babies of other placental mammals. Human mothers could not protect themselves and also feed such dependent babies without help, so they depended on the group for their survival. They were biologically fitted to live as hunter-gatherers within an extended family and social group.

In nearly all cases each mother breastfed, carried, and slept with her baby as she reared her infant within this communal group. She joined in work and play, teaching and protecting her child until he was able to survive safely while away from his mother. To reach this stage, powerful attachments between a mother and her infant were needed. Like all living creatures, human infants have basic survival 'instincts' and drives to get their own needs met; but for humans *there must also have been natural selection in favour of infants and children who were innately social and appealing to the group, since they depended absolutely on this group for their survival* as they grew up and joined in group activities.

Today each healthy baby, girl, or woman, has a long pedigree for success in each of these qualities and achievements. Each baby boy, too, needed to be appealing and rewarding to his mother and others in the group, since without eliciting all this support, he would not have survived. Boys, too, are included in the following discussion, wherever appropriate.

2. Evidence about the values of breastfeeding

Although all baby mammals are fed by their mothers' milk, the composition of milk in different mammals varies – adapted to their particular way of life. The milk of those who carry their young and feed them frequently is different from the milk of mammals that hide their young while they seek food and therefore feed them at longer intervals. The composition of human breast milk places us at the extreme end of those who carry their young and feed them frequently.

Human milk is uniquely matched to the needs of human babies. Authoritative reports cite much evidence to support their recommendations for a long period of breastfeeding, continuing for as long as is desired by both mother and baby, perhaps for years, but supplemented with other foods from no earlier than six months of age.

These reports show that when compared with formula feeding, breastfeeding provides many benefits, including lower risks of many disorders in both mother and infant, in the short-term and throughout their lives.

The experiences involved in healthy breastfeeding strengthen the love between a mother and her baby, and they also help in the early 'wiring' of the child's brain to build lifelong connections between its nerve cells. As well as contributing to higher intelligence, these early experiences also help to 'set the base' for many later patterns, such as those for effective learning styles, behaviour patterns, good emotional and general fitness levels, resilient responses to stress – all building sound foundations for future wellbeing and healthy relationships.

It is more accurate to see these 'benefits' of breastfeeding as helping the infant to achieve the natural and *normal* level of health. Against this standard we can see that formula feeding actually increases various risks. Fortunately, some of the benefits and other features of a healthy breastfeeding experience can also be enjoyed during formula feeding – for example, peaceful skin-to-skin contact. One advantage is that a baby can also be fed by father, helping him to feel more involved with his baby, though the father-baby bond can be strengthened in ways that do not compromise breastfeeding.

3. Evidence of the importance of attachment between mother and baby

Like all mammals, humans have needed secure bonds of attachment between mothers and their babies for them to survive. These were essential if the infant was to be protected and breastfed, so mutually satisfactory breastfeeding and attachment normally enhance each other. If the attachment was inadequate, that infant perished and failed to pass on her genes. An infant's primary and most secure attachment is normally with the mother, and secure attachment to mother, and/or other loving mother figures during infancy has been shown to be the best basis for healthy child development.

Disruption of infant-mother attachment by complete separation of an infant from the mother rouses powerful emotions, with risks of serious and sometimes prolonged emotional disturbance. These risks are lessened if the infant is cared for by a motherly person with whom he or she has first formed a good secondary attachment. These normally occur with other relatives or carers if they are dependable and love the child.

In the 1930s, a group of doctors associated with the Tavistock Clinic in London adopted a biological approach to understanding the material that was brought to them by their patients in analytical treatment, as described in their publications from 1932 to 1950. Between 1940 and 1980, John Bowlby, working later at the same clinic, built on their work and used a biological perspective to develop attachment theory. He documented this in his major three-volume work about attachment, separation, loss, and depression. In this trilogy he defined the significance of attachment, and the effects that can follow immediately and later in life, when there is a loss – even a temporary loss – of the primary attachment figure. Mary Ainsworth then developed a test to assess the quality and security of the infant's attachment to his mother, and this led to much research confirming the validity of Bowlby's work.

4. Comparative behavioural and brain-imaging studies in humans and other mammals

As they care for their babies, human mothers show mothering behaviours that correspond to those studied in other mammals. When they are mothering their babies, live brain-imaging techniques in human mothers and in some other mammals show similar activity, deep in the same parts of the 'mammalian brain' in the limbic system.

Much of this is brought about by neuro-endocrine processes that produce strong ties between the bonding pair. "For most mothers, interacting and engaging with one's own infant is a rewarding and pleasurable experience that promotes mother-infant attachment, ensures optimal care for the developing infant, and motivates maternal behavior, even in the face of extreme fatigue and competing needs for attention" (Swain et al., 2007).

Finding a place to 'nest' before having a baby is the first of the mothering activities that are common to all mammals. These systems, and the behaviours that underlie mammalian mothering, have been tested, refined, and have worked well for millions of years, providing mothers and their babies with the rewards needed to reproduce successfully. For humans there was neither the need to re-design this pattern, nor even the possibility of doing so – whether to fit a misconceived ideology, or for any other purpose.

Yet many affluent Western societies have made it so difficult for mothers to find and maintain somewhere to 'nest' – the very first step in mothering – that many couples must shorten or sacrifice other basic patterns of mothering behaviour, even though these have been possible for most human societies and all other mammals.

Since two-income couples can bid up the price of a home, most young parents need two incomes from paid employment if they are to compete successfully in the housing market. Through 'social engineering', equality feminism brought about a situation in which it became ever more difficult for a woman to both afford a home and also breastfeed and enjoy her infant. More and more women in the West cannot *afford* to do both.

Natural reward systems can be seriously disrupted when an infant is separated from her mother. Experimentally, these mothering reward systems can be abolished by damaging a specific nucleus in the brain. Drugs such as cocaine, and perhaps other addictive substances, can 'hijack' and block the reward systems that support mothering. It appears that this may be how such substances become so addictive; the infant cannot then give her mother any further satisfactions, and neglect and child abuse may follow.

5. Research into effects of early centre-based childcare during infancy

In the mid-20th century there was a lack of hard evidence about the many possible ill-effects of early childcare. But *absence of evidence* was often regarded as *evidence of absence* – a very different matter. Despite the many difficulties of studying the effects of early non-maternal childcare, research has now produced some robust conclusions. Early nurture with normal mothering and breastfeeding leads to better outcomes in many ways.

Centre-based childcare by unrelated carers during infancy carries a number of immediate and long-term risks for the child's healthy behavioural and emotional development. Various aspects of the childcare experience affect these risks – such as the quality and quantity of the care; but in the real world "universally available, high quality, affordable childcare" is an unachievable, fictive goal – an abstraction.

The more hours spent in early daycare, the greater the risk of adverse effects. Long daily separations, and other aspects of the childcare situation, can lead to insecurity in the infant's attachment to his mother, and adverse effects can continue through childhood and beyond. In addition, long hours of separation *diminish the mother's own sensitivity to her child* during the time that they do have together. There is evidence that emotional disturbances arising out of insecure early attachments can adversely and seriously affect relationships in adolescence and adult life.

Rewarding secondary attachments may occur in childcare if the carer has time, is affectionate, dependable and continues to be available, but this is not possible in most real-life childcare.

By school-age, while some children may show benefits, the effects of early childcare lead to increased risks of aggressive and disobedient behaviour in the playground and classroom. Such behaviours not only disrupt the class, but induce similar behaviour in non-daycare classmates. This presumably makes teaching more stressful for teachers and on a national scale is likely to have adverse consequences for society as a whole.

Increased release of the hormone cortisol into the blood is part of the body's normal response to stress, and it helps to arouse bodily reactions to cope with danger. The level of cortisol in the blood can be assessed by taking a swab from the saliva in the mouth; normally, this level is higher in the morning and falls during the day. But many infants show that they are under stress in childcare because they have levels of cortisol that *remain abnormally high during the second half of the day* – even if the daycare is regarded as being of 'high quality'.

These elevated levels of cortisol in early childcare are likely to have lasting effects on various body 'settings' and responses to stress. At age 15, adolescents who had been in childcare as infants had cortisol levels that were abnormal, in that they were *lower*, rather than *higher*, when they woke up in the morning. Eminent researchers concluded that these abnormal findings were related to the adolescents' early childcare experiences, and also to early mothering that had been assessed as being less sensitive during infancy. These two effects were judged to act independently, and one effect can add to the other. Longer hours of early childcare also predicted greater risk-taking and impulsivity at age 15.

The evidence shows that the emotional and other qualities of the home environment have the greatest influence on a child's development, and for some young children from deprived or dysfunctional homes, childcare at an early age can offer some benefits – most clearly in cognitive achievements; but it is only to be preferred if the alternative would be worse.

Part 2: When the environment does not match early needs

Departures from the natural patterns of mothering can create early environments that fail in important ways to match the needs of infants. These needs arise from their biology, and this in turn is based on their human genes. Disturbed development can arise when the provisions of the environment fail to match the biologically based needs of mothers and infants *in ways that disrupt important biological mechanisms*. Since this mismatch is between the environment or *ecology*, and the biology based on the *genes*, it is proposed here that it may usefully be termed an 'eco-genetic mismatch'. Many of the adverse effects of non-family childcare can be better understood when seen as arising from this kind of mismatch.

Eco-genetic mismatch can involve risks at any stage in life, but it is especially likely to upset healthy development and behaviour when it occurs during pregnancy, childbirth and early childhood. Damaging eco-genetic mismatch can also arise out of ignorance and cultural customs or ideas that were misconceived because their proponents, however well-meaning, had failed to understand some facts of life that are well-established today. Two such ideologies are still influential in Western societies.

1) Though contrary to all the recorded sayings and actions of Jesus relating to children, the doctrine of original sin, with its strongly negative ideas about the basic nature of the infant, eventually became authorised teaching in Western Christianity from 529 AD. It viewed the child's nature as inherently sinful, with risk of far-reaching and terrible consequences. These are succinctly spelled out in the Anglican *Book of Common Prayer*, officially authorised in 1662. It declared that newborn babies inherit a sinful nature, and are destined for damnation unless

saved by various measures. Since many children died in infancy, these corrective measures were urgent, and they sometimes included breaking the infants' wills through early 'correction,' and violence if need be.

Similar ideas about the basic nature and tendencies of an infant have permeated religious and secular advice about childrearing right into the current era; they have also permeated psychoanalytic theory. Ideas that go with the doctrine of original sin have been sadly counterproductive, sometimes leading to disturbed parent-child relationships, psychological and behavioural maladjustment, as well as child abuse. Moreover, as this cultural process undermined many of the natural rewards of mothering and fathering, it prepared the way for another, compounding set of problems.

2) The much-needed movement to liberate women might have fought for a maternal feminism that also included equal rights for women. Unfortunately, 'equality feminism' focused mainly on equality with men in law and in the workplace. While this often offered women more companionship, with relief from social isolation at home, *it denied any particular value in early mothering.* This was regarded as being no different from 'fathering,' and soon the terms 'parenting,' and the completely non-committal term 'caregiver,' became favoured and politically correct.

Equality feminists based their program for social change on cultural determinism – an ideology that denied the influence of biology in most aspects of human nature and behaviour. *Unfortunately, cultural determinism was itself misconceived because its basic premise was untrue and derived from a hoax.* Instead of seeking support for mothers who were now separated from their extended families by societal changes, equality feminists engineered social policies that pressured women back into the 'workforce' – mostly against their real wishes – as if rearing infants only involves valuable 'work' when you are not the infant's mother.

Ignoring research showing the possibly serious and long-term risks involved, childcare advocates still sometimes talk as if infants – even from a few weeks of age – can be safely reared in childcare centres, with no need for mothering during this time. A powerful and costly childcare 'industry' has grown almost exponentially, with a vested interest in early, long-day childcare. It is generally presented as offering early education, and it often has large public subsidies.

The word 'mothering' has been declared to show 'bias,' and it is therefore generally unacceptable in the many publications that follow the *Style Manual* of the American Psychological Association (1995; 2005). Likewise, the words 'mothering' and 'breastfeeding,' have been widely neglected in the relevant social sciences, and they are usually absent from policy planning and legislation affecting early family life. This neglect and denial indicate many policy makers are seriously out of touch with some unchanging and inescapable facts of life.

Part 3: Conclusions and what can be done

There is much we might do. We could aim to bring our culture and our society – that we *can* change – into better harmony with our biological givens that we *cannot* change, and would therefore do well to accept.

We must learn to work with Nature, not against it. For human health, this involves valuing the unchanging facts of healthy mothering, breastfeeding, attachment and an empathic understanding of babies' feelings. Playfulness and joy are important natural rewards to compensate for the sacrifices that can be involved in mothering and fathering.

Natural patterns of mothering develop best when they are supported by the father, with an extended family or social group also available. It is essential to recognise the importance of these factors in human development if we are to promote good health and wellbeing in young children, mothers and society. In the modern world a nursing mother requires adequate freedom, with financial and social support within a facilitating environment. She also needs to feel respected and valued in her role as a mother. With "open pre-schools" as in Sweden, or "child places" as advocated by Penelope Leach, mothers and family daycare providers can meet and enjoy social supports.

A mother who has been in paid employment needs some income during an extended period of maternity leave. If she wishes to return to outside work when her children are old enough, she may need help in updating her skills. The value of what she has learned as a mother should be recognised for her employment, and that contribution to society should be taken into account in provisions for her retirement.

Since economic arguments and pressures are so often used to get mothers back into the workforce and infants into early childcare, this policy is overdue for a full economic analysis that *takes into account all the externalities and collateral damage that economists find it so easy to ignore and so hard to evaluate.* If they think that this collateral damage matters, but they cannot put a price on it, then they should say so. At present, it is ignored.

While there has been an explosion of interest in early education, it remains very important to distinguish the needs of children approaching school age from those of infants, whose primary needs revolve around sociable early mothering and fathering. These needs are best met by a healthy mother – and hopefully an empathic father – within a supportive environment. Since the support of mothering cannot so readily become an academic or government concern, or a profit-making 'industry,' it has received much less attention.

It is necessary to work with Nature and not against her if we are to promote health and wellbeing in young children, their mothers, and society. We were all babies once, and the fruits of good mothering and early nurture are among the greatest blessings a person can have in life. In offering these to their babies, mothers and fathers are setting the pattern of relationships that can be creative, mutually rewarding, and last for the rest of their lives. This may be achieved with joy and satisfaction. For parents who wish the best for their children and themselves, few things are more important for their healthy future – and for the quality of life on our planet. A normal mother-child relationship is a love affair that needs the right conditions to flourish. Infancy cannot be re-run later.

Notes

Note 1. When is an infant no longer an infant?

From: Cook (1996: 74–75).

There is flexibility in the meaning of the term infant that can be convenient, but could be hazardous. In child development literature infancy has been variously defined and there does not appear to be uniform usage. A long-standing definition (Rheingold, 1968) calls infancy the pre-verbal period of human development. This means that it lasts until the child can not only understand what is said, but can also speak well enough to have a meaningful conversation about what is happening to her. This definition of infant is used throughout the book, meaning the period until the child is clearly verbal.

A standard textbook of child development defines the end of infancy as the stage by which "children can experience the world by thinking about it" when representational thinking and the ability to use symbols first appear (Steinberg and Meyer, 1995: 140). By this definition, infancy may be thought to end a good deal earlier. Yet another definition considers that children under one year are infants, while those between one and three are toddlers. This definition further curtails the duration of infancy. The first tentative attempts at walking on one's own are another developmental marker sometimes used to separate infants from toddlers.

It is important to note that reports, statistics and conclusions often fail to recognise the differences between babies, toddlers and 3 to 5-year-old preschool-age children. The needs of these groups are very different and the ages of the children under consideration should always be specified.

Note 2. Genes, chromosomes and DNA

This material is summarised from various sources.

a. Gene. The unit of inheritance, composed of deoxyribonucleic acid (DNA), which is situated on, and transmitted by, the chromosome, and which develops into a hereditary trait as it reacts with the environment and with the other genes (Macquarie Dictionary).

The hereditary determinant of a specified difference between individuals (Chambers Science and Technological Dictionary, 1991). Genes are recipes for proteins, which are made only when and where they are needed, at which point the relevant gene is "switched on."

b. Genome. The totality of the DNA sequences (i.e., genetic material) for any cell, organism or organelle. Since we have around 3.3 thousand million letters of DNA in our genome, there is plenty of scope for specific differences to emerge. In 2001, the Human Genome Project published the entire sequence of our genome. But it was the genome of just one person (Pagel, 2008).

c. Chromosomes. Rod-like structures, visualised most easily in the nucleus during cell division, made up of a continuous thread of DNA and protein. In the human, each somatic cell nucleus normally contains 23 pairs of chromosomes – 46 chromosomes in all (including one sex chromosome, either X in a female, or Y in a male).

Twenty-three chromosomes are inherited from each parent. One pair of chromosomes are known as the sex chromosomes because they determine the sex of the individual. Individuals with two X chromosomes, i.e., XX, are female and individuals with one X and one Y, i.e., XY, are male. Women pass on one of their X chromosomes to each of their offspring, men pass on either an X to a daughter (who having received another X from her mother is XX) or a Y to a son (who having received an X from his mother is XY).

The Y chromosome passes down the male line of inheritance (nearly always unchanged), while in the female line, only the DNA of the mitochondria (the energy organelles within the cells) passes directly down the female line (generally unchanged). For a more detailed account of these changes, tracing back the maternal line, see *The Seven Daughters of Eve* by Bryan Sykes (2001). The two X chromosomes in a woman and the other (non-sex) chromosomes in men and women are 'shuffled' during the process of forming ova and sperms, so, in each generation, any particular gene may have come from either the maternal or paternal ancestor. (But each of these ancestors must also have been a 'successful' survivor, as in the main argument of this book.)

How they work: DNA (deoxyribonucleic acid) is a giant molecule found in the nucleus of cells. There are multiple lengths of DNA inside each cell's nucleus. Each length of DNA is combined with other substances and folded up very tightly to form a chromosome. They are enormously long and complex, and the DNA molecule is like a long twisted spiral ladder, in the shape of a double helix. The two twisted uprights of the ladder are linked together by chemical bridges that form the rungs. These chemical bridges are of four kinds. The exact linear sequence in which they appear on the ladder is the code of inheritance. The code sequences carry instructions for making the proteins that provide the material for building and maintaining the cells and the entire bodies of plants and animals. Most cells in the body of a plant or animal contain identical DNA molecules.

A gene is a short section of a chromosome's DNA. There are thousands of proteins in cells – each carrying out a particular job. For instructions to be issued, part of the DNA molecule must unwind to expose the chemical code on its rungs. The code is copied onto RNA (ribonucleic acid), which leaves the nucleus of that cell with instructions to make a particular protein. (Adapted from *The Incredible Journey to the Centre of the Atom* by Trevor Day and Nicholas Harris. Orpheus, Readers Digest, Australia. 1996).

d. Mitochondrial DNA and Y chromosomes. The DNA in the mitochondria is passed down the generations from mother to daughter. The mitochondria are small structures that mediate energy, and are within the cell but outside the nucleus. Fathers pass on their Y chromosome to their sons. In both cases these are generally passed on unaltered, but very occasionally mutations occur. Today, for a fee, The Genographic Project will trace the migration line of either of these for any male, but only the mitochondrial DNA can be traced for a female, though her father's Y chromosome could be traced.

e. The genome, controls, and 'junk DNA.' The developing field of epigenetics is defined as the branch of biology that deals with the effects of external influences on gene expression (Gluckman and Hanson, 2006: 66). One aspect is how environmental influences, such as nutrition and stress, may affect genes and the expression of genes, as they are passed on to children and grandchildren. The way in which some adverse conditions encountered by the mother may prepare the foetus for the conditions it is likely to encounter, have drawn attention to this phenomenon. While it may be found that beneficial changes can also be passed down in the genome indefinitely, it seems improbable that this process could fundamentally improve the basic mammalian, primate, human reproductive physiology, or the patterns of breastfeeding and early child nurturing that have been refined through millions of years of trial and error natural selection.

A summary on epigenesis is in *Early Years Study 2* (McCain et al., 2007) from which the following is slightly abbreviated. Genes are a blueprint for a development process that needs instructions about what to do, and when and how to do it. Epigenetics is the study of how genes can be turned on or off by environmental factors. It involves the interplay between early experiences and how, where, and when genes work. Experience activates mechanisms that alter genetic expression, affecting variations in disease, behaviour, and other traits and characteristics that emerge over the lifespan.

The epigenome is a suite of biochemical markers and switches in cells that provide instructions and influence the expression of particular genes. The epigenetic signals are influenced by early environments and experiences. Epigenetic signals from the environment can be passed along to the next generation – without actual changes in DNA. Epigenetics tells us that little things in life can have an effect of great magnitude.

Hidden influences on the genes can affect every aspect of development, including the transcription to proteins. Epigenetics proposes a control system of "switches" that turn genes on or off – and suggests that environmental experiences, like nutrition and stress, can control these switches and cause heritable effects in humans. Heritable changes in genome function occur without a change in the actual gene structure. The importance of this field in brain development is leading to advocacy for a human epigenome project. Epigenetic processes influence the differentiation of neurons and their connections for different functions such as vision, hearing, language, behaviour, and stress reactions.

In June 2007, reports of research by the Encode Consortium – the Encyclopedia of DNA Elements – published in *Nature, and Genome Research*, shed light on the genetic differences separating humans from chimpanzees and other species. While the human genome is made up of about three billion DNA 'letters', only about 3 percent of these are known to contribute to our 22,000 or so genes – the DNA 'sentences' containing instructions for making proteins that control the body's chemical processes. Most of the remaining 97% which does not code for proteins – non protein-coding DNA – has been widely regarded as 'junk DNA' – an evolutionary relic performing no significant tasks.

However recent research including that carried out by the Encode Consortium now shows that much of this 'junk DNA' is chemically active in ways that influence how genes are switched on and off. It appears that genes, junk DNA and other elements, together weave an intricate control network. Junk DNA is copied into RNA – an active molecule that relays information from DNA to the cellular machinery. Mutations in these regulatory genetic regions are likely to explain some of our individual varying susceptibilities to disease. While most of our genes are shared with other organisms, much more of our junk DNA is peculiar to our species. About 98.5 percent of human and chimpanzee genes are identical but as there is more variation in the junk DNA, this could influence traits such as intelligence and language. One theory is that it provides a stock of genetic material from which potentially useful mutations can arise to drive evolution. It may be a kind of 'warehouse' for natural selection.

Note 3. Infants' distress and developmental delay in quality Swedish childcare

From the summary in Chapter 2 of *Early Child Care: Infants and nations at risk* (Cook, 1996: 171–172). (For the fuller account, see: Cook, 1996: 102–106).

Ingrid Harsman, PhD (1994), conducted a rare, if not unique, study of infants' reactions to day care centre placement. In Stockholm she observed 26 infants before, and for five months after, placement in high quality day care centres, commencing when they were 6–12 months of age. A matched control sample of 26 infants exclusively cared for by their mothers was studied for comparison.

In the initial phase of 3–4 weeks the day care centre infants "reacted with a significant negative change in mood and often showed sadness, a low activity level as well as a low tolerance for frustration in the center setting. In addition the day-care infants rejected face-to-face contact with the staff...." 52% of the infants were assessed as sad and depressed in the day care setting. 12% showed a clear-cut negative change in mood but no sadness. From about 7 weeks they showed a "very low level of crying and a low level of infant-staff interaction." Complex and subtle changes in the mother-infant interaction were found, indicative of disruption of mother-infant attunement.

On testing with the Griffiths Mental Development Scale and Development Quotients no differences were found between the two groups before starting day care, but "after seven weeks of day-care attendance, the day-care infants showed a significant drop in speech development" (as assessed with the Hearing and Speech Scale) and for some infants this drop was associated with the observed preceding initial phase of sadness and distress.

"After about 5 months of center attendance... the day care infants showed significantly lower scores on the Personal-Social Scale as well as on the Hearing and Speech Scale if sensitive measures were used (i.e., Development Quotient)." A clear-cut decline in test performance on these scales was associated with prolonged daily separations (30–40 hours per week), low to moderately low quality in maternal and/or day care quality, as assessed by sensitivity to the infant's signals of face-to-face interaction and close physical contact. The negative change in the Hearing and Speech Scale appeared mainly in boys. There are striking similarities between these findings and those seen in the 1996 NICHD Study of Early Child Care, using a quite different measure – the Strange Situation.

Harsman concluded that the results "indicate that prolonged maternal separations may negatively influence the infants' cognitive development and the process of adjustment. Taken together the results imply that many of the infants in this study were vulnerable during the first five months in day care" (Harsman 1994).

There is no reason to assume that this vulnerability disappeared after the five-month study period.

Note 4. Maurice Bevan-Brown, and extract from *Baby's Point of View* by Joyce Partridge

Baby's Point of View by Dr Joyce Partridge, published by Oxford University Press in 1935, was out of print when Dr Bevan-Brown quoted from it in *The Sources of Love and Fear*. At the end of his book he wrote a conclusion that seems as relevant today as it was in 1950.

> What, then, is the conclusion of this matter? For unless this book contributes to a better understanding and practice of child nurture it is of little value. The main conclusion is that we must try to produce a better race of parents than now exists, and better parents than we have been ourselves. 'Good' parents do exist in our generation but they are in a minority. The first requirement for a 'good' parent is to be emotionally mature. The majority of parents are emotionally immature – that is, they still retain in some respects the emotional attitudes characteristic of children. Therefore their children, lacking real parental affection themselves, also remain emotionally immature when they become adult. We must try to break this vicious circle at as many points as possible by educative measures applied to: (1) Parents with young children, (2) Prospective parents, (3) Adolescents, (4) Educationists and (5) Doctors.
>
> The whole matter cannot be condensed into rules, but rules are not without their value. We have contended that the first year of any individual's life is the most critical for mental health. Concerning the first year, I know of no code of rules as good as that given by Joyce Partridge in her little book, *Baby's Point of View*. Unfortunately this is out of print: otherwise I would recommend everyone interested in the care of children to buy a copy. Here are Joyce Partridge's rules (quoted by her permission):
>
> (1) "Try to recognise before your baby is born that, in the matter of sex, the chances are even.
>
> (2) "Don't be afraid to follow the maternal instinct and intuition: in other words, give scope to your love for your baby and don't bring him up by rule of thumb.
>
> (3) "Breastfeed your baby.
>
> (4) "Never leave a baby alone to cry.

(5) "Be as much as possible within earshot of your baby in the early weeks and months of life.

(6) "Never in any circumstances scold a baby of whatever age, and never allow anyone else to scold him for wetting or soiling napkins or for wetting or soiling any other place whatsoever."

Joyce Partridge is a first-class psychiatrist, a Fellow of the Royal College of Surgeons (England), and a mother. I commend her rules to you. It is the daily lot of the psychiatrist to meet and endeavour to relieve people who have experienced years of disability, ill-health, distress, and often of utter misery, all, or nearly all, of which need not have happened if they themselves and their parents had had more understanding. There are two highly emotionally toned words in this connection – '*if only.*' 'If only I had come to you ten or twenty years ago....' 'If only my mother and father had understood these things....' 'If only I had understood these things when my children were younger.' If this little book is able to mitigate in any degree some of this widespread distress, it will have fulfilled its purpose.

Though infancy was a central concern, *The Sources of Love and Fear* covered a much wider scope. In a presidential address to The Medical Society of Psychology in London on Oct 10, 1935, Bevan-Brown had presented *A plea for correlation between the different schools of psychodynamic thought.*

The above extract was cited in 'Fifty years of psychotherapy, but what about early childcare and child mental health?' *Forum: The Journal of the New Zealand Association of Psychotherapists* 1998, 4:97–114. Based on a paper to the 50th Anniversary Conference of NZ Association of Psychotherapy, 1998 (Cook, 1998).

Note 5. Dr Truby King's ideology

Professor Eric Olssen, of the History Department at Otago University in Dunedin, examined the ideology of the Plunket Society and Dr Truby King's underlying purposes, in a paper to the Australian and New Zealand Association of Science (ANZAS). It appeared in two parts in the NZ Listener of May 12, 1979 and the subsequent issue, under the titles: *Breeding for the Empire* and *Producing the Passionless People*. They were also broadcast. A formal presentation is in Olssen, 1981.

Note 6. Abstract and table from "Childrearing, culture and mental health"

In the abstract of my paper "Childrearing, culture and mental health: exploring an ethological-evolutionary perspective in child psychiatry and preventive mental health, with particular reference to two contrasting approaches to early childrearing" *Med. J. Aust. Spec. Supp.*, 1978, 2:3–14, I said:

> A shift of historic significance in some aspects of Western attitudes to childrearing is occurring. In this period of transition, the coexistence of two contrasting approaches to childrearing has given rise to much contradiction and confusion in the advice offered to parents. This paper seeks to explore some mental health aspects of this situation from an evolutionary and historical perspective. The term "phylogenetically" or "ecologically determined maladjustment" has been proposed for that particular kind of disturbance in an organism, or in a population, which is due to the fact that the environmental conditions have deviated significantly from those to which the species has become genetically adapted through evolution.
>
> This concept, which is a corollary of Darwinian theory, has health implications and appears relevant in psychiatry both for understanding psychological disturbance and for promoting better mental health. It is particularly applicable in early childhood. I suggest that childrearing in English-speaking societies is emerging from an era in which many widely held beliefs, values, attitudes, and practices have been so out of harmony with the genetically influenced nature and needs of mothers and their developing children that they have contributed to conflict, stress, and emotional and behavioural disturbance in the infant and developing child.
>
> Attitudes of basic distrust towards the human biological "givens," combined with a belief in coercion, have characterised this approach to childrearing, which is here termed the "basic distrust orientation." It is undesirable that developing countries, seeking beneficial, scientifically based advances, should also inadvertently and unnecessarily import some of these tenets and practices that may be prejudicial to good mental health.
>
> The basic distrust orientation is contrasted with a "trusting cooperative" approach to early childrearing that appears to be more in harmony with

the nature and needs of developing children and their parents. These principles are relevant to the diagnosis and therapeutic management of emotionally disturbed children. They also suggest guidelines for the promotion of mental health. It is necessary to understand and respect the biological "givens," together with the potentials of such in-built regulatory mechanisms as have evolved, and then to cooperate with them, rather than work against them in the approach to early childrearing, family life, and the social settings in which they occur. In many ways this can be, and is being, done now.

Table: Comparing a trusting, cooperative approach to childrearing with a distrustful, directive approach

Though many parents, including those of a majority of disturbed children, still display the basic distrust orientation today, it no longer represents the childrearing ideas of some other parents and of many professionals who are concerned with child development. Intermingled, to an increasing extent, is a different approach that has been softening the rigid authoritarianism of earlier times.

It may be termed a trusting, cooperative approach, and some of its characteristics, and ways in which it contrasts with traditional attitudes, are outlined in the table below. From an orientation of basic trust in the biological givens influencing the needs and behaviour of the developing human being, infants are seen as being immature, dependent creatures, who seek gratification and satisfaction according to their needs. They often behave in ways that are influenced by mechanisms whose function is to ensure that their needs are adequately met. Gratification is seen as leading to satisfaction and contentment rather than to "spoiling."[55]

Next page:

Table: Two contrasting approaches to early childrearing, derived respectively from attitudes of distrust and trust towards the genetic influences underlying the needs and behaviour of human infants.

---

55. Cook, P.S. (1978). Childrearing, culture and mental health: exploring an ethological-evolutionary perspective in child psychiatry and preventive mental health, with particular reference to two contrasting approaches to early childrearing. *MJA* 1978; 2: S3-S14. © Copyright 1978. *The Medical Journal of Australia* – reproduced with permission.

Ideas	Contrast	A Distrustful Directive Approach
Ideas influencing parents' perception of, and responsiveness to, the infant	*Basic attitude:*	Distrust and non-acceptance towards the biological 'givens' influencing the needs and behaviour of the developing human being
	The infant is seen as:	(a) being selfish, demanding (b) wanting as much gratification and indulgence as he or she can get (probably too much)
	Gratification behaviours perceived as:	self-willed, demanding, manipulative, cunning (which may confirm belief in inherent potential for badness)
	Gratification behaviours lead to:	danger of 'spoiling' if more than the right amount is given
Ideas influencing parents' requirements of their infants	*Basic parental goal:*	to control and direct the child's behaviour, and produce a 'good' child (who will be obedient and conform)
	Childrearing method:	(a) mould the child to a predetermined pattern; secure control by regulating habits, and training to accept authority and discipline (b) teach 'right from wrong' and demand obedience; extinguish 'naughty' behaviour and insist on or reinforce 'good' behaviour (c) child's point of view often misunderstood or ignored, and requirements often disregard the child's feelings and capacities, so that hostility and negativism tend to be aggravated, and unless these are repressed, control requires more force (d) disapproval more frequent and may be reinforced by threats, punishment, and sometimes violence, or inculcation of shame (e) timing: start training early (perhaps from birth)
	Apparent outcome:	(a) increased risk of conflict, frustration, and stress in unsatisfying relationships (b) sensitivity may be blunted; externally imposed discipline may break down in rebelliousness (c) emotional maturation at risk; maladjustment and psychopathology

A Trusting, Cooperative Approach
Trust and acceptance towards the biological "givens" influencing the needs and behaviour of the developing human being (a) being immature, dependent (b) wanting as much gratification and satisfaction as he or she needs (an adequate supply) influenced by possessing mechanisms whose function is to ensure that his or her needs are adequately met satisfaction and contentment; spoiling not a danger
to enjoy a good relationship with the child, and help to produce a 'whole,' healthy person (who is likely to be sufficiently 'good' also) (a) satisfy young child's needs, and develop a cooperative, mutually satisfying, affectionate relationship, in which the potential of the child and parents unfold, blossom and gradually mature. The developing capacities for self-regulation are respected and encouraged (b) teach avoidance of common dangers and gradually encourage disposition to consider and respect the needs and feelings of others, through experiencing this consideration within the family (c) child's point of view more likely to be understood, and requests consider the child's feelings and capacities, so that hostility and negativism tend to be minimized; the child's feelings are accepted in the expectation that sufficient (self) control will be achieved as appropriate to the child's age; (the options of exercising authority and sufficient force are still available if essential) (d) inconsiderate behaviour discouraged, but the quality of relationships tends to make punishment inappropriate and it may be seldom or never required (e) timing: await maturation and encourage development
(a) mutual satisfaction in interpersonal relationships with joy and delight (sometimes) as a natural reward for health-promoting activities (b) sensitivity intact; adequate self-discipline develops as appropriate to the age (c) emotional maturation facilitated; mental health

Note 7. Margaret Mead, Samoa, and why Derek Freeman *was right after all*

7 A. The documentary film by Frank Heimans, *Margaret Mead and Samoa*

In some of the lamentable attempts to defend Margaret Mead by *ad hominem* attacks on Freeman, there has been a remarkable and inexcusable neglect of the extensive documentation of first-hand accounts by many eminent people who knew Mead, as shown in the multi-award-winning documentary film *Margaret Mead and Samoa*, made by Frank Heimans in 1987-8. This film shows early photographs, biographical details, and archival footage of Mead and some key people in her life. There is also much filming in Samoa, and many interviews with academics in anthropology. The DVD of this film is readily available to anyone, and yet, along with the powerful critique by G.N. Appell in 1984, it is not even referenced by some critics, who ignore them as if they did not exist. Some of the reviews and awards that this film has received, together with a pdf of the complete film script, may be seen at www.members.optusnet.com.au/pcook62

The wide range of participants in this film, including Mead's daughter, Catherine Bateson, may be seen in the acknowledgements at the end of the film. As of 2010, many were still active in senior academic positions. Below are some quotes from the film.

Who could possibly have fallen for that stuff?
Phyllis Grosskurth, Mead's close companion and biographer, says:
> I think the fascination of the book was its focus on sex, idealized sex and America was at a stage where it was becoming sex-obsessed, and she catered really to that. Listen to this passage: 'Familiarity with sex and the recognition of a need of a technique to deal with sex as an art, have produced a scheme of personal relations in which there are no neurotic pictures, no frigidity, no impotence, except as a temporary result of severe illness, and the capacity for intercourse only once in a night is counted as

senility'. I mean, who could possibly have fallen for that stuff?[56] (Heimans, 1988: 12 min.).

He attacked the Goddess of Anthropology

Robin Fox,[57] Professor of Anthropology, Rutgers University, NJ, says:

> What Derek did, you see, was a double whammy. He didn't just attack it in the theoretical way, he attacked it in the person of the Goddess, of the super-celebrity, who had made anthropology, who was anthropology, who was the symbol of anthropology to the world and who was the prime promulgator of this doctrine to the world on behalf of anthropology. So he did a thing that was doubly bad. He didn't just say 'You know, this religion is theologically problematical', he said 'God is wrong', or rather in this case 'the Goddess is wrong'. She couldn't be, you see, she couldn't be, because if she was wrong, then the doctrine was wrong, then the whole liberal humanitarian scheme was wrong, and I think this is a wrong connection. I think the liberal wing here made a wrong connection. You don't need that position in order to defend the goodness of man, but they do, and they did (Heimans, 1988: 23mins).

I haven't read the book, but I know he's wrong

The film also shows Professor Marc Swartz, of the University of California, San Diego, saying:

> One of the leading anthropologists came out immediately after the first word of Derek's book was out and said, 'I haven't read the book, but I know he's wrong'. That's a bit depressing in a field that thinks it's a science (Heimans, 1988: 24 min.).

American anthropologists didn't realize what they were taking on.

Robin Fox then says:

---

56. In 2010, Phyllis Grosskurth is listed as a professor emeritus at the University of Toronto.
57. Robin Fox is an Anglo-American anthropologist known chiefly for his work on marriage, human and primate kinship systems, and evolutionary anthropology and sociology. As Professor of Anthropology, he founded the department of anthropology at Rutgers University, NJ, in 1967, and remained as a professor there for the rest of his career. Listed as Advisor, Social Issues Research Centre.

American anthropologists knew very little about Derek Freeman as a person and didn't realize what they were taking on. I think they felt a few dismissive reviews and he would curl up and die and go away and retire back to Pogo Pogo, or Bongo Bongo, or wherever it was he'd come from. They didn't realize that they were taking on a very tough character. I mean, anyone who knows Derek knows that when he has got his teeth into something, he does not let go – he's going to get it right though heavens fall. So American anthropology suddenly found itself with this one-man tornado, taking it on, and for every twenty indignant letters or articles in the '*American Anthropologist*', or speeches, Derek came back with twenty more, equally powerful, and I think this has rather shaken them. I think they weren't prepared for something of this magnitude, they just thought he'd go away. Well, Derek doesn't just go away (Heimans, 1988: 27 min.).

Samoan aggression

Narrator Margaret Throsby says: "In 1973 Richard Goodman, a student of Samoa for many years, writes his own independent refutation of Mead's book. He arrives at many of the same conclusions that Freeman reaches". Richard Goodman:

Well, what I uncovered was that Samoans have a huge amount of aggression in them, due to the way they're brought up as children and treated as children, punished as children; that they repress this aggression and anger, that they displace it. It comes out in very interesting and peculiar ways. They simply aren't that happy, they have a mask of happiness (Heimans, 1988: 29 min.).

Not aggressive? "Kill the ref." And they did – twice.

Tim O'Meara, Assistant Professor of Anthropology, University of North Carolina, says:

In the area of Samoa that I lived, there was one occasion of extraordinary violence, which happened at the National Cricket Tournament in Apia, in the capital city. Our team went to the cricket tournament and were not doing very well in the cricket tournament and they thought they would, should, be doing better; and [during] one game they became enraged by the referee's calls. They thought they were biased and the crowd began yelling 'Kill the ref', and they did. They beat him to death with their cricket bats. One occurrence that I have read about, and I believe it was in 1928 – a very similar occurrence – happened in Apia in the National Cricket Tournament when a referee was beaten to death by the players with their cricket bats for bad calls. Exactly the same thing that happened in 1982 (Heimans, 1988: 29 min.).[58]

7 B. Margaret Mead tells of her lies, in a book called *All True!*

After publishing in early 1999 the hardback edition of *The Fateful Hoaxing of Margaret Mead*, Derek Freeman was tidying his papers for the archives when he belatedly found an old reference that had escaped everyone's attention. In 1931, in a rare and now little-known book *All True! The Record of Actual Adventures that Have Happened to Ten Women of Today*, Mead's own account was published in her story *Life as a Samoan Girl* (Mead, 1931, 116-118).

In the second (revised) edition of his book, published as a paperback in late 1999, Freeman quotes Mead from this story, as she says: "In all things I had behaved as a Samoan, for only so, only by losing my identity as far as possible had I been able to become acquainted with the Samoan girls, receive their whispered confidences and learn at the same time the answer to the scientists' questions."

In her 1931 story Mead was writing about an evening on the island of Ofu at the end of the day when she had apparently received these "whispered confidences". She gave a vivid description of a reception that was held in honour of herself and her companions, and she describes how Misa, the high chief of the village came in full regalia to join the celebration.

By now Mead had been given a Samoan name, and she was dressing and living as a Samoan. At this reception, she was enjoying the "dancing, music and the light-hearted repartee" when unexpectedly the village chief, whose his wife had died, arose and said to her "Misa is rich. He will marry your highness and accompany you on your further travel around the world…" Suddenly, Mead had to quickly think up an answer that would neither insult him nor ruin the rapport and persona that she had so carefully established. Though she says no one believed

---

58. In 2011, Tim O'Meara is listed as Assistant Professor, Department of Sociology and Anthropology, University of North Carolina.

his offer was serious, it did need a formal and culturally correct reply. She looked round at the circle of dark expectant faces, and wrote that she feared "all the flimsy structure was going to collapse about my head".

Finally, she said that when she left her home in America she had declared that she was going all round the world by herself. She added: "All the people laughed and said that a mere girl could not go around the world by herself. Were I to accept his lordship Misa's most honorable invitation and were he to accompany me, all the people would laugh and say that they had been right. And I would be ashamed because I who was young had boasted of something which I could not perform." Mead wrote that the crisis was past and the tension relaxed, as she had given the courteous answer (Mead, 1931, 116-118).

So having largely concealed the fact that she already had a husband, and having three times accepted the status of ceremonial virgin, she seemingly boasts about having given a reply that was completely fabricated, and she sees nothing incongruous about recording this in a book called *All True!*

One of these "girls" was Fa'apua'a Fa'amo, and an extract of her 1987 account confirming this story is in Chapter 9 (Heimans, 1988: 43mins). The interview may be seen in Heimans' DVD, and the post-production film script may be seen on: www.members.optusnet.com.au/pcook62.

7 C. Mead's 'hunches' that went on to influence feminism

Freeman says Mead was much given to having "hunches", and recorded one that involved her conclusions in *Sex and Temperament in Three Primitive Societies* (1935).[59] She wrote that the most "bizarre" of these societies was the Tchambuli, whose "formulation of sex-attitudes contradicts our usual premises." On March 21, 1933, she wrote from Tchambuli to her colleague Ruth Benedict, "I've had a tremendous spurt of energy and I've gotten the key to this culture from my angle – got it yesterday during hours of sitting on the floor in a house in mourning. Now it is straight sailing ahead, just a matter of working out all the

---

59. This book became a major influence on the feminist movement, since it claimed that females were dominant in the Tchambuli Lake region of the Sepik basin of Papua New Guinea, without causing any special problems. But this apparent lack of male dominance may have been due to the outlawing of warfare by the Australian administration.

ramifications of my hunch." These "ramifications" in turn flowed into her influential 1949 book, *Male and Female*. Freeman wrote that many such anecdotes shed light on how her fertile mind worked. He emphatically denied that she was guilty of scientific fraud, but rather that, on hearing what she very much wanted to hear, she eagerly believed it (Freeman, 1999: 146).

7 D. Derek Freeman's health

Since his death in July 2001, attempts to defend Margaret Mead by attacking Derek Freeman have continued, as if the historical facts that he unearthed can be countered by disparaging his motives, persistence, personality, or mental stability. One academic wrote that he was "a difficult man with a mysterious psychological illness", and various ill-informed and derogatory personality diagnoses were touted – as if such *ad hominem* attacks invalidate historical evidence that can be independently verified.

In the hope of bringing such hurtful and untrue psychological abuse to a close, Freeman's wife, Monica Freeman, has authorised me to set down some facts. In addition to having diabetes, Derek Freeman suffered from bipolar disorder – a condition that afflicts many people. In earlier years, his mood might be depressed for some weeks, after which it would be normal for perhaps quite a long period. Then it might become elevated, and he would become very active and lose sleep. Following this, his mood would again return to normal. He was more likely to become overactive if he encountered a situation that, professionally, he had good reason to believe was wrong. His bipolar disorder gradually lessened and abated through the 1980s. As a psychiatrist who came to know Derek Freeman quite well from 1998 until the time of his death, I was impressed with his integrity, fairness and careful concern for accuracy. During that time I saw no signs of psychiatric or personality abnormality.

7 E. Cultural relativism and women's rights

Lest it be thought that the ideologies derived from cultural determinism are no longer relevant, note that well into the 21st century, Ayaan Hirsi Ali, the courageous Somali author of *Infidel: My Life*, blames Western feminism's adoption of cultural relativism for the way in which it seldom criticises, and mostly turns a blind eye to, the abuse and oppression that women suffer in some Muslim societies. A Google search of "Ayaan Hirsi Ali" *and* "cultural relativism" together, finds many thousands of references.

Note 8. De Beauvoir – Two concerns

8 A. "No woman should have that choice"

Professor James Tooley (2002: 76), in *The Miseducation of Women*, outlines his findings after he researched the background, and many lesser-known aspects of the ideas, writings, and lives of some key women who influenced the women's liberation movement. He analysed the pathways and policies that have failed to meet many of the needs of women. In a remarkable chapter, "Romantic Illusions," he cites many lesser-known sections in the writings of these women, who played crucial roles in the directions taken by the movement for the 'liberation' of women.

Describing the effects for girls of a government policy document that mandated an identical curriculum for girls and boys, Tooley describes some adverse effects of equality feminist influences in the education of girls in the UK. The document states, with evident satisfaction, that "the liberation of women from the cult of femininity and domesticity and the traditional family... cannot now be reversed." He comments: "Let us repeat: these are feminists – writing in the traditions of the early Freidan, Greer, and Steinem – who provide support for government policy on education; the traditions in which they write coincide with the educational landscape today."

Tooley discusses three problems with these policies: the degradation of domesticity; "a curious romanticizing" of the world of men; and "the nagging doubt that, in their praise of independent women, the feminists have missed out something about the mutuality, the interconnectedness, of the happiness of men and women." (Tooley, 2002: 60). In tracing the roots of the degradation of domesticity, he says: "The need to liberate women from 'domestic drudgery' to their rightful position at the workplace, can usefully be traced back to Simone de Beauvoir's tirade against the housewife of 1949 in *The Second Sex* – ideas then translated to an American and then wider Anglo-Saxon audience by Betty Freidan in *The Feminine Mystique* of 1963."

Tooley presents reasons for thinking that much of what de Beauvoir wrote in *The Second Sex*, was "to please, to entertain, to seduce and – perhaps most centrally – to retain Sartre.... She did what Sartre told her to do." (Evans, 1996: 70). Tooley commented:

> The odd thing is, if *The Second Sex* had actually been written by Jean-Paul Sartre, rather than, as seems likely, inspired in part by the difficulties of a conventional relationship *with* him, it would have been dismissed long ago as the ranting of a misogynist chauvinist, in a long tradition of abuse of women. Instead, it has been held up for acclaim by feminists. When she died in Paris in 1996, Simone de Beauvoir was 'almost universally' proclaimed as the 'mother' of contemporary feminism, 'its major twentieth century theoretician, one of the greatest twentieth century philosophers and writers.' And *The Second Sex* is 'widely regarded as the major feminist text of the twentieth century'... 'one of those rare classic statements on the human condition whose power only grows as its many dimensions are discovered and interrogated.' All this about a book that eventually succeeds in denigrating all that women stand for, in favour of a picture of the woman becoming as much like a man as possible. Or, to put it another way, of de Beauvoir becoming as much like Sartre as possible, to retain his affection.

Tooley cites de Beauvoir's "chilling prescriptions," uttered in 1975, of how to create the independent woman:

> 'No woman should be authorised to stay home to raise her children. Society should be totally different. Women should not have that choice, precisely because if there is such a choice, too many women will make that one. It is a way of forcing women in a certain direction.'[60]

Or, as she put it in *The Second Sex*:

> 'What is extremely demoralising for the woman who aims at self-sufficiency is the existence of other women of like social status, having at the start the same opportunities, who live as parasites.... A comfortably married or supported friend *is a temptation in the way of one who is intending to make her own success.*'

---

60. Tooley, 2002, 76, quoted Graglia, p.274 from 'Sex, society and the female dilemma: a dialogue between Simone de Beauvoir and Betty Friedan", *Saturday Review*, 14 June 1975, p.18. Manne (2005: 33, 321) cites this as de Beauvoir's reply when Friedan had said to her that she "believed women should have the choice to stay home to raise their children if that is what they wished to do," and de Beauvoir had answered "No, we don't believe that any woman should have this choice etc." Manne references this as cited from Sommers (1994), *Who Stole Feminism?* p. 257.

With great candour, she tells us that the temptation of being a housewife is enough to stop young women from pursuing their independent path: 'The hope of some being one day *delivered from taking care of herself*, and the fear of having to lose that hope if she assumes this care for a time, combine to prevent her from unreservedly applying herself to her studies and her career' (de Beauvoir, [1949] 1993: 733–734, cited from Tooley, 2002: 76–7, his emphasis added).

8 B. "I am astonished when I realise how thoroughly I have been cheated."

Hazel Rowley, in *Tête-à-Tête: The Lives and Loves of Simone de Beauvoir and Jean Paul Sartre,* describes how de Beauvoir devoted her life to living an exemplary modern relationship partnership, as she and Sartre had agreed, with no secrets between them. She also followed his suggestion to make her own life, and the recording of it, her project, so that all might benefit from their pioneering experiences. She evidently hoped for an exemplary love life, on equal terms with Sartre. Yet he insisted that they each retain complete sexual freedom, and *he never allowed her to actually live with him, and he probably pressured her into aborting her child* (Tooley, 2002: 73).

Despite mutual promises of having no secrets from each other, de Beauvoir later discovered that he concealed many of his liaisons with other women. Tooley says: "If Sartre hated the things women desired he certainly did not eschew the company of women. Or, to be more precise, sexual relations with women. Very early on in his relationship with de Beauvoir, he told her that monogamy was out; that they must both have additional sexual relationships. In practice, this meant him having as many women as he could lay his hands on, and her having the occasional fling to compensate when he was tied up with others." It was Sartre's idea that she should write a book about women (Tooley, 2002, 73, 75).

It is not so well known that de Beauvoir later came to feel that she had been most selfishly exploited by Sartre. In a section "De Beauvoir cheated," Tooley describes the background to her anguish and profound disillusionment as she reviewed her life and achievements at the age of 54. She wrote: "Nothing has taken place.... As I look back, wondering, on the credulous adolescent that I was, I am astonished when I realize how thoroughly I have been cheated." (Tooley, 2002: 71, quoted from de Beauvoir, 1993: 685–6, translated by Leighton, 1975: 111).

In 2008, in *Glued Together by Their Lies – A Dangerous Liaison*, Carole Seymour-Jones, with the cooperation of de Beauvoir's adopted daughter, presented a devastating account of some discreditable and less well-known aspects of the lives and loves of Sartre and de Beauvoir. She documents how, personally and politically, the reality was sometimes sordid, and often so very different from what they claimed to hope for, prescribed for others, or how they intended to be remembered. In reviewing this book, Gillian Tindall comments: "Just how far the Sartre-Beauvoir compact became a travesty of all their claims to honesty and freedom now becomes clear in this excoriating study.... Sartre, for all his libertarianism, was sexually a cold fish, preferring the initiation of virgins or other exotic conquests to sex with a familiar equal. De Beauvoir, of course, knew this, and developed a lifelong fear that their much-trumpeted union would not survive. Her solution was to provide him with girlfriends whom she could control. Several of them were young *lycée* pupils of hers, and on more than one occasion, there were formal complaints from parents that Mlle de Beauvoir was a sinister influence and probably a lesbian. Of the half-dozen women annexed to 'the family' in this way, one later committed suicide, two became drug addicts, and another was so permanently traumatised by betrayal and abandonment, that de Beauvoir for once felt pangs of guilt" (Seymour-Jones, C. 2008, reviewed by G.Tindall).

The family owners of Sartre's papers denied both Rowley and Seymour-Jones any access to these records as they wrote the biographies of two people whose ideas and lives have profoundly influenced the perspectives and experiences of so many others.

All this invites the question: "Does the way philosophers live their own lives, and how they relate to other people in their lives, have any relevance to the validity of their ideas, philosophies, and prescriptions for the lives of others?" Perhaps Jesus' succinct advice in the Sermon on the Mount is relevant here: "Beware of false prophets that come to you in sheep's clothing, but inwardly they are ravening wolves. Ye shall know them by their fruits" (Matthew 7:15).

Comment

It is worth reflecting on some implications of what de Beauvoir is revealing when she insists "women should not have that choice." She is using a formula underlying much purportedly well-meaning inhumanity down the ages: "I know what is good for you, and I shall see that you get it (whether you like it or not) – because I care about you, or love you."

This has sometimes appeared in history as a perversion of the injunction to *love your neighbour*. What could be more loving than saving someone's soul from suffering in Hell, even if the method was against the will of the person concerned? This perversion was used by the Spanish Inquisition, to justify torture for the greater good of saving the victims' souls. It sometimes justified slavery, since being enslaved in *this* life and then baptized was a small price to pay for the blessing of being saved from eternal suffering in Hell (Wright, 1970: 31).

Here, the end justifies the means. When combined with the quest for "the greatest good of the greatest number," it could be twisted by Marxists and other tyrants, who might claim that gulag imprisonment and the murder of countless millions were necessary cleansings to achieve their vision of greater social wellbeing. It can also be – and often has been – used to justify beating children – 'this is for your own good.' We have seen that Susanna Wesley used it to advocate beating even infants, "whatever pains it cost" till it breaks their wills.

In 1957, the eminent London psychiatrist, William Sargent, wrote *The Battle for the Mind: A Physiology of Conversion and Brain-washing.* He described various techniques of brainwashing and suggested they could serve both good and evil purposes. He urged their use for good, and said that churches might learn to employ them to convert people to Christianity.

This was cogently disputed by Ian Ramage, an Auckland Methodist theologian. In 1967 he wrote *The Battle for the Free Mind*, and argued that such coercive manipulation is exactly what the authentic call of Jesus is not. It is not based on brainwashing techniques, but is a voluntary response to the offer of unconditional love. For many who heard John Wesley's message, and [ab]reacted dramatically in response (as described by Ramage), it may well have brought up feelings of deeply repressed early pain and longings when – for the first time in their lives – they felt they were being offered the *unconditional love* that should be every baby's birthright.

Note 9. Why daycare centres cannot offer "high quality" daycare for infants

The research on a 1:4 staff-child ratio for children aged under two years was summarised as follows by the Cross Sectoral Task Force (2006), in the *Report on the implementation of a 1:4 staff-child ratio for children aged under two years in NSW children's services.* Sydney: New South Wales government.

Report Section 2. Research

Current research on the issues of staff-child ratios and quality care shows that:

- good quality early childhood education has positive outcomes for children in both cognitive and social domains;
- the quality of children's services is influenced by staff-child ratios;
- staff-child ratios and group size are significant factors in quality care; and
- the research recommends a ratio of 1:3 for children under three....

"This research shows that the aim of setting any ratios for staffing is to create conditions that maximise or enhance the quality of relationships between adults and children, between children themselves and between the adults working in the service. Positive relationships create the most favourable climate for children to thrive, to develop and to learn. The staff-child ratio in child care centres is widely regarded as one of the major indicators of quality care.

"Many early childhood educators, on the basis of research on social attachment and early brain development believe anything less than a 1:3 ratio for babies under two years of age is insufficient to allow staff to interact effectively with each young child. The reasons for this are varied but include:

- lower ratios enable staff to develop effective meaningful relationships with the children in their care; and

- [lower staff ratios] create a less stressful environment for child carers in which to work.

"Research shows that as the number of children per staff member increases, staff spend more time in restrictive and routine communication with children but less in positive verbal interaction.

"Recent research by The Australia Institute, which focused on the quality aspects of care included a national survey of long daycare centre staff. The survey posed a range of questions about key aspects of quality care. 'Staff to child ratios are at the core of the ability to provide quality care and a number of survey questions explored this issue.' The survey confirmed that:

> Most child care workers believe that current legal minimum staff-to-child ratios are too low. That is, there should be fewer children under the care of each staff member. The majority of respondents identified lack of 'one to one' time with children as the most negative aspect of low staff-to-child ratios.
>
> Child care workers are most concerned about the negative impact poor staff to child ratios have on developing relationships with individual children.

"The US Department of Health and Human Services commissioned a research brief to review and provide an analysis of the research literature focused on 13 key licensing indicators of quality in childcare. These 13 indicators have been used by many states in the US in the development of their respective licensing indicator systems.

"The research brief highlighted the latest pertinent research studies related to the 13 key indicators. Staff-child ratios was one of these indicators.

"The research brief found that a review of all the major research in childcare 'clearly demonstrates the importance of maintaining appropriate child-staff [sic (it should be "staff-child" throughout)] ratios' and that 'child-staff ratios and group sizes are two of the best indicators for determining the quality of a childcare program and they significantly effect many other health and safety issues.'

"Defining lower child-staff ratios as 1:3 for babies and 1:4 for toddlers, the literature review showed that in centres where there is [sic] lower child-staff ratios:

- there was a reduction in the transmission of disease because caregivers are better able to monitor and promote healthy practices and behaviors;
- there was [sic] fewer situations involving potential danger and child abuse;
- caregivers are enabled to have more positive, nurturing interactions with children and provide children with more individualised attention;
- infants displayed less apathy and distress and greater social competence;
- babies engaged in more talk and play and displayed more gestural and vocal imitation than children in classrooms with higher child-staff ratios;
- babies are more likely to have positive interactions with caregivers, be properly supervised, and be engaged in activities rated as good or very good;
- there is more developmentally appropriate caregiving and sensitivity, more contact (e.g., talking, playing, touching, and laughing) and more responsive and stimulating behaviour and less restriction of children's behaviour;
- there are higher rates of secure attachments between toddlers and their caregivers;
- there are more verbal communication [sic] between caregivers and children, which appears to foster language development in children;
- adults and children talk to one another more and caregivers engage in more dialogues and fewer monologues;
- caregivers engage in more educational activities (e.g., teaching, promoting problem-solving) with children."

Comment: The real meaning of all this

It logically follows from each of these research findings, that by staffing ratios alone, regardless of any claims or grading of 'high quality,' the following adverse effects of childcare will apply in any daycare centre having a 1:5 staff/child ratio for infants under 2 to 3 years of age, as compared with a centre having a 1:4 or 1:3 staff/child ratio:

- there is an increase in the transmission of disease because caregivers are less able to monitor and promote healthy practices and behaviours;
- there are more situations involving potential danger and child abuse;
- caregivers have fewer positive, nurturing interactions with children and provide children with less individualised attention;
- infants display more apathy and distress and less social competence;
- babies engage in less talk and play and display fewer gestural and vocal imitations than children in classrooms with lower child-staff ratios;
- babies are less likely to have positive interactions with caregivers, be properly supervised, and be engaged in activities rated as good or very good;
- there is less developmentally appropriate caregiving and sensitivity, less contact (e.g., playing, touching, and laughing) and less responsive and stimulating behaviour and more restriction of children's behaviour;
- there are lower rates of secure attachments between toddlers and their caregivers;
- there are fewer verbal communications between caregivers and children, which appears to impede language development in children;
- adults and children talk to one another less and caregivers engage in fewer dialogues and more monologues;
- caregivers engage in fewer educational activities (e.g., teaching, promoting problem-solving) with children.

Note 10. The Child Psychiatrists' Daycare Memorandum of 1971 – Extract from Appendix II, *Early Child Care* (Cook 1996, 1997)

In 1971 the New South Wales child psychiatrists of the Royal Australian and New Zealand College of Psychiatrists published a memorandum on some aspects of the welfare of infants and children under three years whose mothers are in full-time employment (Nurcombe, 1971). They concluded that "full-time work of mothers of children under three years of age is undesirable," and that "it is doubtful whether there could be any circumstances in which mothers of children under three years might be encouraged to go to work for national reasons." They drew attention to "the importance of satisfactory experiences and relationships during infancy for subsequent healthy development, and also to the weight of opinion that much emotional disturbance in children and adults originates in the first few years of life."

Urging recognition of the vulnerability of children at this age, they said that it should be an accepted principle in an affluent society that every mother who wishes to look after her own infant for the first three years should be enabled to do so, and should have the right to choose whether or not to work outside the home, without severe economic pressure to do so. Provision for suitable part-time relief from constant care, with socialising experiences for toddlers and their mothers on a part-time basis was urged.

Note 11. A two-year-old's mother goes to the maternity hospital

Extract from the beginning of *A two-year-old's mother goes to the maternity hospital,* followed by the Summary as it originally appeared at the end of the paper (Cook, 1962). The article began:

The situation that may arise when an infant's mother goes into hospital to have another baby was recently described in the following letter:

> Dear Doctor,
>
> With reference to our discussion regarding my little two-year-old nephew, Paul, who was staying with me recently whilst his mother (my sister) was in hospital, I would very much like to thank you for your suggestion that it would be at least worth a try to telephone the Matron and explain my problem to her in the hope that she would grant special permission for Paul to see his mother. This I did in desperation after nights of no sleep and days of wailing, "Mummy wumming home?" The child eventually would not eat or hardly drink his milk and was fretting continuously. In fact I even had a job to get him to let go of my hand long enough to go to the toilet.
>
> Although his five-year-old brother was here with him, and sleeping in the same room also with us, I could not impress on him at all that mummy would soon be home with a little baby.
>
> His brother had lots to interest him on the farm and played outside all day, but we could not get Paul to go with him to see the calves which I thought would interest him, unless I was there too and holding his hand, or at least he gripping mine. Might I add that he had his own cot, high chair and toys here, so that it was not a case of sleeping in a strange bed.
>
> I tried to take his mind off his mother sometimes by singing nursery rhymes, playing games and making toys. His dad telephoned the children practically every other night about 6 p.m., and I would let Paul hear him speak. This settled him for five minutes and then once again he would commence wailing, "Mummy wumming home?" Of course he had known beforehand he was going to stay with me whilst his mummy was in hospital and was quite excited at the prospect until the second night here. I did not mention to my sister that I was having difficulty with him

fretting. She used to draw pictures for them and I used to read her frequent letters to them both.

My husband and I took Paul only, the same day that we telephoned the Matron, who said that she would try it just once, but was of the opinion that these mothers could prepare their children for such an event if they tried. Naturally she could not let us up to the ward but she had my sister brought to a room downstairs and much to my amazement my nephew didn't say a word. He just looked bewildered and wanted to sit on my knee again after a while instead of his mother's. The Matron mentioned that she could see that the tension was there and very kindly wheeled an older baby than my sister's in to show him. He showed some interest and still did not speak. We were there in all about half an hour during which time my sister talked to him whilst he sat on my knee. As we did not wish him to see his mother taken back in a wheelchair, we left first and as soon as we were outside he started to talk and pointed to the birds and trees.

That night he was a different child, even coming home in the car he'd point to prams and say, "bubba." Instead of perpetually wailing, "Mummy wumming home?" he jumped up and down whenever he said it. It was a relief to get some sleep without disturbance and it was interesting to note that after that visit he would never cry when he woke up but just lie quietly in his cot and play or ask to come in my bed when I eventually woke. He told his brother, "Mummy bubba" and even called the calves "bubba." He would play outside all day and just come in now and again to tell me something. I thought you may be interested to hear the results. My husband suggested that I write and thank the Matron, I feel I should write and thank you, too, for your suggestion.

Yours faithfully, etc.

Since knowledge about the effects of maternal deprivation on young children has been publicised, the visiting of children in hospital by their parents has become widely accepted as sound practice. Yet application of the same principles to the situation occurring when the mother goes to the maternity hospital has received less attention. The general public and even members of the professions concerned seem unaware of the emotional hazards that may arise through the separation of a mother from her toddler at this time. With the increasing trend towards hospital confinements it is important that these risks should be recognised and suitable prophylactic measures taken.

....

Summary

Attention is drawn to the emotional stress to which a child of under two or three years of age may be subjected when the mother goes to hospital to have another baby. He may be separated not only from his mother but also from his father and siblings if he goes to stay with relatives. Such an experience may arouse in a child intense feelings of a kind which could disturb his capacity to make satisfactory relationships. When a period of separation from his mother precedes the child's introduction to the new baby he is faced with a double set of problems. These contribute to the causation of emotional disturbances of varying severity and duration. It is urged that the potential hazards of such arrangements should be more widely recognised by professional workers and the general public. Three illustrative cases are cited. In the first, the child's acute anxiety subsided immediately he was allowed to visit his mother. In the second, the experience precipitated a psychotic illness. The third child developed a prolonged sleep disturbance and indications of feelings of insecurity. Though he eventually improved, at the age of six he reacted to a separation and the birth of another sibling by developing faecal incontinence.

Note 12. "It takes a child to raise a village" – as actualised by Paul Ritter

The idea that "It takes a child to raise a village," described in *Early Years Study 2*, has been a concern of Paul Ritter, an architect and town-planner, and for many years he has been interested in creating urban environments that more nearly meet the needs of family and community life, and are safe for children.

In 1959, Ritter and his wife, Jean, wrote *The Free Family – A creative experiment in self-regulation for children*. Lloyd deMause cited this book in *The History of Childhood* by saying it was one of only three accounts then available that described children "brought up according to the 'helping mode' of childrearing" (1974: 54). [The other two were *The Free Child* by A.S. Neill (1952), and *The Children on the Hill* by Michael Deakin (1972).]

In 1975, Gollancz published *The Free Family and Feedback 1949– 1974: A Creative Experiment in Self-regulation for Children*. This was a reprint of the original 1959 book, with a 25-year follow-up by the parents, and then came six chapters contributed by six of their seven children. This is unique, and copies of the book are highly valued.

As an architect and town-planner, and supported by an excellent developer, Ritter designed a development with 500 dwellings that was an urban application of the principle – "it takes a child to raise a village". Crestwood Estate at Thornlie, in Perth, Western Australia, is far ahead of its time. It was influenced by the Garden City approach to planning – initially a concept of a self-sufficient town, balancing agriculture, residential and industry requirements. Crestwood incorporated the Radburn approach, with separation of pedestrian and vehicular traffic. Each house was individually designed, with small gardens, minimally fenced. Each has safe access to all the parkland, and communally shared facilities. Underpasses achieve separation from vehicular traffic for pedestrians, allowing them safe access to the various parkland areas, but dogs must be on a leash. The environment available to homes in Crestwood is in marked contrast to that in the surrounding suburbia, and they are much sought-after. (The difference can be seen with Google Earth, online.)

References

This book includes updates of various earlier publications by this author. Some of this material, with further references, may be found at:
www.naturalchild.org/peter_cook
Also at: www.members.optusnet.com.au/pcook62, and, www.newsweekly.com.au/books/0813336937.html

Others are in *Early Child Care: Infants and Nations at Risk*, available in digital format from this author. Parts of the text are available online. In some instances detailed referencing is not given in this book if a major topic is fully presented and referenced, as, for example, in *Becoming Attached* by Robert Karen, or *Mother Nature* by Sarah B. Hrdy.

Adderly, B., Gordon, J. (1999). *Brighter Baby*. Washington: Lifeline Eagle.

American Academy of Pediatrics (2005). Breastfeeding and the use of human milk. *Pediatrics*, 115, 496–506.

American Psychological Association (1995; 2005). *Publications Manual*. Washington, DC. Chapter on bias.

Augustine of Hippo. De Civitate Dei XIV, 26. Cited from Watts, A.W. (1958) *Nature, Man and Woman*. London: Thames and Hudson, 138.

Appell, George N. (1984). Freeman's refutation of Mead's *Coming of Age in Samoa*: The implications for anthropological inquiry. www.gnappell.org/articles/freeman.htm Revised from the original 1984 article in *The Eastern Anthropologist* 37: 183-214.

Austveg, B., Sundby, J. (1995). Empowerment of Women: the case of breastfeeding in Norway. Oslo: Norwegian Breastfeeding Association.

Australian Association for Infant Mental Health (2004). Position Paper 1 Controlled Crying. aaimhi.org.au/documents/position%20papers/controlled_crying.pdf.

Australian Breastfeeding Association (2008). Submission to the Inquiry into Paid Maternity Leave, Productivity Commission, GPO Box 1428, Canberra.

Bailey, D.S. (1959). *The Sexual Relation in Christian Thought*. New York: Harper.

Bartick, M. et al (2010). The burden of suboptimal breastfeeding in the United States: A pediatric cost analysis. *Pediatrics,* 125, 1048-56.

Bauer, I. (2001). *Diaper Free! The gentle wisdom of natural infant hygiene*. Saltspring Island, BC, Canada: Natural Wisdom Press.

Baxter, J., Cooklin, A.R., Smith, J. (2009). Which mothers wean their babies prematurely from full breastfeeding ? An Australian cohort study. *Acta Paediatrica* 98, 1274-1277.

Belsky, J. (1998). In Hope, D. Spare the non-maternal care and nurture the child. *The Australian*, June 4.

Belsky, J. Cited by Manne (2005:216), referenced as quoted in Garrison, 'Researchers in child-care study clash over findings'; also quoted in Robertson, *The Daycare Deception*, 56.

Belsky, J. (1998b). Personal communication.

Belsky, J. (2001). Developmental risks (still) associated with early child care. *Journal of Child Psychology and Psychiatry*, 42, 845–860.

Belsky, J. (2003). The Dangers of Daycare. Editorial, *The Wall Street Journal*, July 16. [Belsky's intended title was "The Politicized Science of Childcare," as posted with original text at www.iscfsi.bbk.ac.uk]

Belsky, J. (2002). Quantity counts: Amount of child care and children's socioemotional development. *Journal of Developmental and Behavioral Pediatrics*, 23: 167–170.

Bevan-Brown, M. with Allan, R.S. and Cook, E.F. (1950). *The Sources of Love and Fear*. Wellington: AH and AW Reed, 10.

Biddulph, S. (2003). *Raising Boys: Why Boys Are Different – And how to help them become happy and well-balanced men*. Sydney, Australia: Finch.

Biddulph, S. (2005). *Raising Babies: Should under 3s go to nursery?* London: Harper Thorsons.

Biddulph, S. (2007). Paid care for babies a pale imitation of parental love. *Sydney Morning Herald*, July 16.

Blurton Jones, N. (1972). Comparative aspects of mother child contact. In N. Blurton Jones (Ed.), *Ethological Studies of Child Behaviour*. Cambridge: Cambridge University Press.

Bowlby, J. (1940). The influence of early environment in the development of neurosis and neurotic character. *Int. Journal of Psychoanalysis*, 21: 1–25.

Bowlby, J. (1944). Forty-four juvenile thieves: their characters and their home life. *International Journal of Psychoanalysis*, 25, 19–52, 107–127.

Bowlby, J. (1951). *Maternal Care and Mental Health*. Geneva: World Health Organization. Abridged version, *Child Care and the Growth of Love*. Harmondsworth, Middlesex: Penguin, second edition, 1965.

Bowlby, J. (1969). *Attachment and Loss. Vol 1, Attachment*. London: Hogarth and the Institute of Psychoanalysis.

Bowlby, J. (1973). *Attachment and Loss. Vol 2, Separation, Anxiety and Anger*. London: Hogarth and the Institute of Psychoanalysis. Appendix II: Psychoanalysis and evolution theory.

Bowlby, J. (1980). *Psychoanalysis as a natural science*. The Freud Memorial Inaugural Lecture. London: University College, delivered October 21, as Freud Memorial Visiting Professor 1980–1981.

Bowlby, J. (1981). *Attachment and Loss. Vol 3, Loss: Sadness and Depression*. Harmondsworth, Middlesex: Penguin, 9, 13, 442. First published in 1980, London: Hogarth and the Institute of Psychoanalysis.

Bowlby, R. (2007). Stress in daycare. Available: socialbaby.blogspot.com/2007/04/richard-bowlby-stress-in-daycare.html

Breazeale, T.E. (2001). *Attachment parenting: a practical approach for the reduction of attachment disorders and the promotion of emotionally secure children*. Thesis submitted to the faculty of Bethel College for the degree of Master of Education, 2001. www.visi.com/~jlb/thesis/attachment.html

Brunton, P.J., Russell, J.A., Douglas, A.J. (2008). Adaptive responses of the maternal hypothalamic-pituitary-adrenal axis during pregnancy and lactation. *Journal of Neuroendocrinology,* 20(6), 764–776.

Bunting, M. (2004). Are nurseries bad for our kids? *The Guardian*, July 8.

Calvin, J. (1559). *Institutes of the Christian Religion*. Book II, Ch.1, Section 8. Geneva.

Cook, P.S. (1962). A two-year-old's mother goes to the maternity hospital. *New Zealand Medical Journal* 61, 605–608.

Cook, P.S. (1970). Antenatal education for parenthood as an aspect of preventive psychiatry: some suggestions for programme content and objectives. *Medical Journal of Australia*, 1, 676–681.

Cook, P.S. (1975). Childrearing, culture and mental health: the basic distrust syndrome and its influences. In Pilowsksy I. (Ed.), *Cultures in Collision*: Congress of the World Federation for Mental Health. Adelaide: Australian National Association for Mental Health (1973).

Cook, P.S., and Coombs, J. (1975). Obsolescence is obsolete in an inflated society. *The Australian*, May 6.

Cook P.S. (1977). Attachment and separation: what everyone should know. Royal Far West Children's Health Scheme, Sydney, 1977. Revised March 2000. www.naturalchild.org/peter_cook/attachment.html

Cook, P.S. (1978). Childrearing, culture and mental health: exploring an ethological-evolutionary perspective in child psychiatry and preventive mental health, with particular reference to two contrasting approaches to early childrearing. *Medical Journal of Australia, Special Supplement,* 3–14. www.naturalchild.org/peter_cook/childrearing.html. *The table from this paper in Note 6 is © 1978,* The Medical Journal of Australia – *reproduced with permission.*

Cook, P.S. (1995), *Wear-out products, prosperity and environmental degradation: effects on the economy, the consumer and the environment.* A talk broadcast in the Ockham's Razor Program by the Science Unit of the Australian Broadcasting Corporation on Radio National, December 9, 1995. www.members.optusnet.com.au/pcook62/index_files/page0004.htm

Cook, P.S. (1996). The early history of the New Zealand Association of Psychotherapists and the related movement of primary prevention in mental health: some recollections. *Australian and New Zealand Journal of Psychiatry* 30, 405–409.

Cook, P.S. (1996, 1997). *Early Child Care: Infants and nations at risk.* Melbourne: News Weekly Books (now Freedom Books). [The 1997 reprint has some corrections and a postscript, summarizing the next NICHD report to 36 months. Chapter 1. The species-normal experience for human infants – a biological and cross-cultural perspective can be seen at: www.naturalchild.org/peter_cook/ecc_ch1.html]

Cook, P.S. (1998). Fifty years of psychotherapy, but what about early childcare and child mental health? *Forum: Journal of the New Zealand Association of Psychotherapists,* 4, 97–114.

Cook, P.S. (1999a). Rethinking the early childcare agenda. *Medical Journal of Australia,* 170, 29–31. www.mja.com.au/public/issues/jan4/cook/cook.html

Cook P.S. (1999b). Home truths absent in early childcare debate: We need parent-friendly options. Opinion. *The Australian,* March 24. Sydney. www.naturalchild.org/peter_cook/home_truths.html

Cook P.S. (1999c). *Margaret Mead, Samoa and the sexual revolution – A summary-review of The Fateful Hoaxing of Margaret Mead* (Freeman, 1999). News Weekly, 2564, 12–14 (part 1) and News Weekly 2565, 17–18 (part 2). Melbourne. www.newsweekly.com.au/books/0813336937.html Also at http://www.members.optusnet.com.au/pcook62/pcook62/The_Fateful_Hoaxing_of_Margaret_Mead.html

Cook, P.S. (2000). The Tragedy of the Commons versus a sustainable environment. Talk for the Ockham's Razor programme, recorded by the Science Unit of the Australian Broadcasting Corporation, Sydney (but never broadcast). www.members.optusnet.com.au/pcook62/index_files/page0006.htm

Cook, P.S. (2002). Make mothers matter: childcare is just that – not parenting. Opinion. *The Australian,* July 24, Sydney. www.naturalchild.org/peter_cook/mothering_matters.html

Cook, P.S. (2004). Feminism, childcare, and family mental health: have women been misled by equality feminism? *Byronchild* (later called *Kindred* magazine) Sept: 28–31.Mullumbimby, NSW, Australia [no longer in production] naturalchild.org/peter_cook/feminism.html

Cook, P.S. (2005a). Simplified parenting for mental health – a framework www.naturalchild.org/peter_cook/simplified_parenting.html

Cook, P.S. (2005b). Equal opportunity for babies: breastfeeding as a strategic priority. *Byronchild* (later called *Kindred* magazine), Sept 18–19. www.naturalchild.org/peter_cook/equal_opportunity.html

Cooklin, A.R., Donath S.M., Amir, L. (2008). Maternal employment and breastfeeding: results from the longitudinal study of Australian children. *Acta Paediatrica*, 97, 620–623.

Cross Sectoral Task Force (2006). *Report on the implementation of a 1:4 staff-child ratio for children aged under two years in NSW children's services.* Sydney: New South Wales Government.

Darwin, C. (1859). *On the Origin of Species by Means of Natural Selection or the Preservation of Favoured Races in the Struggle for Life.* London: Murray.

Darwin, C. (1874). *The Descent of Man and Selection in Relation to Sex.* London: Murray.

De Beauvoir, S. [1949] 1953 *The Second Sex*. London: Jonathan Cape.

De Beauvoir, S., as cited by Tooley (2002: 71), in his section, *De Beauvoir Cheated*, and referenced by Tooley as 'Quoted from de Beauvoir, pp.685-6, translated by Leighton, 1975, 111 (emphasis added), 550.'

deMause, L. (1974). *The History of Childhood*. London, Souvenir Press.

Dicks, H.V. (1939). *Clinical Studies in Psychopathology*. London: Edward Arnold, (Revised second edition, 1947: 1).

Dmitrieva, J. Steinberg, L, Belsky, J. (2007). Child-care history, classroom composition and children's functioning in kindergarten. *Psychological Science*, 18, 12, 1032–1040.

Duffy, M. (1995). Is childcare bad for kids? *The Independent Monthly*, 88, 36–42. Melbourne, Australia.

Duijts, L. et al. (2010). Prolonged and Exclusive Breastfeeding Reduces the Risk of Infectious Diseases in Infancy. *Pediatrics*, 126, 1, 1825.

Eaton, S.B., Shostak, M., and Konner, M. (1988). *The Stone-Age Health Program: Diet and exercise as nature intended*. Harper and Row: London.

European Commission. Directorate Public Health and Risk Assessment (2004). E.U Project on Promotion of Breastfeeding in Europe. Protection, promotion and support of breastfeeding in Europe: current situation. Luxembourg: European Commission.

Evans, M.D.R., and Kelley, J. (2001). Employment for mothers of pre-school children: evidence from Australia and 23 other nations. *People and Place*, 9, 28–40.

Evans, M.D.R., and Kelley, J. (2002). Changes in public attitudes to maternal employment. *People and Place*, 10, 42–57.

Fox, I. (1996). *Being There: The benefits of a stay-at-home parent.* Barron's Educational Service: New York.

Fox, J.J. (2000). Testimonial supporting an Australian Honours award for Derek Freeman.

Fraser, A. (2007). It's child's play: ABC posts a 75 per cent increase as international expansion pays off. *The Australian,* Aug 28, 21. Sydney.

Freeman, D. (1983). *Margaret Mead and Samoa.* Harvard University Press. Reissued in 1996 as *Margaret Mead and the Heretic: The making and unmaking of an anthropological myth.* with a new foreword by Derek Freeman. Melbourne: Penguin. (Published for the launch of *The Heretic*, a play by David Williamson).

Freeman, D. (1999). *The Fateful Hoaxing of Margaret Mead: A historical analysis of her Samoan research.* Boulder, Colo. Westview. [It is important to note that, whereas the hardback edition of this book was published earlier in 1999, it was the paperback, published later that same year – and effectively a second edition – that Freeman regarded as the definitive version of this book. Within pages 141–146, the paperback contains two important new paragraphs that total nearly a page of material. These describe Mead's own 1931 account that corroborated Freeman's conclusions. Freeman discovered this final clinching evidence after publication of the 1999 hardback first edition, where page 148 is blank, and then the publisher used this blank space to accommodate the new material. Apart from this, all the other page numbers remain the same, and nowhere is attention drawn to these highly significant changes. Most libraries are likely to have only the hardback first edition, which lacks this final confirmation from Mead herself. Freeman presented his updated evidence in detail, and defended his argument against critics, in the Forum in *Current Anthropology*, 2000. A careful reading of this second edition paperback shows the quality of Freeman's work, and should itself be enough to dispel *ad hominem* critiques.]

Freeman, D., Orans, M., and Cote, J.E. (2000). Was *Coming of Age in Samoa* based on "A fateful hoaxing?" Forum on theory in anthropology. *Current Anthropology*, 41, 609–623.

Friedan, B. (1963). *The Feminine Mystique.* New York: W.W. Norton and Co.

Friedan, B. (1981). *The Second Stage.* New York: Summit Books, Simon & Schuster.

Galletly, C. (2008). Motherhood is good for the brain. *The Weekend Australian* July 5–6, 15.

Glover, E. (1960). *The Roots of Crime: selected papers on psychoanalysis*, Vol. 2. London: Imago.

Gluckman P., and Hanson, M. (2006). *Mismatch: why our world no longer fits our bodies.* Oxford: Oxford University Press.

Goodall, J. (1994). *With Love: Ten heart-warming stories of chimpanzees in the wild.* Zurich: North-South.

Gordon, T. (1970). *Parent Effectiveness Training: The tested new way to raise responsible children.* New York: Wyden. www.gordontraining.com/store.html

Graglia F.C. (1975). Sex, society and the female dilemma: a dialogue between Simone de Beauvoir and Betty Friedan. *Saturday Review*, June 14, 18. Cited from Tooley, 2002: 76.

Greenspan S. (2001). *The Four-thirds Solution: Solving the childcare crisis in America today.* Cambridge, Massachusetts: Perseus.

Greer G. (1972). *The Female Eunuch.* New York: Bantam Books.

Greer G. (1999). *The Whole Woman.* London: Transworld, 2–3, 260, 415.

Greven, P. (1991). *Spare the Child: The religious roots of punishment and the psychological impact of physical abuse.* New York: Alfred Knopf.

Gribben, T. (1979). *Pyjamas Don't Matter (or what your baby really needs).* Melbourne: Sun Books.

Grille, R. (2005). *Parenting for a Peaceful World.* Alexandria, New South Wales: Longueville Media.

Hadfield, J.A. (1950). *Psychology and Mental Health: A contribution to developmental psychology.* London: Allen and Unwin.

Hadfield, J.A. (1962). *Childhood and Adolescence.* Harmondsworth, Middlesex: Penguin.

Haire, D. (1972). The cultural warping of childbirth. *International Childbirth Education Association News*, Milwaukee: International Childbirth Education Association.

Hardin, G. (1968). The Tragedy of the Commons: The population problem has no technical solution; it requires a fundamental extension in morality. *Science*, 162, 1243–1248. www.garretthardinsociety.org/articles/art_tragedy_of_the_commons.html

Hardin, G. (1972). *Exploring New Ethics for Survival: The voyage of the spaceship Beagle.* Viking Press. 1972. Penguin, 1973.

Heimans, F. (1988). *Margaret Mead and Samoa*. Film (51 minutes), Produced by Cinetel Productions Ltd, Sydney, in association with the Australian Broadcasting Corporation and The Discovery Channel. [A DVD of this film made by Frank Heimans may be purchased from Cinetel Productions, 15 Fifth Avenue, Cremorne, New South Wales, 2090, Australia, 61 2 9953 8071. Price: For personal use only: A$50, plus p&p; for educational and commercial use: A$150, plus p&p. See www.cinetel.com.au. Some of the reviews and awards this film has received are reproduced in a document that may be seen at www.members.optusnet.com.au/pcook62. Frank Heimans has also kindly permitted the complete post-production script to be made available at this website.]

Hope, D. (1998). Spare the non-maternal care and nurture the child. *The Australian*, June 4, 1998. Sydney. [Jay Belsky had been accused of inducing "mother guilt" when he claimed that childcare could damage youngsters. Here, Deborah Hope gives Belsky's reply when she asked him if he had changed his mind.]

Horin, A. (2007). Taskforce advice on child-care rejected. Sydney. *The Sydney Morning Herald*, Jan 1, p.3.

Hrdy, S.B. (1999). *Mother Nature: Natural selection and the female of the species.*

Hrdy, S.B. (2009). *Mothers and Others: The evolutionary origins of mutual understanding.* Cambridge, Mass. Harvard University Press.

House of Representatives Standing Committee on Health and Ageing (2007). *The Best Start: Report on the inquiry into the health benefits of breastfeeding.* Canberra. Commonwealth of Australia. www.aph.gov.au/house/committee/haa/breastfeeding/report.htm

Huff, D. (1973). How to Lie with Statistics. Harmondsworth, Middlesex: Penguin.

Hunt, J. (2001). *The Natural Child: Parenting from the heart.* Gabriola Island, BC, Canada: New Society Publishers.

Illingworth, R.S. (1957). *The Normal Child: Some problems of the first five years and their treatment.* London: Churchill, 234.

Johnston, D.J. (2004). Statistics, Knowledge and Policy. OECD World Forum on Key Indicators. Palermo, November 12, 2004.

Joint Commission on Mental Health of Children. (1969). *Crisis in Child Mental Health: Challenge for the 1970s.* Washington, DC: 264.

Karen, R. (1994). *Becoming Attached: Unfolding the mystery of the infant-mother bond and its impact on later life.* New York: Warner.

King, F.T. (1925). *Feeding and Care of Baby.* London: Macmillan.

Kinsley, H., and Lambert, K.G. (2006). The Maternal Brain. *Scientific American*, 294, 72–79.

Kramer, M., Aboud, M. et al. (2008). Breastfeeding and cognitive development: new evidence from a large, randomized trial. *Arch Gen Psychiatry*, 65[5], 578–584.

Krauthammer, C. (2000). *The Washington Post*, May 12, A47 (as cited by Tooley, 2000: 51).

Kroeber, A.L. (1917). "The Superorganic". *American Anthropologist*, 19: 208, 213. See also reference to Kroeber's "abyss," C. Stringer and R. McKie, African Exodus London, 1996. (as referenced in Freeman, 1999: 239).

Lacey, T.A. (1962). Saint Augustine, *Encyclopaedia Britannica*. Chicago: Encyclopaedia Britannica.

Lally, R., Torres, Y., and Phelps, P. (1994). Caring for Infants and Toddlers in Groups: Necessary considerations for emotional, social and cognitive development. *Zero to Three*.

Leach, P. (1994). *Children First: What society must do – and is not doing – for children today*. London: Michael Joseph.

Leach, P. (1997). Infant care from infants' viewpoint: the views of some professionals. *Early Dev Parent,* 6, 47–58.

Leunig, M. (1995). Thoughts of a baby lying in childcare. Cartoon in *The Age*, July 25, 1995.

Liddiard, M. (1928). *The Mothercraft Manual* (6th edition). London: Churchill.

Liedloff, J. (1975). *The Continuum Concept*. London: Duckworth.

Leighton, J. (1975). *Simone de Beauvoir on Woman*. London: Associated University Press.

Manne A. (1995). A reflection upon re-entering the world. *Quadrant Magazine*, June 1995, PO Box 82, Balmain, New South Wales 2041.

Manne A. (1996). Electing a new child. *Quadrant Magazine*, Summer (Jan/Feb) 40: 8–19. PO Box 82, Balmain, New South Wales 2041.

Manne, A. (2005). *Motherhood: How should we care for our children?* Sydney: Allen and Unwin, 33, 195–9, 257.

Manne, A. (2008). Love and Money: the Family and the Free Market. *Quarterly Essay*. 29, 1–90. Melbourne, 17, 20. Also, citing Hochschild, A. (1997). *The Time Bind: When work becomes home and home becomes work*. New York: Metropolitan Books, 44.

McCain, M., and Mustard, J.F. (1999). *Reversing the Real Brain Drain: The Early Years Study.* Report to the Government of Ontario: Ontario, 6. Full Report available: www.children.gov.on.ca/htdocs/English/documents/topics/earlychildhood/early_years_study-1999.doc.

McCain, M., Mustard, J.F., and Shanker, S. (2007). *Early Years Study 2: Putting Science into Action.* Report for the Council for Early Child Development. Toronto, Ontario, 47. Full Report available: www.founders.net/fn/news.nsf/24157c30539cee20852566360044448c/5e0d29958d2d7d04852572ab005ad6a6!OpenDocument.

McHarg, I. L. (1971). The environmental crisis. *Architecture in Australia.* Aug, 638–646.

Mayle, P. (1978). *Baby Taming.* New York: Harmony. (1979) Melbourne: Sun Books.

Mead, M. (1928). *Coming of Age in Samoa: A psychological study of primitive youth for Western civilisation.* New York: Morrow.

Mead, M. (1930) *Social Organization of Manu'a.* Honolulu: Bernice P. Bishop Museum. *Cited in Chapter within quote by Appell, 1984.*

Mead, M. (1931). *Life as a Samoan Girl.* In: *All True! The record of actual adventures that have happened to ten women of today.* New York: Brewer, Warren and Putnam.

Moloney, J.C. (1949). *The Magic Cloak.* Wakefield, Massachusetts: Montrose.

Morgan, P. (1996). *Who Needs Parents? The effects of childcare and early education on children in Britain and the USA.* London: Institute of Economic Affairs, 109.

Mustard, F. (2007). From his contribution to *A Message from the Authors* in McCain, M., Fraser, M. J., and Shanker, S. (2007). *Early Years Study 2: Putting Science into Action,* 11.

National Childcare Accreditation Council (1993). *Putting Children First: quality improvement and accreditation system handbook.* Sydney: National Childcare Accreditation Council.

National Geographic (August 2007). *Geography: Who Gives Parents a Break?* Map of the world showing the amount of guaranteed leave for mothers, 2006. Source: McGill Institute for Health and Social Policy and the Project on Global Working Families.

National Health and Medical Research Council (2003). *Dietary Guidelines for Children and Adolescents in Australia incorporating the Infant Feeding Guidelines for Health Workers.* Canberra: National Health and Medical Research Council.

National Institute of Child Health and Development: Early Child Care Research Network (2006). Childcare effect sizes for the NICHD study of early childcare and youth development. *American Psychologist,* 61, 99–116.

National Institute of Child Health and Development: Early Child Care Research Network (2007). Are There Long-Term Effects of Early Child Care? *Child Development,* 78, 681–701.

National Institute of Child Health and Development: Early Child Care Research Network (2009). Early family and child-care antecedents of awakening cortisol levels in adolescence. *Child Development,* 80, 907-920.

Neill, A.S. (1962). *Summerhill.* London: Gollancz, 102.

Nurcombe, B. (1971). For the New South Wales Branch of the Child Psychiatry Section of the Royal Australian and New Zealand College of Psychiatrists. Memorandum on some aspects of the welfare of children aged under three years whose mothers are in full-time employment. *Medical Journal of Australia,* 446–448.

Nyland, B. (2003). The child-care centre as a developmental niche. Paper given to the Australian Institute of Family Studies conference, February 8.

Ochiltree, G. (1994). Effects of child care on young children: forty years of research. Australian Institute of Family Studies, Melbourne, 69, 116.

Olssen, E. (1981). Truby King and the Plunket Society. An analysis of a prescriptive ideology. *The New Zealand Journal of History,* 15(1), 1–23.

Pagel, M. (2008). Our world is growing apart as people adapt to their environment. *The Weekend Australian* Feb 16–17, 23. www.theaustralian.news.com.au/story/0,,23221327-7583,00.html?from=public_rss

Partridge, E.J. (1936). *The Management of Early Infancy.* Paper to the Medical Society of Individual Psychology, London. Nov 12.

Partridge, E.J. (1937). *Baby's Point of View.* London: Oxford University Press.

Prescott, J.W. (2005). Prevention or therapy and the politics of trust: Inspiring a new human agenda. *Psychotherapy and Politics International,* 3(3), 194–211.

Productivity Commission (2008). *Paid Parental Leave: Support for Parents with Newborn Children.* Draft Inquiry Report, Canberra. Commonwealth of Australia. Available: pc.gov.au/projects/inquiry/parentalsupport/draft

Ramage, I. (1967). *Battle for the Free Mind.* London: Allen and Unwin.

Read, G.D. (1942). *Revelation of childbirth: the principles and practice of natural childbirth.* London: Whitefriars Press, Heinemann.

Renfrew, M. J. (2009). Breastfeeding promotion for infants in neonatal units: a systematic review and economic analysis. *Health Technology Assessment,* 13(40):48.

Rheingold, H.L. (1968). Infancy. In: *International Encyclopedia of Social Sciences.* New York: Macmillan and the Free Press.

Ritchie, J., and Ritchie, J. (1970). *Child-rearing Patterns in New Zealand.* Wellington: Reed. 48.

Ritchie, J., and Ritchie, J. (1981). *Spare the Rod.* Sydney: Allen and Unwin.

Ritter, P., and Ritter, J. (1959). *The Free Family: A creative experiment in self-regulation for children.* London: Gollancz.

Ritter, P., and Ritter, J. (1975). *Free Family and Feedback 1949–1974: a creative experiment in self-regulation for children.* London: Gollancz.. [This is the original 1959 book, plus a 25-year follow-up in which the parents, and then each of their six children, contribute a chapter discussing his or her upbringing.]

Rob, M., Reynolds, I., Finlayson, P.F. (1990). Adolescent marijuana use: risk factors and implications. *Australian and New Zealand Journal of Psychiatry*, 24, 47–56.

Roberts, Y. (2005). Official: babies do best with mother. *The Observer*, (London) October 2. observer.guardian.co.uk/uk_news/story/0,6903,1583072,00.html

Roberts, Y. (2008). Mum is the missing word. *The Guardian*, July 2. Reprinted in *The Australian*, July 3. www.guardian.co.uk/commentisfree/2008/jul/02/familyandrelationships.women

Robertson, J. (1953). *A two-year-old goes to hospital* [film]. For details, see Karen, 1994.

Robertson, J., and Robertson, J. (1973) Substitute mothering for the unaccompanied child. *Nursing Times,* Nov 29.

Robotham, J. (2008). Study shows stress affects brain growth. *Sydney Morning Herald*, Feb 18.

Room, A. (Ed.) (1999). *The Cassell Dictionary of Word Histories.* London: Cassell Reference.

Rowley, H. (2006). *Tête-à-Tête: The lives and loves of Simone de Beauvoir and Jean-Paul Sartre.* New York: Chatto and Windus.

Sage, L. (2002). *Moments of Truth: Twelve twentieth-century women writers.* London: Harper Collins, 154, 160.

Sears, W. (1991). *Christian Parenting and Child Care.* Nashville: Thomas Nelson. 116–7. (The table is reproduced in Cook, 1996, 189.)

Seymour-Jones, C. (2008). *Glued Together by Their Lies: A Dangerous Liaison.* Century. Reviewed by Gillian Tindall, <u>Literary Review</u>, April 4-5, 2008.

Shankman, P. (2009). *The Trashing of Margaret Mead: Anatomy of an anthropological controversy.* Madison: University of Wisconsin Press.

Smith, J. (2004). Mothers' milk and markets. *Australian Feminist Studies*, 19(45), 369–379.

Smith, J.P., Ingham, L.H. (2005). Mothers' milk and measures of economic output. *Feminist Economics* 2005, 11(1), 41-62.

Sommers, C.H. (1994). *Who Stole Feminism? How women have betrayed women.* New York: Simon and Schuster, 257. Cited from Manne, 2005:33, 321.

Spock, B. (1974). What I said in February about raising children – and what I did not say. *Redbook*, June, 22.

Steinberg, L., and Meyer, R. (1995). *Childhood.* New York: McGraw-Hill.

Suttie, I., and Suttie, I.J. (1932). The mother: agent or object? Part I in *Medical Psychology*, Vol 12, Part II, 12; 7-108. Part II in *Medical Psychology* Vol 12 Part III: 199–233.

Suttie, I. (1935). *The Origins of Love and Hate.* London: Kegan Paul. Preface by J.A. Hadfield in 4th Impression, 1948.

Swain, J.E., Lorberbaum, J.P., Kose, S., and Strathearn, L. (2007). Brain basis of early parent-infant interactions: psychology, physiology, and in vivo functional neuroimaging studies. *Journal of Child Psychology and Psychiatry*, 48, 287. (The words cited are selected from the long abstract.)

Sykes, B. (2001). *The Seven Daughters of Eve.* London: Bantam/Transworld.

Theile, D. (2005). The problem with sociology: morality, anti-biology and perspectivism. *Quadrant*, 49(10); 11, Suite 2/5 Balmian, New South Wales.

Tooley, J. (2002). *The Miseducation of Women.* London: Continuum, 71.

UNICEF/Innocenti (2005). UN Secretary-General: *Global Study on Violence Against Children.* www.unicef.org/protection/index_3717.html

Uvnas-Moberg, K., & Petersson, M. (2005). Oxytocin, a mediator of anti-stress, wellbeing, social interaction, growth and healing. *Z Psychosom Med Psychother,* 51(1), 57-80.

Weber, M. (1905). *The Protestant Ethic and the Spirit of Capitalism.*

Wallace, A.R. (1893). Woman and Natural Selection. *London Daily Chronicle*, Dec 4. London. www.wku.edu/~smithch/wallace/S736.htm

Watson, J.B. (1928). *Psychological Care of the Infant and Child.* New York: Norton, 81–82.

Watts, A.W. (1958). *Nature, Man and Woman.* London: Thames and Hudson.

Werner, E.E. (1972). Infants around the world: cross-cultural studies of psychomotor development from birth to two years. *Cross-Cultural Psychology*, 3, 111–134.

Wilson, E.O. (1998). *Consilience: The unity of knowledge.* New York: Alfred Knopf, 203, 211.

Acknowledgements

Like other writers, I am grateful and indebted to many people from whom I have learned over the years – often from children and their parents. In particular, I express grateful thanks to:

Professor Jay Belsky, for generous help over the years, and for his advance comment.

Steve Biddulph, for writing the Foreword.

Professor Forrester Cockburn, for his advance comment.

Elliott Barker, MD, for his encouragement and advance comment.

Michael Denton, MD, PhD, for proofing Chapter 1 and Note 2 on Genes, Chromosomes and DNA

Julie Smith, PhD, Research Fellow, Australian Centre for Economic Research on Health, Australian National University, for help in updating Chapter 2 on breastfeeding.

Professor Derek Freeman, for quotations from *The Fateful Hoaxing of Margaret Mead: A historical analysis of her Samoan research*, and for his dedication and uniquely valuable contribution. Also for his checking the accuracy of my 1999 Summary-Review of his book. Thanks also to his wife Monica for checking Chapter 9 and Note 7D.

Frank Heimans, for quotations from his 50-minute documentary film/DVD *Margaret Mead and Samoa*, and permission to reproduce its post-production script on www.members.optusnet.com.au/pcook62

Professor James J. Fox, Director of the Research School of Pacific and Asian Studies at The Australian National University, for permission to put in the public domain his testimonial recommending national recognition of the contribution of the work of Professor Derek Freeman.

The Medical Journal of Australia for permission to reproduce in Note 6, the Table in Cook, P.S. (1978). Childrearing, culture and mental health: exploring an ethological-evolutionary perspective in child psychiatry and preventive mental health, with particular reference to two contrasting approaches to early childrearing. *Medical Journal of Australia*, Special Supplement, 3–14. www.naturalchild.org/peter_cook/childrearing.html

The Council for Early Child Development, Toronto, for quotations from the two *Early Years* studies.

Ronald G. Every, DDS, who, in the 1960s, displayed to me how the dentition in humans and other mammals, and also the associated structures and their functions and *behaviour*, all evolved together – down to the minutest detail, and always to some advantage.

Kevin Scally, BDS, who in some ways builds on and continues Every's work, including demonstrating that the phenomenon of thegosis has evolved independently in a range of phyla, and can be considered to be a common evolutionary strategy to enhance and maintain the dentition. Some of this may be seen on his website www.8.co.nz Then go to projects thegotics.

J. A. Hadfield, and Allen & Unwin for quotations from *Psychology and Mental Health*.

Jan Hunt, who has encouraged me, and with her son Jason Hunt, has made some of my writings available on the website of The Natural Child Project: www.naturalchild.org/peter_cook

Penelope Leach, PhD, for quotation from *Children First*.

Michael Leunig, for his 1995 cartoon *Thoughts of a baby lying in a child care centre*.

Anne Manne for quotations from her book *Motherhood*, and also from two essays.

The Tavistock Institute of Human Relations, The Institute of Psychoanalysis, and Dr John Bowlby for his words and personal encouragement.

Professor James Tooley, for quotations from *The Miseducation of Women*.

June Ward, for quotations from *The Sources of Love and Fear* by her late father, Dr M. Bevan-Brown.

Professor E.O. Wilson, for quotation from *Consilience*.

George N. Appell, PhD, for quotatons from his 1984 review *Freeman's refutation of Mead's Coming of Age in Samoa: The implications for anthropological inquiry*.

John W. Travis, MD, for much expert and enduringly patient editing and advice.

Jenny Cullen for the frontispiece, *Creativity, Women and Parenting*.

Helen Cushing, for expert editorial help.

And to all in my extended family my debt is lifelong and profound.

Every effort has been made to locate holders of copyright material, however, the author and publishers would be interested to hear from any copyright holders not here acknowledged, so that full acknowledgement may be made in any future editions.

Peter S. Cook

Author's note

As a medical student, I attended the conference at which the New Zealand Association of Psychotherapists was formed in December 1947. I described this in "The early history of the New Zealand Association of Psychotherapists (NZAP) and the related movement for primary prevention in mental health: some recollections" (Cook, 1996). Additional details of that occasion were in a paper to the Reunion Conference in Christchurch, celebrating the 50th anniversary of the founding of the NZAP. My presentation, "Fifty years of psychotherapy, but what about early childcare and child mental health?" was published in 1998 in *Forum: The Journal of the New Zealand Association of Psychotherapists,* 4, 97–114.

In 1951, while working in paediatrics, I read John Bowlby's *Maternal Care and Mental Health*, published by the World Health Organization, and it confirmed my interest in studying adult and child psychiatry. Subsequently, many clinical experiences led me to a particular interest in primary prevention. For this reason I have tried to write in ways that can be understood by a general reader.

While studying psychiatry in London in the early 1950s, I heard what I call "The Hilliard Principle." It is important and should be more widely recognized. Dr Hilliard was the medical superintendent of the Fountain Hospital for the care of the mentally handicapped in London, and was a renowned authority in this subject. Rehabilitation of patients from such hospitals back into the community was then a novel idea, but he believed in it. Essentially, his advice was: "Start with the easiest one. Then, when you have shown success in rehabilitating one into the community, try the next easiest one, and so on. As the idea catches on, you will have more and more successes, and the idea will become established."

It seems to me that this Hilliard Principle, starting at the easiest and most cost-effective aspect of a problem, has wide relevance and should be more generally recognized and applied, especially if there is an underlying cultural problem – as there is in our society's current 'denial' of mothering. Vast effort and money are put into efforts to help those who are most damaged in our society – often with very limited success – while much less effort and expenditure in strategic areas might prevent many such troubles.

Dr Elliott Barker took this approach when he formed The Canadian Society for the Prevention of Cruelty to Children. As deputy medical superintendent in an institution for the 'criminally insane' in Canada, he once knew a hundred murderers by their first names. But he became convinced that their psychopathy, and the fundamental defect in their development of true empathy, was resistant to treatment, and often irremediable. He concluded that early prevention, by encouraging empathic parenting from birth, was the most cost-effective way forward. His steps toward this are outlined in Chapter 12.

In the 1970s I was involved in two Memoranda published by the New South Wales branch of the Child Psychiatry Section of the Royal Australian and New Zealand College of Psychiatrists. The first was "The admission of mothers to hospital with their young children," published in *The Medical Journal of Australia*, October 3, 1970. It was then adopted, with slight modifications, as a Position Statement of the RANZCP. This led to the formation of The Association for the Welfare of Children in Hospital, and it achieved much success toward improving the care of children in hospital throughout Australia. The Association's website is: www.awch.org.au/about.html.

Soon afterwards, the New South Wales child psychiatrists published a "Memorandum on some aspects of the welfare of children aged under three years whose mothers are in full-time employment" (*Med. J. Aust*, 1971, 446–448). It became the basis of another Position Statement of the College. An extract from that Memorandum is reproduced in Appendix II of my *Early Child Care*, and above in Note 10.

An early version of one theme in this present book was presented at the 1973 Congress of the World Federation for Mental Health, and published in the Proceedings. In 1978, a much more developed version was published as a Special Supplement in *The Medical Journal of Australia*: "Childrearing, culture and mental health: exploring an ethological-evolutionary perspective in child psychiatry and preventive mental health, with particular reference to two contrasting approaches to early childrearing" (Cook, 1978). Its abstract is included as Note 6. The full text may be seen at www.naturalchild.org/peter_cook/childrearing.html.

After retirement, I was prodded into activity by a 1994 book about the effects of childcare on young children. It advocated much more provision for early childcare, which it said should be of "high quality." This led to the publication of my *Early Child Care – Infants and Nations at Risk* in 1996, with a critique of that 1994 book in Chapter 6. An updated reprint of *Early Child Care* appeared in 1997, and it remained in print for ten years. It may become available as a PDF on my website.

In 1999, *The Medical Journal of Australia* published my "Rethinking the early childcare agenda." This detailed five reasons why the early childcare agenda is misconceived, and it was followed by an opinion article in *The Australian* that began with these five reasons and then outlined what we could do about it (Cook, 1999a; 1999b).

An earlier version of *Mothering Matters* was officially published as *Mothering Denied* in April 2009, and it was made available from my website for download under restricted conditions. In this revised and updated second edition it has been renamed because some people misunderstood the meaning of the original title, but this book retains the subtitle, *The sources of love, and how our culture harms infants, women, and society*. It is a sequel to, and in some ways a development of, my 1996 *Early Child Care – Infants and Nations at Risk*, and it also complements the 1978 paper. Other articles relating to this theme, and some publications about sustainable conservation topics, are listed on my website. Most are readily available, or obtainable through a medical library.

Peter S. Cook

Queenscliff (Sydney), New South Wales, May 2011.

Postscript

As new techniques emerge, and human knowledge of genetics expands, there is reason to expect that new information will extend and validate our understanding of the history of our species as mammals, and the basic patterns of human mothering. Mothering is a complex, biologically based process that is much influenced by environmental circumstances. It is a vital activity that has been evolving for longer than 100 million years.

As primate infants evolved increasingly large brains, it became necessary for them to be born at progressively less mature stages of development. In humans the degree of this helpless dependency is greatest at the very stages when the brain is developing most rapidly. Although we usually have no conscious memories of important experiences that occur during this time, we have increasing evidence that they are of profound and lifelong importance. The many consequences that stem from this fact cannot be deleted by any society, no matter how sophisticated its culture.

In comparative studies of early mothering and the brain effects of suboptimal early nurturing, research is increasingly filling in more details, but the main thesis of this book – some of which was published by this author in 1973, and more fully in 1978 and 2006 – has been supported by much new evidence in the past 30 years. The trend is toward providing more information about the importance of getting the environment right for children in their very early years, especially from the time of conception onwards.

This book discusses many strands of verifiable evidence, but the emotional repercussions of adverse or traumatic experiences during infancy are seldom consciously remembered. However, that does not mean they are not influencing relationships, attitudes, and behaviour during childhood and adult life. Sigmund Freud wrote *The Psychopathology of Everyday Life* in 1901, and much has been said about it since. But the ways and means through which early emotionally significant experiences influence personal and public life, and historical events, must become more accurately and widely understood if the twenty-first century is to run a creative course.

We still have much to learn about resilience. In 1951, Bowlby pointed out that not all children who drank milk infected with tubercle bacilli contracted tuberculosis, but that did not invalidate the evidence that it was dangerous for other children. As more extreme examples, a few people seem uninjured even by nuclear radiation or infection with HIV, but this does not mean that others will not be harmed.

Understanding the nature of the problem and making the correct diagnosis is generally fundamental in reaching the best remedy for any disorder or malfunction. The ancient and basic principles of medicine remain valid: *Primum non nocere* – first and foremost, do no harm. Prevention is better than cure.

Appendix 1. Do effects of early childcare extend to age 15?

National Institute of Child Health and Development: Early Child Care Research Network (2009). Early family and childcare antecedents of awakening cortisol levels in adolescence.[61]

Abstract

This study examined early-observed parenting and child-care experiences in relation to functioning of the hypothalamic-pituitary-adrenocortical axis over the long term. Consistent with the attenuation hypothesis, individuals (n = 863) who experienced: (a) higher levels of maternal insensitivity and (b) more time in childcare centers in the first 3 years of life had lower awakening cortisol levels at age 15. Associations were small in magnitude. Nonetheless, results were (a) additive in that both higher levels of maternal insensitivity and more experience with center-based care uniquely (but not interactively) predicted lower awakening cortisol, (b) not accounted for by later caregiving experiences measured concurrently with awakening cortisol at age 15 or by early demographic variables, and (c) not moderated by sex or by difficult temperament.

....

Comment

The cost to the National Institute of Child Health and Development of the total Early Child Care Research Network Study to age 15 was apparently around US$132 million, but this may not include all the costs. As at the date of publication of this Report, an Internet follow-up survey after the adolescents have finished high school was being carried out, so 15 years may not be the final follow-up age, but this 15-year study is the final that will be funded by the NICHD.

It is noteworthy that in this massive NICHD study, no records were made of the breastfeeding experiences or histories of any of the children.

---

61. Published in: *Child Development*, 80, 907-920.

As described in Chapter 2, Kramer et al. (2008) proved that children who were being fully breastfed at three months, when followed up at six and a half years of age, scored an average of 7.5 points higher in verbal intelligence tests, and 5.9 points higher in overall IQ tests, compared with the children who were not fully breastfed at age three months. Moreover, teachers rated the children fully breastfed at three months as being more advanced in reading, writing and solving mathematical problems.

Also, the massive US dollar health costs of suboptimal breastfeeding, calculating the cost during infancy and early childhood alone, make it the more surprising that the child's breastfeeding history was simply not regarded as a variable to be taken into account in this huge NICHD Study (Bartick, 2010).

As described in Chapter 2, the many benefits of breastfeeding were well recognized before the design of this NICHD project was settled.

Many such studies, together with the Norwegian experience outlined at the end of Chapter 2, give a glimpse of the costs in health and human ability that follow when our societies depart in major ways from human needs that are laid down in our genome, as outlined particularly in Chapters 2 and 6 (see also Appendix 3).

Appendix 2. The dollar costs of suboptimal breastfeeding in the US

The Burden of Suboptimal Breastfeeding in the United States: A Pediatric Cost Analysis[62]

Abstract

Authors. Melissa Bartick, MD, MSc (Department of Medicine, Cambridge Health Alliance and Harvard Medical School, Boston, Mass.), Arnold Reinhold, MBA, (Alliance for the Prudent Use of Antibiotics, Boston, Mass).

Background and objective. A 2001 study revealed that $3.6 billion could be saved if breastfeeding rates were increased to levels of the Healthy People objectives. It studied 3 diseases and totalled direct and indirect costs and cost of premature death. The 2001 study can be updated by using current breastfeeding rates and adding additional diseases analyzed in the 2007 breastfeeding report from the Agency for Healthcare Research and Quality.

Study design. Using methods similar to those in the 2001 study, we computed current costs and compared them to the projected costs if 80% and 90% of US families could comply with the recommendation to exclusively breastfeed for 6 months. Excluding Type 2 diabetes (because of insufficient data), we conducted a cost analysis for all pediatric diseases for which the Agency for Healthcare Research and Quality reported risk ratios that favored breastfeeding: necrotizing enterocolitis, otitis media, gastroenteritis, hospitalization for lower respiratory tract infections, atopic dermatitis, sudden infant death syndrome, childhood asthma, childhood leukemia, Type 1 diabetes mellitus, and childhood obesity. We used 2005 Centers for Disease Control and Prevention breastfeeding rates and 2007 dollars.

Results. If 90% of US families could comply with medical recommendations to breastfeed exclusively for 6 months, the United States would save $13 billion per year and prevent an excess 911 deaths, nearly all of which would be in infants ($10.5 billion and 741 deaths at 80% compliance).

Conclusions. Current US breastfeeding rates are suboptimal and result in significant excess costs and preventable infant deaths. Investment in strategies to promote longer breastfeeding duration and exclusivity may be cost-effective.

---

62. Published in: *Pediatrics*, 2010;125:1048-56.

Appendix 3. Six months breastfeeding lowers infancy infection risk

Prolonged and Exclusive Breastfeeding Reduces the Risk of Infectious Diseases in Infancy

In Chapter 2, the study by Kramer et al. (2008) was outlined showing, with the most powerful evidence possible, that exclusive breastfeeding for 3 months caused higher intelligence and better school performance at 6 1/2 years. Or to put it more accurately, it showed that the introduction of other milks or foods during the first 3 months of life caused a fall in the child's IQ (averaging 7.5 points in verbal IQ and 5.9 overall IQ) and poorer school behaviour, as assessed at 6 1/2 years.

Such strong evidence has not been available to the World Health Organization and other health authorities to support their recommendations of exclusive breastfeeding for 6 months, and continuing through infancy (often or generally with supplementary foods) for as long as mutually desired by mother and child (outlined in Chapter 2). So the WHO called for research to strengthen evidence of the benefits of 6 months exclusive breastfeeding, rather than just 4 months.

In June 2010, *Pediatrics* published the study, "Prolonged and Exclusive Breastfeeding Reduces the Risk of Infectious Diseases in Infancy", by L. Duijts and colleagues. It is part of a large prospective longitudinal study being conducted in Rotterdam, from foetal life onwards. The authors begin by saying that respiratory and gastrointestinal tract infections are the leading causes of sickness in young children and exclusive breastfeeding seems to decrease the risk of these infectious diseases in infancy. The object of the study was to examine the associations between (i) the duration of 4 to 6 months of exclusive breastfeeding, and (ii) infections in the upper respiratory, lower respiratory, and gastrointestinal tracts during infancy.

All the babies they studied were breastfed for 6 months, but while some were exclusively breastfed for 6 months, the others, after exclusive breastfeeding for 4 months, had various combinations of additional foods. The authors then recorded all the doctor-attended infectious illnesses in these infants up to the age of 12 months, as assessed by questionnaires completed for 4164 subjects.

They found that exclusive breastfeeding until the age of 4 months, with partial breastfeeding thereafter, was associated with a significant reduction in respiratory and gastrointestinal illness in infants. But the study also provided evidence that exclusive breastfeeding for 6 months tended to be more protective against the infections than exclusive breastfeeding for only 4 months.

The authors concluded "Our findings support health-policy strategies to promote exclusive breastfeeding for at least 4 months, but preferably 6 months, in industrialized countries."

EPILOGUE

... but man, proud man,
Dressed in a little brief authority,
Most ignorant of what he's most assured,
His glassy essence like an angry ape,
Plays such fantastic tricks before high heaven
As make the angels weep.

Shakespeare, *Measure for Measure* **II, ii**

www.ingramcontent.com/pod-product-compliance
Lightning Source LLC
Chambersburg PA
CBHW072001290426
44109CB00018B/2091